A Year in
The Cuyamacas

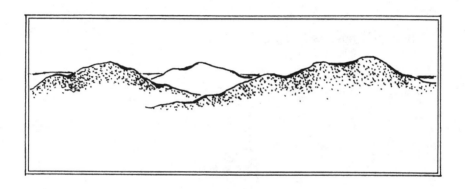

By Leland Fetzer

August, 1998

With Illustrations By
Donald Covington

To Jerry and Nancy Traven from the author.
Happy reading about Cuyamaca Woods

Lee Fetzer

Tecolote Publications
San Diego, California

1998

ISBN 0-938711-52-0

Library of Congress Catalog Card No. 98-60165

Printed in the United States of America.

Tecolote Publications
San Diego, California

Table of Contents

Acknowledgements

I could not have written some of the essays in this book without the assistance of local informants, experts, and others. Although the list is too long to cite in full, I want at least to acknowledge the essential role these people played in making this book. On the other hand, I apologize to those who do not find their names here, but lack of space demands some economy.

In no special order: Richard Zerbe, Kay Howley, Stan Scott, the late Loie Lewis (Mrs. Alfred M. Lewis), Mr. and Mrs. Warren Rhodes, Willis Fletcher, Charles LeMenager, Richard Chandler, Felix and Margaret De Rooy, Jessie Phoenix, Douglas Cargile, Dr. Don Hunsaker, Mary Tschumperlin, Mary Ward of the San Diego County Parks Department, and Mitch Tendler, particularly.

Special thanks must go to Jim Nowland, who helped steer me through the land title maze at the San Diego County Recorder's Office; John Silbernagel, who remembers very well the early years of the non-subdivision, Cuyamaca Woods; and Charles F. Sawday, who kindly shared with me his memories of his grandfather, first settler in the Cosmit.

Also playing an essential role in the book were the staffs of Love Library at San Diego State University; the Archives of the San Diego Historical Society, especially Sally West and her very helpful assistants; Special Collections at the University of California Library (La Jolla); the San Diego County Highway Department; and the Cartography Department of the San Diego County Planning Department.

My special thanks also to Katie Price and Lisa Curtis of the Writing Program at the University of Iowa; their contribution is apparent on nearly every page of the book, at least to me.

Thanks go to Carol Bowers who contributed her editing skills to ridding the book of many infelicities and who saw the book through the press. What's more, her tactful advice at crucial moments was right on.

Thanks, too, to Don and Karon Covington, friends of long standing, but especially to Don who supplied the whimsical designs that enliven the book's pages.

My children, Anne and her husband, Tom Scott; Eric and his

wife, Linda; and Tom F. had a hand in this book, but most important was my wife, Lois, who encouraged the mountain project and has been sympathetic almost always to her husband's eccentricities and enthusiasms. This book is dedicated to her.

Note: Beginning in February, 1995, I published a monthly column in the *Julian News* under the heading "A Year in the Cuyamacas." Fourteen of the shortest essays in this book appeared in the column. I have revised all of them and some I have re-named.

Introduction

In 1988 my wife and I bought two and a half acres of wooded land on the front of North Peak in the Cuyamaca Mountains at an altitude of 4,300 feet about fifty miles from San Diego and eight miles from the nearest town, Julian. The place is reasonably remote, reachable only by a mile's drive off a paved county road, Engineers Road, over gravel and dirt lanes through the trees. We bought it to find living room and as a station to observe stars, weather, and nature. Later on, we began to talk about building a cabin.

A few years having passed, it occurred to me to write some brief essays about the district centered at the cabin that we in fact built. My idea was to compose an introduction to the natural history of the region; at the same time I would be learning about a place that I in fact did not know very well. I began buying books and committed myself to a course of reading about local natural history.

However, after I had written a half dozen essays I became dissatisfied with my project. While learning and writing about nature was gratifying, the results were too confining. Increasingly, I sensed an urge to paint a broader picture of life on the mountain. Nature essays–birds, geology, trees–I decided, were not enough to capture the spirit of North Peak and its woods and what it meant to live there every month of the year, my real concern. At the same time, my goal of informing the reader about the facts of plants and animals on the mountain increasingly became an exploration of my own experiences and emotions about what I saw around me in the woods. Imperceptibly, the lessons in natural history had become personal essays, although I never allowed myself to forget that I was not writing about myself, but the land, above all.

One reason I broadened the book's intention, is that the cabin does not rise in wilderness where nature makes an exclusive claim on the land. In the district humans have lived for thousands of years, leaving their marks. If I walk ten minutes from the cabin I note deeply worn Indian morteros. One hundred and twenty years ago ranchers and lumbermen came to the mountain, leaving fences and stumps. Our century brought paved roads, and because

North Peak stands above an expanding metropolis, developers arrived with plans for subdivisions and vacation homes. Now, first and second homes dot the landscape; our cabin is one of them.

No, if I wanted to do justice to the district, man and his works would have to find a place in the book. To the nature essays I decided to add some pieces on local history. Expanding the idea, I decided to include a few essays about initiating the cabin; I can't think of a better occasion for man and nature to meet than building a house in the woods.

The same goal led me to include a pair of sketches about my neighbors. These I focused on the question of why they chose to live in mountain woods; secondary questions I asked were how they prospered in their remote homes and if isolation enriched them. I leave the reader to decide if they live lives worthy of emulation.

The authentic subject of this book is a westward-tilting triangle of land about forty miles from San Diego as the crow flies with its corners at Cuyamaca Rancho State Park; Pine Hills, an older subdivision southwest of Julian; and Boulder Creek Road that snakes west of Cuyamaca Peak. Each leg of the triangle is about ten miles long, and so the triangle encloses about fifty square miles of slopes gentle and precipitous, birds, reptiles and mammals, silted-up farm ponds, meadows, chaparral, roads, a few year-round streams, small and large houses, many oaks and pines, forgotten prospect holes, Indian dwelling sites and reservations, rusted barbed wire, and perhaps three hundred residents, man, woman, and child, a sum that swells considerably on week-ends. At the heart of the triangle stands our newly-built cabin.

I have found great pleasure in exploring this plot's places, known and obscure, and then writing about them. Perhaps, reading these essays, you might share some of that pleasure with me. I would be happy, too, if this book encourages others to write about a tract of western land they prize; the West needs its known places and all too often suffers for their absence.

I wonder how many people have gone to the library to read about something on their local woods and found books about the Arctic, the tropics, the oceans and space, but nothing much about their local woods.

David Rains Wallace

November

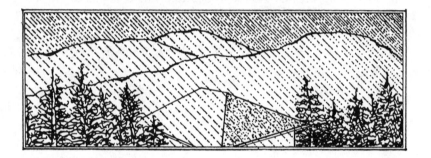

November

Created only in the last few decades, artificial satellites allow us to see the full expanse of the North Pacific, the source of our west coast winter storms. Beginning in earnest in October, over the ocean appear emphatic comma-shaped clouds, each with a tail descending from a tightly curled dot, the center of the storm, the low. Spinning counter-clock-wise, the two thousand mile spiral of moist air moves slowly east and south towards the California coast and us.

These winter storms have an awesome inevitability. Most of the year they lurk far to the north, but as the northern hemisphere cools in autumn, they slip further and further south. Usually in November the first of our winter storms comes ashore, not in British Columbia, not in Humboldt County, not at San Francisco Bay, but at Santa Barbara or even Ventura. As the huge roll of rain-heavy clouds hits the coast, the long tail of the beast slaps Los Angeles, Orange County, and finally at our corner of the country. The winter rains have arrived, in their slow series.

I hear rain dancing on the cabin roof, but I'm not surprised because I know it has been on its way for hours. The man says, "Rain has begun falling at Point Conception," and later, "Heavy rain is falling in downtown Los Angeles," and finally, "Northern San Diego County reports steady rain." The first great Pacific storm of the year is marching down the coast, rain drumming on roofs and avocado groves and roads and on the woods of North Peak.

We have holidays for everything in America, from National Secretary Day to National Wear a Hat Day, but I can't understand why we don't declare a National Rain Day, which people would celebrate with special enthusiasm in Southern California. Rain fell last in March, dust has accumulated for seven months, and only fog or rare clouds gave variety to an otherwise everblue sky. When the first rain hits why aren't people dancing in the streets? Why aren't people kissing each other in the downpour and saying, "At last! I thought it would never get here!" "Marvelous!" "Glorious!" "Let's have a holiday!"

The reason rain jubilation doesn't break out in Southern California, I think, is because most of us here don't really care about rain. We have arranged our lives so artfully, especially by utilizing our

3

automobiles to the fullest, that most of us hardly notice rain. I get up in the morning and see rain is falling. I reach my car through the garage door in the kitchen. I drive to work on streets shining black in the rain, never slowing down for a moment. After parking my car, I sprint to my workplace, wearing not a rain coat, but a light jacket. If the rain falls in a deluge, I put up an umbrella borrowed from my wife and dash across the parking lot. As to needing water in Southern California, it flows out of a pipe 365 days a year. We ignore the rain and live as we always do, blind to an annual miracle, the coming of life-giving moisture to a thirsty, dry, dusty land.

People who actually are aware of rain and its significance belong to two groups, it seems to me: those who watch rain because their livelihoods depend on it, or those who have a keen interest in nature, for reasons known only to themselves. The first group consists mostly of farmers and ranchers, the second of nature lovers. They may also be plumbers or presidents, playgirls, or podiatrists.

Born a city boy, I remember the first time I met a representative of the first group, those who watch rain because their livelihood depends on it, in a downpour. We rented an apartment in San Antonio from an elderly retired couple who once operated a small ranch in arid South Texas. When a torrential rain fell one afternoon, our landlady, unlike every woman I had ever known, did not take shelter. She put on a clean cotton dress and worked in her garden. Within minutes rain soaked her to the skin, her dress becoming as wet as any bathing suit. No matter, she puttered about the garden, placing pots and pans under spouts to collect rain water for her house plants. Rain streamed down her face, saturated her hair, soaked her red sneakers, but she ignored it all. From the porch where I had found shelter, I could hear her humming to herself over the pounding of the rain on the house's tin roof. This was surely a woman who knew the value and importance of rain, and perhaps its beauty.

I doubt if she loved rain as the living moist breath of the planet; no, rain made grass grow, filled stock ponds, and put meat on cattle. I knew cattle were dear to her heart, for on the mantel, where others might have shown family portraits, she and her husband displayed the statuette of a Hereford steer, standing foursquare. This animal had supported them in an unforgiving land, given them a good life, and helped raise their children. It deserved to be the family god.

As a former farm wife, for her nature played an everyday role, but not one us urban nature lovers might expect. Sitting with her one day on a backyard glider, I pointed out a caterpillar crawling up a hackberry. Quicker than I could say *Field Guide to Western Insects* she leaped to her feet and with a broad thumb squashed the interloper against the tree, its vital fluids splashing bright orange in every direction. After washing her hands at the garden hose she returned to the glider, having given me a vivid demonstration of how farmers tend to see insects, except bees, as the Enemy.

If the storm moves in during the day, I can watch its progress. Across the horizon from southwest to northeast stretches an advancing blanket of clouds, contrasting cleanly with the empty half of the sky where the sun still shines. The bruised purple edge of the clouds is ragged; above it scud dark wisps and wild cloud hair. The sunny half of the sky shrinks; the dark cloud blanket takes its place. When the clouds are overhead, rain drops spot the windows and tap on the roof. In a few minutes a cold rain that persists for hours or days is falling.

Sometimes, though, winter rain is warm because air from the South Pacific joins the northern storm; people say the pineapple express has flown in from Hawaii. Not common, this influx of warm wet air brings the season's heaviest rain. If it is warmer outside than in the house during a winter storm in San Diego, I expect rain to be heavy, unbroken, and loathe to depart. The air is so mild that no snow falls anywhere in the county, even on the summit of Cuyamaca Peak at six thousand feet, only incessant warm rain. On television they talk about the possibility of local flooding.

After the first storm in November has left us, I emerge from the cabin to see a sunny sky and to feel a fresh northwest breeze. The rain gauge indicates that something like two inches of rain fell, about average for an early storm. Oak leaves sparkle and drops are still pattering from the needles on the Coulter pines. Vegetation has taken on a darker and richer hue, after only an afternoon of rain. To the eye the ground is voluptuously dark with the texture of velour. When I walk on the woodland path the soil is resilient, giving way willingly under my feet. I see no mud and no rivulets and no gulleys near the lane; these will come later. Every drop that fell instantly soaked into soil that has known no rain for six months. Autumn earth is like a creature with open mouth eager for every drop of rain from the sky.

I am something of an expert on the texture of autumn soil in the

5

mountains. During the last few years I have planted a plenitude of daffodil bulbs and many fruit trees in the fall. This has required a crash course in soil characteristics; I have been compelled to be a fast learner. Daffodil bulbs are in the stores in September; for the first few years I eagerly purchased a hundred at a time and hastened to the mountains to plant them. Here I discovered I could not force a shovel into the autumn soil in spite of all my efforts. The shovel, even though I lay all my weight on it, would only skip across the earth. After some exertion I would succeed in digging a scrape only a few inches deep. In it the big plump King Alfred bulb would lie forlorn, half exposed, shamed. I would cover it with dry leaves and dry humus and hope. I was trying to plant bulbs in soil like plaster, the result of months of hot high summer sun and no rain to soften it and stir it to life.

I had a similar experience when I attempted to dig a hole to plant young fruit trees. I could not force the shovel into the ground and had to resort to the aid of a digging bar. It loosened the soil sufficiently so that I could remove it with a shovel, but this doubled the time and effort needed. When I hit rocks, and I always did, they held onto the dry flinty soil like they possessed invisible fingers. Grunting and groaning, I pried them from the hole, cursing the mountain and all its ways.

Oh, but what a difference after the rain came! Now a shovel slips sweetly into the soil, exposing damp fragrant humus. When I hit rocks they lift free from the damp soil as though they want to flee the earth to become stone walls or to form ranks alongside woodland paths. Ten minutes of mild effort deliver a hole big enough for an apple or even a cherry tree. When a neighbor asked for advice about planting daffodils (a native of coastal California, he did not know what to do with bulbs he'd never seen) I gave him advice acquired through bitter mountain experience: buy early, plant late.

As the winter progresses the soil becomes wetter and yet wetter. When I dig a hole, after piercing leaves and humus, I discover that the red sub-soil is saturated and has become a red soup, something resembling what the Russians call Moscow borsch. Digging a hole now becomes difficult because the soil is heavy, glistening with moisture. Springs begin to seep from cut banks, and in these places the earth slumps, too heavy with water to stand upright. The rain brook in the ravine runs high and all night. Seeing it, I can hardly believe that most of the year it is only a line of dry stones down the draw.

Then the final scene begins in this drama of the rain. The first delicate blades of grass emerge in the sunniest places, sprouting from seeds that have lain still and unchanging for six months. Is there anything more beautiful than fresh new blades of grass growing in rain-swollen soil? Simple in shape, like slender sails on canoes, richest green, greener than the greenest shamrocks, they declare in the simplest language: have no worry, the year of growth, of fresh vegetation, of animals plump and sleek and fecund has begun.

Birds Obscurely Understood

Just about any winter day when I drive along Engineers Road I surprise band-tailed pigeons feeding on acorns on the shoulders of the pavement. In flocks of four to thirty birds, lifting into the air with their wings flapping like window blinds, they quickly disappear; speed is their best friend in an emergency. They are gone before I get a good look at them, and so for me they remain a kind of mystery bird, poorly seen and poorly understood. It wasn't until I began to do a little reading about the ways of these birds that I discovered the experts don't understand them very well either.

I suspect when most city people see them in the Cuyamacas they assume they are domestic pigeons foraging from farms and ranches. They are about the same size and weight and certainly they are pigeon-colored. Because they are so skittish, they don't give travelers much time to see the identifying gray and black bands across their tails and the white crescent at the nape of the neck as they evaporate into the oaks.

Biologists report that the males are a little more brightly colored than the females. Furthermore, there are two races of bandtails, one resident in Utah and Colorado mountains, and a Pacific coast race nesting from British Columbia into Baja California. To add to the difficulty of understanding our birds, in addition to residents, we have migrants coming south from Oregon, Washington, and British Columbia to pass the winter in Southern California. The bandtail I flush from Engineers Road may be a snowbird from Vancouver Island or a native North Peak resident.

Their occurrence is hard to predict. Philip Unitt in his book on San Diego County birds says, "Resident in the sense that the species is present through the year, but subject to irregular movements or migrations which are still obscurely understood." Migrants are no less elusive. Another expert on the birds, Robert G. Jeffrey, says that "Bandtails are very adaptable to changing food conditions, a trait that contributes to their being characterized as erratic."

Once when walking in the woods in early spring I surprised a pair of bandtails fluttering in a Kellogg oak. Apparently busy building a nest in one of its lower branches, they fled as I came closer. My curiosity aroused, I read at home that they do in fact begin nesting as

8

early as March. After building a crude twiggy nest, the female lays a single white egg, rarely two. Later she repeats the process, but no one seems to know precisely how many broods the pair raises each year. At first I assumed this was another of their surprising eccentricities–after all, why not have one large brood, getting it all over, like many of us humans.

I discovered, however, there is a principle explaining this seeming eccentricity. If a species of birds enjoys a long summer with a reliable food supply, then the bird is inclined to have a series of small broods, like bandtails, but if the season is short, a species will have one large brood, going for broke, so to speak. In the bandtails' habit of raising several small broods there is a kind of avian family planning, guaranteeing that they need raise only a single nestling at a time with adequate food and generous care from both parents.

Bandtails have another puzzling habit: they congregate at mineral springs. Jeffreys, in his work on bandtails, lists seventeen mineral springs in three western states where the birds collect in large numbers. Hunters are well aware of this habit, and to protect the pigeons Jeffreys recommended that the states purchase the springs to protect the birds; he made the recommendation in 1977 and I don't know if any action was taken. It seems the birds crave some unidentified mineral that plays a part in their digestive processes. Along the coast, they congregate to drink sea water for the same purpose.

Bandtails have long been game birds in California. In the nineteenth century sportsmen found a challenge hunting them at springs and in grain fields where they gather in large numbers. However, conservationists became convinced the species was in danger, particularly because of market hunters. There was the awful example of passenger pigeons, once incredibly numerous, whose last representative was shot in the wild in 1899. In the winter of 1911-1912 one market hunter in Santa Barbara shipped two thousand bandtails to markets in Los Angeles and San Francisco.

As the result of this well-publicized event, in 1913 government officials removed bandtails from the list of California game-birds. The closed season continued until 1932. However, game wardens often had to drive the birds away from cultivated fields and orchards, especially in mid-winter when wild crops of buds and berries were in abeyance. At present, the season is nine days long and split: in far northern California counties hunters pursue the birds in September

9

and in the rest of the state they take to the fields and woods in quest of bandtails in December. The limit is two birds per day. The seasons are late so hunters do not kill parent birds still rearing young.

Band-tail pigeons sometimes come to feeders my neighbors maintain. Here they have the reputation for taking over, driving smaller and more timid birds away shamelessly. Perhaps some day I might set up a feeding station myself and then perhaps I'll get a good look at bandtails. In the meantime I find consolation for my inability to observe them closely by reminding myself that even the experts say their movements are "obscurely understood" and "erratic."

If I had any doubts about their restlessness, they ended when I read that in September of 1973 observers saw one of these fidgety birds on Sugarloaf Key, Florida, by anyone's standards a very long way from its little gray home in the west.

Battle in View

In 1906 the American philosopher William James taught at Stanford University. This was his introduction to California and he did not like what he saw. James, who had divided his life between the eastern United States and Europe, wrote to a friend: "...the social insipidity is great here and the historic vacuum and silence appalling."

James wrote what many visitors have noted about California, that it lacks history to lend life depth and resonance. It's difficult to argue with this attitude. The Eastern U. S. has its Colonial and Revolutionary history, and the South and the Border States their Civil War battles. These are hard to match in California. But some of us have been favored by history. We, for example, seated in comfortable chairs on the deck of our mountain cabin with the help of binoculars can see the site of a historic battle, the Battle of San Pasqual, on the north slopes of Starvation Mountain. How many people in the older parts of the country can see a battlefield without leaving their homes?

Nearly 150 years ago, on December 5, 1846, if we had been sitting on our deck we could have seen a party of about two hundred armed men arriving at the Stokes ranch on Ramona's northern edge. If we had extremely good vision we could see that they wore two kinds of uniforms: a larger group were U. S. Dragoons, under the command of General Stephen Watts Kearny. Riding emaciated and exhausted mules and horses, they were trail-worn themselves; they had just completed a seventy day march from Santa Fe, New Mexico, to Warner's Ranch. At Ballena near Highway 78, Marine Lt. Archibald Gillespie with twelve sailors and some volunteers had joined them, after marching up from San Diego. Kearny commanded this very small army.

After spending the night at the Stokes Ranch, Kearny decided to attack a party of armed Californios whom scouts had seen at the Indian village of San Pasqual, a few miles to the northwest. This was the first of several mistakes which Kearny made in the next few days; first of all, the battle should never have been fought because Kearny's men were bone-tired after their long march.

At 2:30 a.m. on December 6, 1846, in total darkness (another mistake) Kearny led his troops into terrain that the enemy knew

11

well. From our deck we could have seen the American troops file out of Santa Maria Valley down toward the floor of San Pasqual Valley. In spite of their fatigue, Kearny insisted that his men lead the attack.

The Californios under Andres Pico who waited for them at San Pasqual were not organized troops at all. They were ranchers who had spent much of their lives in the saddle and they carried long lances ideally suited for cavalry attacks. Today, I suppose, we might call them guerrilla fighters. Given the way the battle was shaping up–horse combat on a plain well-known to the Californios, in darkness–they were battle ready.

When the Americans reached the valley floor, a misunderstanding had grave consequences. General Kearny gave the command "Trot!" Since his troops were already dispersed, some of the dragoons heard this as "Charge!" and surged ahead. One of the ironies of this (and perhaps most battles) is that the soldiers who charged first into battle took the heaviest losses; it was the boldest who died. The battle soon disintegrated into a series of broken combats across the flats near the stream. The Californio horsemen found the situation ideal because they could maneuver at their own discretion.

Pico, who by now could see more American troops filing down the ridge into the valley, knew he was outnumbered. He collected his forces and retreated to the west out of the valley. Later, when the battle was re-fought in official circles, Kearny claimed that this signified that his forces had won the Battle of San Pasqual.

But judging from the casualties, the Californios could claim victory. Twenty one Americans died, most of them run through by Californio lances. Fifteen more men were wounded. The Californios left no dead on the battlefield; no one knows if they had any wounded, but it seems likely.

From our deck we could have seen Pico and the Californios, having passed the entrance to the Wild Animal Park, retreat rapidly toward Escondido and Rancho Bernardo. The Americans paused to bury their dead, covering the grave sites with rocks to discourage coyotes. Eventually, the remains were removed to the cemetery at Point Loma and buried under a stone from San Pasqual inscribed "They Fought a Good Fight." Later that day from our deck we could have seen the shattered American troops slowly follow the Californios out of San Pasqual Valley, fearing the enemy might counterattack any time.

12

That night they lay over on Mule Hill, a rocky knoll on the shore of Lake Hodges; we couldn't see them because Starvation Mountain (elevation 2140 feet) screens our view. A few days later a party from San Diego rescued them from their precarious perch. Although they had to kill and eat some of their mules, all the survivors made their way to the town without loss of life.

So ended the Battle of San Pasqual, the largest skirmish in the Mexican-American war north of Mexico. To me it seems a battle that should not have been fought, and certainly not under the conditions that existed on the early morning of December 6, 1846. It remains a shadow on the career of Stephen Watts Kearny to this day.

Not much of a battle, you might think. But let me point out that while the bloodshed was small, it was much greater than at a battle to which historians have devoted great attention. According to Thoreau, in the Battle of Concord there were "Two killed on the patriots' side, and Luther Blanchard wounded!" At our battle the casualties were much more numerous.

I leave only one question for researchers to decide: could Thoreau see the site of the Battle of Concord from his house at Walden Pond? We have our history, too, and the historic silence is not always so appalling, at least for those of us who live high on North Peak.

Three Long Mountains

Every year after New Year's Day I make a pilgrimage to the Cabrillo Monument high on Point Loma at the entrance to San Diego Bay. I choose the day carefully: it has to be after a rain when the air is as clear as it ever is on the Pacific coast and my view is unlimited in every direction.

After I leave my car near the monument, I turn to the west to watch for spouts of gray whales migrating south to their calving grounds. A puff of spray blossoms every few minutes–a whale coming up for air; sometimes a black forty-foot shape emerges from the water and then sinks out of sight. I'm reassured to know California gray whales are returning in numbers from near extinction.

But after getting my fill of the annual whale spectacle, I take a deep breath and survey the horizon. South, the Coronado Islands rise bleak out of the sea off the Baja coast. West, beyond the spouting whales the Pacific Ocean stretches to Japan. North lies the broad back of San Clemente Island and the lesser rise of Santa Catalina. Northeast stretch distant chains of snow covered mountains–San Antonio, San Gorgonio, San Jacinto, and lesser peaks ringing the Los Angeles basin. Closer, Palomar Mountain straddles northern San Diego County. And to the east lie the silhouettes of three long mountains that make up the Cuyamaca range. For all the world they look like the whales behind my back–three great mountain whales swimming south toward the warm waters of Scammons Lagoon.

The leader is the most imposing, with a perceptible hump, reaching a summit at 6,512 feet where stands an abandoned fire watch tower. This is Cuyamaca Peak. In its wake follows Middle Peak, more modest in aspiration, its rounded crest swathed in a rumpled carpet of Jeffrey pine, western cedar, and sugar pine. The hindmost is North Peak, at nearly six thousand feet altitude, also wooded. Its summit displays a crown of electronic towers and gadgetry.

South to north the range stretches about fifteen miles. The three peaks sit slightly at an angle to the southeast-northwest trend in the coastline and the other ridges of the Peninsular Range. This declares that it was not a northwest trending fault that adjusted the spine of the range, but that rain and snow and wind in their working molded it. A respectable western mountain range, comparable to the

14

Mohawks or the Henry Mountains, the Cuyamacas can't compete in heft with the Sierras or the Rockies, but still they rise more than a mile above salt water less than an hour's drive away. If Cuyamaca Peak was in New Hampshire, its summit would rise two hundred feet higher than Mt. Washington, and people would write poems about it.

When I look at the Cuyamacas I see that nearly the entire range, where vegetation does not mask it, is composed of a dense dark stone. This dark stone was once molten rock welling up from deep below the earth's surface in the unstable zone where two massive plates–the North American plate and the Pacific plate–collide. This molten rock rose into the earth's crust, but never reached the surface. Geologists call this dark igneous rock Cuyamaca gabbro.

This finely crystalline, shining, nearly coal-black rock is extremely hard, as anyone knows who has tried to drill a hole in it, as the Builder has, or to smash an outcrop of it that threatened the oil-pans of passing cars, as I have. Slow to weather, its exposed surface eventually turns a dull red as the iron in the gabbro oxidizes, producing the characteristic red soil underlying the woodland's humus. The gabbro's toughness and durability have preserved it when lesser rock has failed.

When I look more closely at the range I can see another rock, brown, perhaps, and apparently stratified, but its layers tilted and turned. In places they whirl in arabesques so the rock resembles old-fashioned taffy. This rock I can see across the lower reaches of North Peak and in the hills further to the north, but also in fragments elsewhere. If I had the inclination to fly over the range I could see that this undistinguished rock sweeps further north and east of the range in a broad horseshoe, forming an outcrop nearly a mile wide and about twelve miles long. Always it rests directly on the Cuyamaca gabbro and other igneous rocks that constitute the core of the range; no other stratum rests on this brown rock's surface anywhere. What I see is a quite different rock formation, perhaps the oldest formation in San Diego County. This is the famous Julian schist. It is famous because it is the source of nearly all the gold which has been dug from the Cuyamacas in the last 130 years.

Geologists conclude that the Julian schist was once sands, silts, and, rarely, small lava flows, but heat and pressure have so altered these deposits that it is difficult to discern the original stratification. What's more, faulting and uplift have often tilted the horizontal sands and muds into a nearly vertical position. Consequently, while the deposits were firstly sedimentary, geologists feel entitled to classify this formation as metamorphic—sands and muds altered into schist and its more flamboyant relative, gneiss.

While geologists agree that Julian schist is mostly a sedimentary rock metamorphosed by heat and pressure, they disagree on the question as to when these sand and silt strata first flowed across a quiet inland plain. In 1951 Donald L. Everhart listed the time periods to which the Julian schist had been assigned as Lower Triassic (?), Carboniferous, Triassic, Juratriassic, "possibly several ages" in the Paleozoic and Triassic, "most likely" late Paleozoic and Triassic and "probably late Paleozoic extending into the Triassic." Today geologists sometimes give the period of its origin as "Jurassic (?)." A recent publication, *Geology of San Diego County*, by Harold J. Clifford, et al, dates the schist cum gneiss to the Triassic, designating it the San Diego variant of the Bedford Canyon formation from the Santa Ana Mountains.

There exists only one clouded record of a fossil find in the Julian schist, although apparently paleontologists have found fossils in the Bedford Canyon formation, according to Clifford (p. 50). Writing in 1922, F. S. Hudson recounts that:

> A fossil was found by Mr. D. D. Bailey of Julian in the small area of metamorphic rock that lies in the granite about a mile southeast of Banner. This was submitted by Mr. H. L. Huston of San Francisco to Dr. J. P. Smith, who pronounced it "a slender ammonite that is without much doubt Triassic."
>
> The fossil is an imprint of an ammonite on the surface of an angular pebble of dark gray, quartzitic rock. It was found as float. The writer in company with Mr. Bailey visited the locality where this was found... Several hours' search was not rewarded by the finding of any fossils, but considerable rock similar in appearance to the matrix of the fossil specimen was seen.

F. S. Hudson's ammonite has since been lost. In the subsequent seventy years geologists have searched fruitlessly for fossils in the Julian schist. To succeed, while it would not compare in importance to finding the lost remains of Peking Man, it would certainly guarantee fame for the finder in the annals of Southern California geology.

Of course, the reason that no one has found any fossils in the

16

schist, excluding Hudson's (assuming that it existed), is that time and conditions in the earth so drastically altered its rock. Another factor which complicates the dating of the Julian schist is that only the igneous mass underlies it and nothing remains of the strata which must have lain above it. These younger rocks wore down and their by-products disappeared into the Pacific Ocean. The Julian schist remains, so to speak, a lithic orphan, both its predecessors and followers wiped from the face of the earth.

Long after the Julian schist was deposited and uncounted strata, now lost, accumulated above it, the next major event in the history of the Cuyamaca mountains began. In the Mesozoic era 160 million years ago molten magma rose from deep in the earth toward the surface in an area stretching from near Oregon to Baja California. This immense reservoir of molten rock formed two separate pools, the Sierra batholith (the name for such a feature) and the Southern California batholith. Of the latter, the Cuyamaca pluton (a small distinct section of a batholith) was only a part. The most casual eye can see granitic rock over much of San Diego county—this is rock from the Southern California batholith. The mass welled upward in an uneven fashion, more rapidly in some places than in others, but one thing is certain: this molten rock never reached the earth's surface. Because it was so heavily insulated by the sedimentary rock above it, the batholith cooled slowly. The magma had ample time to crystalize, giving it the typical grainy texture of igneous rock.

The Cuyamaca pluton rose in at least two waves with different chemical compositions. The first surge became Stonewall granodiorite, the second Cuyamaca gabbro. The distinction between the two was heightened by the fact that the advancing pluton enveloped differing strata as it moved upward. Such differentiation is typical for all the rocks in the batholith.

Today's geological record shows that the pluton reached the much older Julian schist; no one can say what strata it absorbed before it touched the schist. But touch the Julian schist it did, much altering its rock. You can see the contact zone where they meet at many sites in the mountains, especially at road cuts. But it would be wrong to think of this contact as a neat orderly line drawn across the countryside. The contact is very irregular, with blocks of the schist falling into the magma and magma surging into the schist. So confused is this contact in places that geologists sometimes refer to this area as a "mixed zone," tacitly admitting that is impossible to assign it to either the schist or the batholith's igneous rock.

In the last stage of its cooling, upwards through the magma rose super-heated water and gases holding in solution elements such as silica and precious metals. This water and gases filtered through faults or fractures in the magma, cooling as it advanced, and left in dikes and veins solid minerals, to the delight of miners, for gold was sometimes a component of these super-heated waters.

A principle the Cuyamaca prospectors understood very well was that if they wanted to find gold they searched the broken and cracked schist encircling the north end of the range. Of course, the schist sometimes appeared in isolated remnants in otherwise barren rock. For example, the Stonewall mine, richest by far in the district, is located on a lobe of schist far from the mines around Julian. Prospectors even found color in isolated sites on the west and south of the range, so unpredictable are the occurrences of the fragmented auriferous Julian schist. The most remote of these is at Boulder Creek below and west of Cuyamaca Peak. From Point Loma I can see the location of these forgotten mines, all abandoned today, but once holding high hopes for their developers at the turn of the century.

Probably another reason miners made their richest strikes (aside from the Stonewall Mine) on the northern skirts of the range was because this is where numerous faults run northwest through the Julian district, the most prominent being the Elsinore fault in Banner grade, and the Chariot Canyon fault. This zone must be ancient, for the faults appear to have served as highways along which the gold-bearing vapors rose towards the surface. The central block of the Cuyamacas, particularly where gabbro dominates, is almost fault-free and therefore miners found no wealth in this district.

Mineralization occurred below the surface of the earth under huge pressures; no one today can say with certainty what lay above the pluton, but crowning it were apparently many thick layers of sedimentary rock, including what became the Julian schist. These sediments formed a featureless plain without a hint of the slowly cooling igneous mass buried deep below it. Evidence for the existence of this ancient sedimentary plain is the curious table lands still apparent east of the Cuyamaca summits, such as the Cuyamaca reservoir site, East Mesa, and the sandy flats in the Laguna mountains.

The up-welling of the two great batholiths–Sierran and Southern

California–would eventually transform the landscape as we know it today in those two regions, although they were as yet below the surface of the earth. Events of the later Pleistocene epoch–a second major event in the history of the mountains–also altered the face of the land, but in a very different way. During this epoch in the earth's history faulting and uplift commenced in central and southern California and northern Baja. This resulted in the emergence of long massive tilted mountain blocks tending to rise from west to east. At their eastern edges the blocks terminated in great faults still existing today. Yet further east, wedges of the earth's crust dropped as the western blocks rose. As a result a block of land rose as the Sierra Nevada, low to the west, ending with a dramatic eastern escarpment at the Owens Valley Fault, followed by the deep trench of the Owens Valley itself.

In the San Diego back country the same process occurred at the same time but on a much smaller scale. The broad plain which dominated the country was heaved upward, less in the west and more in the east. At a line parallel and west of the great San Andreas fault zone the block reached its maximum height along a line marked roughly by today's Sunrise highway. To the east the land fell away to create the depression whose lowest point is the Salton Sea, the equivalent of the Owens Valley in the north.

This great uplift had a powerful effect on the rocks of the district. Higher elevation and steeper slope accelerated erosion and the many layers of sedimentary rock overlying the Cuyamaca pluton began to wear away, their sands and silts gone to the west. Eventually this accelerated erosion revealed the now cold igneous rocks of the pluton. Stonewall granodiorite, Bonsall tonalite, Rattlesnake granite, and Cuyamaca gabbro emerged into the light.

With them appeared the broken necklace of the Julian schist draped over the northern shoulders of the mountains. When I look today at a gabbro boulder lying near our driveway I pause to contemplate its history. More than a hundred million years ago it was a measure of molten super-heated magma originating at the edge of the Pacific plate abutting the North American plate. It rose as part of a molten mass through the country rock until it contacted the oldest sedimentary rocks, including the ancestor of the Julian schist. For a million years it cooled unseen under the earth. Then the Pleistocene mountain building hoisted it thousands of feet. Millions of years of

19

erosion followed until this broken boulder was finally exposed to the afternoon's sun. I hold it in my hand and admire its sparkling black crystals.

There is a significant difference between the Cuyamaca montane block and the much larger Sierra uplift: even the casual observer sees that the highest summits of the Sierra stand at the eastern brink of the block, and so the hiker on Mt. Whitney peers dizzily down on the sagebrush of the Owens Valley. Erosion on the Sierra block has been regular and even, for the most part. But in the San Diego mountains the pluton cooled into a variety of igneous rocks with differing grains and temperaments, the densest being black gabbro. As the block eroded, the gabbro stoutly resisted the elements while the other rocks surrendered more tranquilly to the demands of rain, wind, snow, and ice. Consequently, the three hard gabbro peaks stand much higher than the eastern lip of the block, the Laguna mountains. They stretch in their thin line well to the west of the faults that cut the block's eastern edge.

No doubt this is why they catch my eye, three long whale-like mountains silhouetted as the highest points on the horizon east of San Diego and its crowded coastal plain.

December

December

Should I drive to the mountains today? I had a few chores to do at the cabin and perhaps this was the time to finish them off. But still, the weather looked uncertain, and I'd better check the newspaper: "A ridge of high pressure over the western U. S. will keep the weather fair throughout the region today." For the mountains the forecast was even more encouraging: " Skies will be sunny with a few high clouds today."

My irresolution ended, I decided a trip to the mountains it would be. But as I left the city I still had some misgivings about the weather because I could not see the mountains at all, thanks to a heavy bank of clouds that extended almost into the lowlands. When rain began to fall as I drew closer to the Cuyamacas I knew that someone at the weather bureau had miscalculated. If the meteorologist had looked out the window instead of relying on Dopplers and computers and faxes from Los Angeles he might have seen rain falling twenty miles from the city.

As I mounted to the four thousand foot level the rain turned to snow, plain flakes that whipped and soared in the mountain wind. Once or twice the truck's wheels whipped and soared a little too, when they sought purchase on snow-covered ice on the road. By the time I saw the cabin there was three inches of snow everywhere, even plastered on trees and boulders as the ceaseless mountain wind carried everything before it.

This was the first snow of the year and I was at the cabin to see it. If I'd thought the weather would be so unsettled I would have never left the city. The dog shared my enthusiasm, seemingly infected by the same elan the falling snow gave me. A native Californian, she had never seen snow, and casting off her middle-age inhibitions, she reverted to childhood ways. Running wildly, she slid on her belly over the snow-covered ground, or she spun like a big shaggy rug in the middle of the road, or she bit off mouthfuls of shallow snow and threw them into the air, huffing and puffing, her breath streaming into the universal grayness. Now and then she would dart into the woods, shaking snow off the shrubs and trees. It merged with the flakes falling from the sky, adding to the general confusion.

I hadn't seen snow falling for years. I'd forgotten how exciting it is to see flakes spinning and twirling and flying parallel with the ground against a dark background of pines and gray sky, all to the wind's roar. I'd forgotten how brilliantly white new snow covers the ground, its brilliance reflecting the light from a hidden sky. I understood why the Russians describe a snowfall as the Virgin's Robe, covering everything equivocal with its blinding whiteness. Snow brought a new world with its own light and the ceaseless spin of whirling snowflakes. How beautiful it was! It made me so excited that I wouldn't go indoors to my chores, but instead go for a walk up the lane, scuffling through three inches of heavenly purity on the muddy road.

Snow was still falling, or rather I should say, swirling, for the wind blew briskly, and the flakes went in every direction. The air was mild—the thermometer showed 35 degrees at the cabin—even my sneakered feet were warm. But this was not the day for a long trek, just a winter stroll to savor a rare sight for a Southern Californian, a snowstorm, and the first of the season, at that!

The lane stretched ahead, uniformly white, lined with oaks and pines holding scraps of ermine. Kellogg oaks had long ago lost their leaves and stood up stoutly to the storm. Their wood is brittle, but it's not winter snow that breaks off the branches; it's the spring snow that catches the trees half-dressed and brings shattered branches and wilted leaves to the ground. Small tough leaves on the few live oaks at this altitude each held a few flakes of snow, with more arriving.

Only one tree looked as though it belonged in the north woods and snowdrifts and biting cold. A solitary white fir couched in a damp north-facing hollow, the lowest representative of its kind on the mountain that I know of, held all the falling snow that reached it, so that with snow on every branch it looked as though someone had decorated it for the holiday season. White fir grows all over the west under much sterner conditions than this and for my tree a Southern California snowstorm presented no challenge at all. Its stiff branches could support a huge burden of snow, which, if it grew too heavy, the tree would simply shrug off.

Alongside the road, grasses showed straw yellow, leaving Edward Weston streaks in the snow when the wind blew them in circles. Chaparral sages displayed pleasing combinations of gray with snow-white trim. Red rose hips, now very plump, making me realize how they got their name, each held a dollop of fresh snow, but I think the wind would blow them off sooner than later. Still the snow fell, dashing and turning and skipping along the ground, emerging from a cardboard sky.

On the way back, when the dog was exhausted from many forays into the roadside brush, I saw I wasn't the only walker in the snow. Observing small neat prints, slightly bigger than a cat's, but with claw marks, I didn't have to be told that these were the tracks of a gray fox; I'd heard its cough several times late at night and its scat was common enough along the lane, since it chooses this conspicuous site to mark its territory. If this was not enough, one of my neighbors had photographed the fox early one morning when it stood fearless outside the window of his house.

Gray foxes have a knack for living with human beings. Mostly vegetarian, they rarely bother domestic animals, unlike coyotes which have a fondness for devouring house cats, as angry San Diego suburbanites can testify. Not requiring much living space, they rear their young in vacant lots in San Diego. I've seen kits playing on sidewalks under street lights.

They maintain a low profile, even in busy neighborhoods. For every hundred people who instantly recognize a coyote's howl, I doubt there are five who can identify the night time cough of foxes, which may be locally as common as coyotes. Perhaps this is true because coyotes chorus at sun-up and sun-down when people are usually about, but foxes sound a solitary call in the smallest hours. Also, a fox's hack cannot compare with the eerie resonance of coyote howling, and so escapes notice.

Foxes are beautiful animals. Once, on the fringes of the city, taking a short cut across a vacant lot in daylight hours, I confronted a large gray fox. After I, and he, recovered from the shock, he retreated fifty feet and turned to inspect me, as I did him. As large as a coyote or a small German shepherd, he sported a sweeping black-tipped tail (so he was no coyote). The unusual color of his pelt impressed me, a distinctive blend of wolf gray and vulpine red. Admiring him as he stood, I recalled that I knew that pelt. When I was a child I had seen it on stylish women, worn over the shoulders and held against the face.

This was a memory from the 1930s, when wearing fox fur was fashionable. Today, I understand, once more there is a market for

25

gray fox fur. This is regrettable. Any animal as beautiful as a gray fox should be allowed to wear its own fur.

For some reason, dogs nearly ignore foxes. Even now, my dog showed no interest in following the fox's trail, although its spoor was fresh. I've observed that when city foxes call at night, she and other neighborhood dogs never respond, unlike the frantic alarm they raise when cats yowl nearby, to say nothing of their ferocious response to the cries of coyotes.

The day after my walk in the snowy woods, I glanced in the newspaper to see where the weather bureau had gone wrong. The day forecasters predicted fair weather, .72 inches of rain fell in San Diego, something like 7% of the city's annual rainfall, while snow fell in the Cuyamacas. The newspaper quoted the weatherman's *mea culpa*: "We were watching this low and all of a sudden it really intensified. The tropical flow from the southwest got caught up in it and bang! Here it is. It just went nuts." These are his words, as reported in the *Union*.

I thought that if this had been the Soviet Union under Stalin the forecaster, in spite of his disarming manner, would have been packed off to a concentration camp as an enemy of the people, a wrecker, and an agent of Foreign Imperialism, but that's not the way we do things here. Let's give him another chance. An occasional glance out the windows towards the Cuyamacas during unsettled weather might be advisable, however.

Not that I bear the man any ill will. Because he predicted fair weather I went to the mountains. Because the season's first snowfall was so enticing I succumbed to its song, excused myself from my chores, and had a glorious walk down the lane in new snow. All in all, it was a very successful December day in the mountains.

Why the Road Goes Thisaway
and Not Thataway

On my frequent drives northward from Descanso on Highway 79 as I passed through Cuyamaca Rancho State Park across the Sweetwater River bridge, I would ask myself: why at this point doesn't the highway continue north up the obvious route through upper Green Valley? Why does it turn to the northwest and follow Cold Stream toward Paso Picacho Campground and Cuyamaca Lake?

If you pause on the bridge you can see that if the road took the Sweetwater route it could proceed in a straight line northeast up an open sunny valley dotted with pines. After crossing a rise it would reach the point where the Cima Conservation Camp road joins today's Sunset Highway and then through rolling meadows east of the lake and so on to Julian. This route is direct, sunny, has a moderate grade, and is shorter than the existing route. This country I know from our hikes with the children years ago, from Harper Canyon to Soapstone Grade, with a wary eye on the Conservation Camp.

On the other hand, Highway 79 as it exists today stays within the shadow of Cuyamaca Peak, has a rather steep climb alongside Cold Stream (better put your truck in third gear) and two hairpin curves marked 15 MPH (put it in second gear or the engine will labor) and so over the rise at Paso Picacho. Also, you must navigate several awkward curves as you drop towards the lake. Unfortunately, this route is often heavily shaded so that ice and snow linger here long; county crews must be prompt to plow the road after a winter storm and sand the icy highway to make it safe. The Sweetwater route seems to have every advantage over the Cold Stream route the highway follows today. Why was it chosen?

A few years ago in reading the *Memoirs* of Ed Fletcher, paragon of the backcountry developers, I came upon the solution to this mystery that had puzzled me for so long. It's an interesting story, I think, and an instructive example of how a man with the right political ties can have his way, with consequences for us even today.

As Fletcher tells it, some time after 1908 when the county had begun an ambitious road building program, the county supervisors appointed a gold medal highway commission; perhaps "gold metal" would be more accurate, for it consisted of probably the wealthiest

27

and most powerful men in the country, John Spreckels (heir to a sugar fortune), E. W. Scripps (publishing), and A. G. Spalding (sporting goods). Following the recommendation of their engineering staff, the commissioners, busy laying out new roads in the county, decided that the Descanso-Julian highway would follow the obvious Sweetwater route through today's park, still my choice today.

But the commissioners had not reckoned on the influence of Ed Fletcher, who for good reasons wanted the highway to go directly to the dam at Cuyamaca, which Fletcher, with mostly Other People's Money, had purchased in 1910. His Cuyamaca Water Co. also owned large tracts of land surrounding the lake. The Cold Stream route he advocated would provide direct access to the lake and the company property around it.

Fletcher had good friends among the county supervisors, particularly Joe Foster, the chairman, who was one of Fletcher's warmest admirers. What's more, as incentives to shift the route to Cold Stream, Fletcher offered to to have his own engineer lay out the alternate route and to donate the right of way through the lands of the Cuyamaca Water Co. free to the county for the construction of the highway. In accordance with Fletcher's request, and accepting his incentives, the supervisors voted, as they were fully empowered to do, to over-ride their highway commission's projected Sweetwater route. They ordered that the Descanso-Julian highway be built up Cold Stream. By the way, this was long before anyone had even thought about the creation of a state park in this region

As Fletcher says in his *Memoirs*, consciously or unconsciously employing a roadway figure of speech: "Spreckels, Scripps, and Spalding had to back up" and accede to the Supervisors' instructions. Following in his way of thinking, I see that I wrote that the Supervisors "over-rode" their highway commission's decision. But whatever the language one thing is clear: now I know why Highway 79 goes thisaway and not thataway through the park.

There's an ironic footnote to this story of influence and power exercised. In 1919 Spreckels, Scripps, and Spalding resigned from the highway commission and the supervisors appointed three new members. They were Ed Fletcher, his good friend, Frank White, and Sherwood Wheaton. Never again would Ed Fletcher lock horns with the highway commission, because with the assured vote of his friend, White, he *was* the commission. We don't know how the three

28

previous members reacted to Fletcher's capture of the commission, but this makes it easier to understand why John Spreckels had such an intense dislike for Fletcher, which the latter, to his credit, did not reciprocate.

Rain and Snow, Sun and Clouds

When I began to search reference books in preparation for writing about the climate of North Peak, I realized I had a problem on my hands: because of its sparse population there is no weather station on the mountain and so I had no weather records I could scrutinize. But fortunately there are two nearby stations with many years of accumulated weather records, which, with adjustments, I could use. These are at Cuyamaca dam in the gap between Middle Peak and North Peak, and at Wynola in the apple growing district below Julian. Cuyamaca dam is about three miles southeast from the cabin and Wynola is about five miles north.

The cabin perches on the cismontane slope of North Peak at an elevation of about 4250 feet above the sea, or about half way between Cuyamaca's 4650 feet and Wynola's 3655 foot altitude. Now, if I take the average between the data from the Cuyamaca and Wynola stations, the results provide a fairly accurate picture of the climate on a west-facing slope thirty five miles from the Pacific Ocean and about four thousand feet above it at the 33rd parallel. This latitude, by the way, is much further south than most people think. If I were to make a trip around the world tracing the 33rd latitude eastward, I would pass through Atlanta; Casablanca, in North Africa, with Europe far to the north; Beirut; Baghdad; Lahore, in northern India; Shanghai in southern China; and the Japanese city of Nagasaki.

These calculations tell me that the slope receives about thirty inches of precipitation every year, three times more than the beach towns; the rise in elevation above the sea adds twenty inches of precipitation to the average at salt water. This four thousand foot lift is the equivalent of about five hundred miles of northern latitude; if I want to find similar rainfall at sea level I must travel to Santa Cruz or Santa Rosa, both of which also have about thirty inches of rain annually.

Statistics also show that North Peak, like all of Southern California, has a pronounced winter precipitation maximum, with twenty seven inches falling between November 1 and June 1, but only three inches of rain in the five summer months. This has important consequences for the plants of the region because they must survive a dry season persisting almost half the year; what's more, these are the hottest months. The two contrasting seasons also determine, in a large way, the life histories of the animals in the region.

With the Cuyamaca and Wynola statistics in hand, we can see that the rainiest month is February, with about five inches of precipitation; the driest is June with less than a quarter inch of rain. The remaining summer months have only a little more, about a half an inch on the average. Some winter precipitation falls as snow, something less than twenty four inches a year, in fact. It does not persist on the ground for more than a week or two. A foot of snow at the cabin is a very unusual sight, eliciting cries of disbelief from residents and visitors alike.

Winter rains with occasional snow sweeping off the Pacific deliver impressive amounts of precipitation. The *San Diego Union* tells us that onto Julian in the first seventeen days of 1993 fell twenty two inches of rain. Rumor has it that five feet of rain fell near our cabin that winter.

These pulses of rain from the Pacific commence in late autumn and continue for seven or eight months, delivering nearly all the moisture which supports life in the mountains. Summer rain falls as rare thunderstorms heavy with noise and flash but little moisture; rain always seems to be falling somewhere else. However, at times summer rain is overwhelming: about every fifteen or twenty years a tropical storm advancing up the warm waters of the Gulf of California collides with the Peninsular Range, of which the Cuyamaca mountains are a part. The six thousand foot rise chills the saturated air so that staggering amounts of rain fall, more than any single winter storm and in a much shorter time. For example, at Campo in southern San Diego County on August 12, 1891, 11.5 inches of rain fell in eighty minutes, a national record for a brief storm.

In the summer of 1976 tropical storm Kathleen swept up the Gulf, her floods annihilating stretches of the San Diego and Arizona Eastern Railroad line in Carrizo gorge and severing Interstate 8 in many places; twenty years later the railroad line has not yet been restored because the damage was so extensive. The same storm brought 3.9 inches of rain to the Laguna mountains on July 27, 1976. That year we often hiked the trails of Cuyamaca Rancho State Park, and we were astonished to see how Kathleen had transformed fire roads into gulleys six to ten feet deep, impassable to vehicles and offering puzzling obstacles to horsemen and hikers alike.

Because they are so rare, a mountain resident might see only a few of these titanic storms during his lifetime. Probably I will never have the opportunity to watch a tropical storm dropping its enormous burden of moisture onto the Cuyamacas, but I once had the opportunity to see what even a small summer rain does to the woodlands. After a brief intense summer storm I wandered along the shaded trails near the cabin. Because they were so compressed and eroded by the passage of human and animal feet, these trails collected the rainwater flowing down the slopes, providing channels for freshets, sweeping all the leaves and twigs from their way. Now the paths were hard and bare roadways through the hills. Even more remarkable were the slopes that held a deep mantle of leaves and mold under a heavy canopy of pine and oak. Here the downpour fell so intensely that it lifted the uppermost layers of humus with its dry leaves and pulled them a foot or so down the slope. A giant hand had swept the trails bare and that same hand seized the carpet of humus and leaves and dragged it downhill, piling it against trees and rocks like a rug against the legs of a dining room table.

Annual temperature swings accompanying the wet-dry cycle give the mountains perceptible seasons, but seasons which would seem moderate to a snowbound citizen of Minnesota or an air-conditioned Miami resident. The coldest inferred temperature on the mountain is three degrees above zero and the warmest is 103 degrees. July, the hottest month, has a mean temperature of 70 degrees. The coldest month, January, has a mean temperature of 41 degrees. I can compare these figures with those from La Mesa, for example, which is much closer to the ocean and near sea level: 71 degrees in July, very close to the mountain's mean of 70 degrees. But in January in La Mesa the mean is 53 degrees. This is twelve degrees warmer than in the mountains. Winter is much colder on North Peak than it is near the ocean.

But when we look more closely at the July data at the two places we see that these means conceal an important fact. In the mountains in July the mean *maximum* is about 87 degrees, while in La Mesa it is 83 degrees. The mean *minimum* is 53 degrees in the mountains and 60 degrees in La Mesa. In a word, in the mountains the days are notably warmer and the nights are notably colder than along the coast, although the means for the two places are deceptively close. To a seasoned mountaineer this suggests he spend more time in the shade during the day, if he can, and sleep under a light blanket at night, even in the summer. Given the moderate mountain temperatures, it seems to me that the better summer climate, in terms of human comfort, is where the oaks and pines grow, not palm trees.

While no statistics are available, one of the striking features of mountain weather to the visiting flatlander is the frequency and velocity of the winds, compared to the tranquility of the coastal strip. (The strongest wind ever recorded at the San Diego airport is a moderate 54 miles an hour; this would be only a stiff breeze in Denver.) Often a west wind blows off the Pacific, sometimes even bringing damp sea air or fog, which for a moment makes me think of wrack and sea sand. Occasionally a south wind sweeps the mountain, particularly in the spring. It soon wears out its welcome when it blows for days on end. Near the cabin I planted three pines, but the persistent south wind blew so violently, twisting and worrying them at ground level, that all three snapped off at the union between trunk and roots. This would not happen near the coast where insistent winds are nearly unknown.

The pines near the cabin declare the force of the wind. The wind has topped some of them, leaving their uppermost branches snarls of dead needles like wild witches' hair. The wind has flagged others so their branches grow in one plane to the southwest. This testifies to the force of the autumn Santa Ana winds escaping the Great Basin on their way to sea. But here, at least, on the mountain crest the winds are not yet hot, as they will be when they descend the front of the range. Fierce though they are, they do not raise the comfort level as the Devil Winds do in the lowlands. In the mountains it is 75 degrees with a gusty east wind, but at the beach, after the air has fallen four thousand feet, rising five degrees in temperature for every thousand feet, it is 95 degrees. Within sight of the sea, a scouring wind rakes the sinuses, the Bougainvillea slaps the glass of the greenhouse, leaves from the Birds of Paradise fly away forever into the surf, and shy housewives consider cutting the throats of their sleeping husbands, or at least so Raymond Chandler believes.

Geographers employing the Koppen system classify the climate on North Peak as Mediterranean, assigning to it the code Csb, the letters designating Mediterranean (C), dry summer (s), as well as short warm summer (b). This climate is rare on our planet, most of it

33

occurring around the Mediterranean Sea and on the California coast, with additions on Chile's coast, extreme southern Africa, and western and southern Australia. By everyone's admission this climate is temperate and benevolent, encouraging an outdoor life. On North Peak I don't worry about freezing to death (but I'd certainly avoid long exposure to cold rain), or perishing of sunstroke. A heavy-handed wind may keep me indoors at times, it's true, and in summer if the wind blows strong from the south and the sky is black and lightning flares close and quick, I check the condition of the cabin roof. But this rarely worries me.

By an oddity, the Koppen system asserts that coastal San Diego County is not Mediterranean at all, but because of its low rainfall technically it possesses a cool steppe climate. Mountain dwellers can justifiably consider themselves as a superior people with a benign Mediterranean climate, who from their alpine homes are entitled to look down on an inferior steppe district. I think this is not the first time that the mountain people have asserted their superiority over their downhill neighbors, nor the last.

Mountain Quail

The bird walked uneasily down the trail, eyes alert–to the side, up, to the side, up–watching for his enemies. From time to time he pecked at fresh wet blades of grass and herbs that had sprung up after heavy winter rains, but he never dropped his head for long; the world is a dangerous place for mountain quail. What is more, this was the one time of the year when he did not have other eyes with him to watch for danger, being now briefly solitary.

Unexpectedly, he hopped onto a rotting stump. Abandoning caution, throwing his head back, erecting his two-feather crest, he opened his beak wide to utter a piercing "Keep!" Down the mountain a mile away, a man sitting in a folding chair on the deck in front of a cabin, reading the paper in the wan February sun, turned to his wife to say, "Sounds like the quail have started courting again." She nodded in agreement.

After precisely eight seconds had elapsed, he repeated his call, "Keep!" astonishingly loud for a bird only a foot long. After another interval, once more he sounded his "Keep!" his crest bobbing with the effort. Hearing the lightest claw steps on the trail, he turned to see a solitary quail, she too having abandoned her covey, advancing down the trail. For the time abandoning all caution, she sought the source of the ravishing love song on this gray damp afternoon. Much resembling the male, she was mostly dove gray with a chestnut gorget and chestnut flanks streaked with white; her top-knot was not quite as long as the male bird's.

Seeing the modest female, he opened his wings to display the white streaks against his chestnut flanks, brighter than hers. She thought he was unbearably handsome.

He hopped off the stump and, approaching closer, began to bend and bow before her. She lowered her head even more modestly and sank to the ground. She could refuse him nothing.

A few days later the pair that now spent all their time together began building a simple nest under a branch that had fallen green from an oak with the first rains of autumn and still held withered leaves. Here on the slope of North Peak they elected to nest in an oak grove, but across from a freshet full from late winter rains was a manzanita and chamise covered sunny hillside. Every morning they

35

left the grove, and hopping over the stream, they found a tiny clearing where they could dry their feathers in the sun; there was no dust anywhere, but later in the year every morning they would revel in the small dusty bowls their breasts made in the sun-warmed earth, turning joyously and flapping their stubby wings.

In the nest the hen began to lay her eggs. Busy with her task, when she rose for the last time she left eleven reddish-buff eggs well hidden below dead branches and leaves. Both the birds began sitting on the eggs, keeping them warm and dry for nearly a month until the first egg tooth pecked its way out of the shell; by the end of that day nine chicks had hatched, but for some reason two of the eggs remained whole and when the parents and their brood left the nest they remained behind, forgotten.

Within a few minutes from the moment they tottered dizzily out of their broken shells, the chicks, streaked brown and tan so they blended in perfectly with dead leaves and litter, could run freely. The hen led them in an unsteady line from the nest they were deserting forever to the brook flowing off the mountain. The chicks drank daintily. Within minutes they were pecking at tiny green leaves forcing themselves out of the clinging springtime mud. They vigorously attacked a beetle that crossed their path, their tiny beaks ample enough to deal it mortal blows, and ants and moths hovering close to the ground.

Within a week the chicks, always close to their mother, grew larger and stronger. Now they made sorties into the brush, but they returned promptly to her side at the sound of her low "skut, skut, skut," instinct telling them where safety lay. However, one of the fuzzy balls for some reason could not run well and so it fell further and further behind the other chicks. Finally, it could not run at all and fell on its back, its claws stroking the air hopelessly. When the brood passed its way an hour later, ants had already found the body. They were disassembling it, carrying it away to their nest under a boulder, having the last word for the raids the chicks had made on their numbers.

One sunny April morning when the chicks were a good third the size of their parents, the whole family was proceeding down a path that followed the stream, now much quieter than it had been in February, when the hen gave her soft alarm call. The male scampered off through the brush and the chicks froze in their places, sink-ing close to the ground. Before them rose a giant, much taller than broad, with two legs, two featherless wings, and huge glassy eyes. The hen continued to cluck softly, although the monster was still advancing towards the family up the trail. Finally, not ten feet away from the hen and the chicks, he stopped, surprised to see a quail so close–usually they fled when he was fifty feet away, an explosion of whirring wings. Less than three paces away, the quail held her ground, fixing her black eyes firmly on him.

The man stopped to ponder. Then he reached into a front shirt pocket to remove a notebook and a pencil. Opening the notebook, he wrote. "April 10. Surprised a mt. quail on the trail near the cabin. Shows no fear. Probably has chicks nearby. Out of consideration for the birds chose retreat." After he was well out of sight and sound, the hen clucked once more and the chicks came running from where they had lain flat on the ground in the oak leaves.

Not much more than a day after this encounter, the family suffered a great loss. They were foraging along the sides of a dirt road, finding ample greenery near puddles fast drying under the hot spring sun. The male was with the chicks in cover, the hen wandering out onto the open abandoned road. Suddenly, with no warning a brown shape hurtled down from a nearby pine and soundlessly seized the hen in its talons.

Grasping the quail tightly, the Cooper's hawk spiraled above the road and flew straight up the mountain to a large clearing overgrown with bracken where the trees were mostly incense cedar and white fir. Descending to a fallen log on the edge of the glade, the hawk dispatched the quail with a few decisive blows to the head. Methodically it began stripping the quail of its feathers. Around the log quail feathers, warbler feathers, pigeon feathers, and feathers of many other kinds and colors floated with every breeze. Satisfied with the results, the hawk flew into a white fir not far away to present the food to its four eager clamoring nestlings; around the nest the area was clean of feathers so as not to attract owls or other predators.

The hen quail gone, the male took her place. It led the young from one place to another, feeding on greens mostly, but also insects when the chicks could catch them. Water had become a problem, now that most of the rain brooks had dried up. But one day the little covey–the male and six chicks, for two of the young had simply disappeared–found a large concrete bowl full of water. At first they

37

were nervous near it because not far away stood an enormous box, whose heavy shadow intimidated them. When they drank at the bowl they could see a dim moving shape within an opening in the cabin, the monster who had frightened them on the trail a month earlier. But at least once a day they had to drink, and the bowl was much closer than the tiny stream that ran in a chain of puddles a mile away down the hill.

One day a stranger joined the covey. It was about the same size as the quail, but it had a white throat and its feet and bill were not at all like a quail's. It fed with them, never going very far away; whatever it was, instinct told it that it was safer with other birds, even if they were not its own kind.

As the covey was drinking at the concrete bowl one day, the man standing in the window of the house started, and then walked briskly to the telephone. "Jim," he said to one of his neighbors who knew the birds of the mountain. "You won't believe this, but I've got a red-legged quail over here." "And what color is its bill?" his neighbor asked, calmly enough. "It's red too!" "Well," came the response, "That's a chukar. The man who lives down the hill in the white house, you know, the one with the swimming pool, has some game birds in cages, pheasants and things like that. Sometimes they escape. One of them, I guess, has joined up with your quail."

He never saw the chukar again. One day it simply abandoned the covey. Perhaps instinct took it to lower ground where it was at home among weed patches and featureless grassy fields. While its kind flourished in the arid slopes of Nevada and Idaho, it could never be happy in the open woods and chaparral on North Peak.

By October the covey consisted of only the father and the six surviving chicks. In the warm mild weather of late autumn their day was simple and the same. After passing the night in heavy brush safe from their enemies, they moved to water, always at least once a day, but in the warmest weather twice. After drinking, they drifted through the woods and chaparral in search of berries and scant green plants. They pecked at green acorns that were close enough to the ground to reach. They scratched for bulblets they could smell below the blanket of oak leaves and pine needles. Sunny mornings they dusted in favorite places in the chaparral. While the dry expanses of dirt roads were attractive, they had learned to avoid open spaces for fear of predators; when in their wanderings they came to a road, they

38

sprinted directly across it, quickly finding cover on the far side.

Making a great daily circle across the mountain's face, never departing too far from the water in the bowl, they sometimes met other quail. One day a second covey chose to join in with them. It too was a family, but had only two adults and three grown chicks. The augmented covey now had eleven birds, a goodly number with twenty-two alert black eyes, the better to see the hawks and owls and bobcats and foxes who sought them as prey.

One hot October day the covey discovered that the bowl no longer held water. No rain had fallen for several weeks and the cabin's owner had gone for a time, leaving no one to fill the bowl; its contents had evaporated, leaving only drying scum. That day the quail began their first mile-long trek down the mountain to Cedar Creek where pools of water still lay black under willows and elderberry bushes.

As they moved in a loose group down the mountain they sensed something frightening near a dirt road along the stream: one of the tall animals and something else, a kind of fox that moved back and forth along both sides of the road. They had seen and smelled these foxes before near the cabins; usually they did not stray far from the tall animals.

The covey ceased their downhill advance and froze in hidden places in the chaparral under the manzanita. The fox suddenly departed from the road and sped straight toward the place where they had taken cover, somehow sensing they were hiding there. When it was thirty feet away from them, six of the quail burst into the air and made a wide circle to return up the mountain to familiar slopes where they would be safe. Tremendous explosions rang out and two of the quail spun into the air as though a heavenly baseball bat had hit them. Immediately, the fox ran to where they had fallen, gathered them both up, and returned to the tall animal.

The quail that had frozen on the ground could hear the tall animal making cooing noises to the fox. Leaving the covey behind, the two of them moved further along the road. But fifteen minutes later they returned, and again the fox darted up the hill. The survivors in the covey had never moved for all this time. Terrified by its foxy odor and the noise it made crashing through the chaparral, all exploded into the air. Once more the shotgun rang out, and one of the quail dropped like a stone into the brush. The fox quickly ran to the spot and collected the dead bird in its mouth. As before, it returned to the man, and the remaining birds, by now running up the slope, heard it making the same strange cooing noises as the fox neared.

That night the hunter's wife took the three quail, now indecently naked, beheaded, and deprived of their vital organs, added a fourth from the refrigerator, and lay them on a plate. From a tin box she removed a piece of stained cardboard on which someone had written with a firm hand:

Quail Vino

2 quail per person
Sliced mushrooms–at least 2 cups
1/4-1/2 cup chopped green onions
Wild rice
2 tbsps. lemon juice
Salt–to liking
Ground pepper
Dry white wine–at least 1 cup
1/2 cup butter or margarine

Brown plucked quail in butter; remove from pan and set aside. Saute mushrooms and onions in pan. Place quail, mushrooms, and onion in a shallow pan and cover with heavy-duty aluminum foil. Bake at 350 degrees for 40 minutes. Remove foil and add wine, lemon juice, a little salt, and pepper. Cook for another 15 minutes or until brown, basting often. Serve hot over cooked wild rice.

That night at the dinner table they agreed that these were some of the best quail they had ever eaten.

Winter's light snows caused the quail no difficulties. Unlike mountain quail in the Sierras they had no need to descend to a mild climate and bare ground. Here, even when it snowed, damp soil lay exposed under the pines and live oaks where they could find food. By now they mostly ate acorns that rested in abundance everywhere on the mountain; when snow covered the ground they flew into oak brush and picked odd acorns off the branches.

As the winter days lengthened, the old male grew increasingly restless. Like the other male birds in the covey, he began to lag behind the other birds scurrying from place to place. One sunny afternoon in February when the covey was far out of sight, he hopped onto a boulder on an open slope. Throwing his head back, his crest bobbing, he opened his beak wide to call "Keep!" After the eight-second pause, he repeated the cry even more vehemently. Again and again he sent his summons across the oaks and pines, the manzanita, the ceanothus. With no response yet to his call, he hopped off the rock and ran spiritedly down the slope, looking for another vantage point from which to sing to the world.

Down the mountain a mile away, the man sitting on the deck before the cabin turned to his wife to say, "The quail are at it again." "Yes," she agreed, and smiled.

January

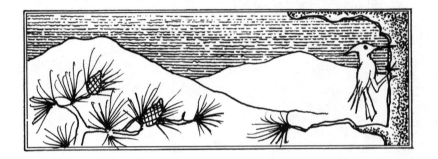

January

January is the coldest month of the year, according to the weather records for the mountains. Some days at noon it doesn't warm up much above freezing, and on an unusually cold night the thermometer stands in the teens. The ground freezes about an inch deep on nights like this, but still if I must dig a planting hole in January I can break through this Southern California version of permafrost with an old worn shovel.

It also vies with February as the rainiest month of the year, with about five inches of precipitation, most of it rain, but some snow falls too. This calculates as about an inch of precipitation every week, but its fall is unpredictable. Some weeks are dry, sunny, and cold; sometimes the rain seems incessant. Sometimes a foot of snow mantles the ground.

In spite of the cold, many native plants are growing now, in January. Pink and white flowers litter the rain-darkened soil under the manzanitas, while some flowers still hold to the plants. Buds on the Kellogg oaks are swelling, beginning to flaunt their unique combination of delicate pink and green. But for the exotic northern fruit trees and grapevines I have planted in the clearing this is the dormant season when growth pauses in expectation of springtime warmth to come. Buds on the vines and fruit trees betray the smallest hint of expansion and unfolding.

For a gardener January is the time to prune his fruit trees and grapes–the most pleasant chore of the year, in one man's opinion. It's light work, requiring only one small tool, pruning shears, which fit the hand comfortably.

If the volume of cuttings from the plants is small, I cut the unwanted branches into short lengths and let them fall to the ground under the trees or vines; in time they will merge with the soil to make more fruit, I think reassuringly. In France they burn vineyard cuttings in quaint portable stoves, but I don't dare burn here–just a whiff of smoke in the woods would bring fire engines to the lane within minutes.

Because my fruit trees are still young, they are easy to prune–cut off a crossing branch here, shorten a long branch there, nip off a watersprout on the trunk, and the little tree is done, ready to meet another summer and, hopefully, yield a small but satisfying harvest

43

of fresh fruit. A few minutes work brings a gratifying change in the tree's shape. It looks healthier and happier.

But pruning grapevines is a different matter. This is an arcane science, with a bewildering terminology, such as cane-pruned as opposed to spur-pruned, head-pruned as opposed to cordon-pruned, and then there are pruning methods such as the Geneva Double Curtain, the Umbrella-Kniffin, and the Chatauqua System. The standard grape-growing text, *General Viticulture* by A. J. Winkler, et al, devotes fifty pages to the question of proper grape pruning.

One reason for the complexity of grape pruning is the vine's habit of bearing its fruit mostly on last year's wood. This means that if no one prunes the vine it will bear its fruit further and further from the plant's trunk, and more and more of the vine will be wood, not fruit. In the Middle Ages European peasants did not prune their grape vines at all, so that vineyards were nearly impenetrable thickets through which the harvesters clambered to collect the fruit. In the 18th century, the most rational and orderly of centuries, French monks came up with the idea of planting vines in rows and pruning them to increase the yield.

Generally, grapes are either pruned to be free-standing, called "vase-pruned" or trained on wires called "cordons." Since the latter system requires a sturdy framework of posts and wires, and setting a post in our rocky soil is a task to be avoided whenever possible, I elect to train my grapevines as free-standing plants, something like heavily pruned miniature trees. This makes it easier to cultivate under them, and to walk through the vineyard sampling the grapes, one of the great rewards for maintaining a vineyard.

I sometimes think, though, that I chose this method of pruning grapes partly because I associate it with some of my earliest California memories. As a teenager I rode the Greyhound Bus to Southern California through San Bernardino and Riverside. This route took me across what a roadside sign near Cucamonga declared was "The Biggest Vineyard in the World," miles of vase trained grapevines. Today, remnants of this immense vineyard survive between industrial parks and subdivisions alongside the freeways east of Los Angeles. That is the kind of vineyard I have in the mountains, only smaller.

This is how I like to prune my fruit trees and vineyard in January. Soft clouds should dot an otherwise clear blue sky. Underfoot

44

there must be no snow because snow means mud and wet boots. This is to be avoided. The ground must be dry to the touch, at least in the sun, and springy to my step. Juncoes must be searching for weed seeds along the lanes. Perhaps I can hear woodpeckers feuding over a granary tree somewhere in the distance, accompanied by the insistent cries of a red-tail hawk soaring somewhere above the leafless vineyard.

After I have pruned the fruit trees, I turn to the grapes. Working down the rows, I lightly prune young vines, leaving five or six buds on each plant. On the older heavier vines, now two feet tall, which stand without a stake to support them, I remove suckers that burgeoned near the ground and heavy shoots that cross over the crown of the vine. I try to leave three or five or seven arms on each plant, preferring, as the books say, an odd number. I don't know why. On each arm I leave five or six buds. If the vines prosper, perhaps my descendants will do the same thing, but for them the vines will be five feet tall.

A good pair of shears easily cuts through a one-inch vine, and grape wood has just the right blend of resistance and yield so that the cuts are always clean. Now, in places where the grapevines were a tangle, I walk freely down the rows. The work goes swiftly and I receive an immediate reward: where there was disorder and wild growth there is now regularity and harmony. Because I am human this is reassuring–for a moment I have control over part of my life and as I look at the renovated vineyard I am convinced that for the nonce I am Master.

After a few hours work on a short winter's afternoon I am finished, confident that the vineyard will not need such concentrated attention until next winter. The buds on the vine that I left are swelling, and at the end of March the first green leaves will appear on the vines. For them there will be plenty of air and space because I pruned in January. If a late frost does not blight the new leaves and flowers, perhaps this year I will have an abundant harvest. But if the summer is long and hot and the birds hungry, the harvest will be small and raisined. But I console myself by saying that no matter what the yield may be, I've had the singular pleasure of pruning grapes on a sunny, mild January afternoon, in the air a red-tail hawk's cry ringing.

Engineers Road, How It Grew

I think the first car my father bought was an Essex. It was in 1930, or maybe a little earlier. Cars were becoming so inexpensive that even families that had barely made it into the middle class could own a car for business, visiting friends and family, and pleasure excursions into the country.

This meant there had to be roads, hard-surfaced all-weather roads, for millions of cars waiting impatiently everywhere in America. In San Diego County, as in all of America, county supervisors found themselves with a new responsibility. Everyone expected that it was up to them to build good roads to connect one town to another, San Diego to Oceanside, Imperial Beach to Chula Vista, Descanso to Julian. By 1919 San Diego County could boast of sixty-three miles of paved road, and by 1929 the total had grown by six fold, to 385 miles.

Of course, many remote districts remained roadless or with only the most primitive muddy tracks. The Sunset Highway, for example, was not dedicated until November 1937; hard to believe when you see the heavy traffic it carries today. And Engineers Road, the only east-west road in the Cuyamacas, that connects Cuyamaca Reservoir with Boulder Creek on the front of the range, early in the century was as yet only an idea growing in the mind of the developer, Ed Fletcher. And grow it did, but slowly.

But first the army had to be called in. About 1918 an army engineers unit began work in the Cuyamaca region—how they came to be stationed there I do not know, but it seems likely that Col. Fletcher's connections with the military might have been a factor. The engineers began work on a dirt road west from Cuyamaca Reservoir on Fletcher's land, with his acquiescence. The road was named in their honor—Engineers Road.

Fletcher no doubt hoped that a road would eventually stretch from Cuyamaca to Pine Hills, because it would be an obvious benefit to him and his backers who had entrusted him with large sums of money for mountain real estate speculation. As of 1910 he was director of the Cuyamaca Water Company which not only owned the reservoir and the former San Diego Flume Co., but also large tracts of land surrounding the reservoir. He had developed the community of Pine Hills, laying out roads and selling land, as well as building Pine

46

Hills Lodge. To complete the picture, in 1910 he bought "between 3,000 and 4,000 acres of land" from Charles Kelly stretching between Cuyamaca and Pine Hills. A road connecting these two points and proceeding through land that he owned would greatly enhance the value of his holdings.

About 1921 (Fletcher's memoirs are often vague about dates), Fletcher ordered further work on Engineers Road, begun some three years earlier. Apparently he bore the cost of this work himself, spending "over $10,000" to quote from a letter that Fletcher later wrote to the County Supervisors. Fletcher himself took part in building the road. As he says in his *Memoirs*, "It was [W. L.] Dedrick who helped me lay out and build the roads around Pine hills, the Engineer Road from Pine Hills to Cuyamaca Lake... now in use today." (1950) By June 1922, it was apparently completed, since the geologist, Frank S. Hudson, in his *Geology of the Cuyamaca Region*, submitted for publication on June 29, 1922, refers to Engineers Road as "recently built."

Although it must have been a very primitive road, the public could use it. Climbing about four hundred vertical feet above the reservoir, it traversed above Kelly Ditch, then dropped toward Cosmit Peak after crossing Azalea Creek. I hope, at this point, that travelers stopped their cars long enough to admire the view into Boulder Creek gorge, the recesses of the San Diego River, El Cajon Mountain, and in the distance Point Loma and the Pacific Ocean. From here it followed Sandy Creek down to today's Fire Station, then swung north to Cedar Creek and Pine Hills.

In the 1930s interest in improving the road grew. Now the county became involved, as well as the U. S. Forest Service and the WPA, which contributed cheap labor. The WPA's presence in the district is memorialized in a way on a concrete bridge on Boulder Creek Road that reads "WPA 1937." By that year the improved road was nearly completed; it was at this time that Fletcher granted the road's right-of-way free of charge to the county. A short time later Engineers Road was finished and opened to the public as a county maintained road.

Fletcher must have profited when the road was open and serviceable. For example, he found reason to buy out one of his backers on the Kelly ranch purchase, paying him $30,000 for the man's original investment of $10,000, a healthy 300% return on the money. To his

47

credit, the developer was strongly opposed to timbering on North Peak, writing that he bought the tract in 1910 from Kelly to save it from the woodman's axe, and he included in his sale contracts a clause stating that trees must never be cut on the land he sold. The handsome stand of pines high on North Peak is a tribute to his views on preservation; today this expanse of woods and bracken meadows is within the northern extension of Cuyamaca Rancho State Park.

When I first drove Engineers Road in 1987 it was still only paved for about half of its length, which meant that crews could not keep it free of snow in the winter. But in the next few years the county extended the asphalt in two stages until finally in the summer of 1994 the paving reached Boulder Creek Road and I could drive Engineers Road's full length without getting mud on my truck's fenders. Many years have elapsed since Ed Fletcher laid out his track over North Peak until the hard-surfaced all-weather road was complete. But that's what a lot of us like about the mountains—there's no need to hurry. Things will get done eventually, even if it takes seventy five years to complete a seven mile road.

Trophy Houses

On the slope of North Peak south of Pine Hills along Engineers Road are about fifty houses hidden in the woods. Some are permanent residences for retired couples, some for working people who tolerate long commutes, and others are part-time summer places. Many are large log houses built from kits, which resemble pioneer log cabins about as much as a Ferrari resembles a Ford model T. But whatever the scale or style in which they are built they all mimic the horizontal lines of the hills. Maintaining the low profile, the owners stain these houses in subdued shades in harmony with what they see as nature's own colors.

As these homes go up, their owners strive to preserve their homes's natural settings. Oaks and pines, growing at the foundations of the houses, are retained to enclose the houses in greenery. Given the acute danger of wildfire, I ask myself if it is prudent to build a house and then permit pines to grow so close that they peer into the windows like Peeping Toms. But I reconsider: if the homeowners so love the settings they risk the danger of fire to remain literally close to the woods, I should respect their wishes. After all, their owners say, if we live here, let's fit into the landscape, even perhaps at a price.

Two houses in the district, and only two, deviate from these principles. Several years ago someone bought a hill above Cedar Creek, cut a long curving drive to its summit, and after constructing an immense retaining wall, put up a large house in the Southern antebellum style, with neo-classic details. True to the plantation style, the owner had the house painted a gleaming white. Then to complete the final effect he had much of the hill scraped clear of the chaparral and access roads cut in loops through the manzanita. The bulldozer scraped off the top soil in these places, exposing the red sub-soil which is nearly as hard and sterile as stone. Aerial photos show this house to be the most conspicuous object on the landscape within ten square miles.

Only recently while walking eastward up a lane in the neighborhood, I discovered that this house has a competitor. From Pine Hills to the north a home builder cut a road down the brush-covered slope toward Cedar Creek. He too constructed a retaining wall like the prow of a battleship, above which he erected a three-story house, in a

49

style which might be described as Near Tudor with a Cape Cod overlay. It too stands naked without friendly trees in the midst of a broad slope of low-lying chaparral.

Irritated, I tried to understand why anyone would erect such obtrusive houses so inappropriate to their settings of rounded hills, chaparral and forest. Clearly their builders had something totally else in mind than my neighbors with their low roofs and weathered decks. I concluded they had built these house with different motives: these were trophy houses, something akin to the trophy wives who have become a prominent feature of American public life.

What is a trophy wife? Acquired usually late in her spouse's life, she is a conventionally beautiful and eminently conspicuous wife whose purpose is to serve as a symbol of wealth and success. Testifying to the high status of her owner, her presence declares that he has achieved prominence (like a hill top?). When he displays her he claims society's envy, not to say imitation. He has more expensive toys than everyone, at least one of them living, and he wants the world to know it.

From this point of view, the two houses, trophies on display, do make a kind of sense, although, of course, this does not lessen their impact on their settings. The key words to understanding this concept, the trophy, are beauty and conspicuousness. No one can visualize a trophy wife who is not conventionally beautiful, and no one could imagine that the owner of such an object would instruct her to maintain a low profile, since by the very nature of it she must be in everyone's eyes. Beauty is hard to define, as thinkers have been saying for, lo, these thousands of years. A trophy wife, of course, must possess those aspects of feminine beauty which are currently in fashion; she must be tall (the better to be seen?), blonde, and slender. On the other hand, architectural beauty is more elusive and debatable, but for our two home owners it seems to be epitomized in Southern neoclassic mansions, Medieval English villages and beach houses on Cape Cod. In principle, there is nothing intrinsically ugly about either style. What is disturbing is that they seem so incongruous in their mountain settings. A Southern mansion belongs in a land of magnolias, cotton fields, and Spanish moss; the other house would be at home in merry olde England or sandy, salty Cape Cod. How have they strayed to a land of rounded forms and a dominating wildness?

But of course this is precisely why they are here. They do not belong, so they cry out for our attention. Questions of architectural propriety are not relevant. Incongruity was what the builders were seeking.

But why should I be so agitated about the presence of these houses, I ask myself. If a professional baseball player chooses to wear a four-carat diamond on his pinkie finger I lose no sleep over it. If a local executive commutes in a Rolls Royce, I may even feel a twinge of envy. When I read that the CEO of a Sorrento Valley bio-tech firm owns a home in the south of France and a vineyard in Napa it doesn't disturb me in the least.

But when I recall the young man in our neighborhood who arose from his bed at 2:00 a.m. to bay at the moon, thereby waking scores of people, including me, or the neighbor's yard-man who dumped trash over our wall, making the cultivation of our garden even more arduous, or the owner of the expensive automobile that occupied two parking spaces in a public parking lot, I know I have a just cause for complaint. The youth, the neighbor's yard-man, the car's owner, impinged on my right to sleep, garden in tranquility, and to find a parking space for my car. They crossed the line.

Similarly, the two houses on the mountain scene scrape my blackboard every time I look at them. They have invaded my visual turf and cause me pain and discomfort. I would be happy if they were some place far from the mountains that would be more beautiful in their absence. I have to live with them but I don't have to like them.

I have found a small consolation, though. By a quirk of the terrain our house and others stand higher than the misplaced hill-top Tara. Can a trophy house be a trophy house when the houses belonging to the lesser breed look down on it from above?

Community Spirit

When we moved to California many years ago we were overjoyed at the prospect of visiting for the first time one of the great wonders of the west, Yosemite, which, like the Grand Canyon and Mesa Verde, we were told, never loses its impact on the visitor. Later, we did in fact walk the trails to see its waterfalls, worried about the bears, and admired the handsome Kellogg oaks growing in the park land along the Tuolomne river. Not only were we impressed by what we saw, we made earnest efforts to learn something about the region's natural history. These Yosemite guidebooks and lectures introduced us to the leading concept of western natural history at the time: the life zone.

According to this system, devised by C. Hart Merriam at the end of the 19th century, all the west's landscapes were classified into six zones through which you advanced south to north or gained altitude, perhaps most spectacularly up the western slope of the Sierra Nevada range. These zones in ascending order are Lower Sonoran, Upper Sonoran, Transition, Canadian, Hudsonian, and Arctic-Alpine.

Even then I was uncomfortable with the scheme. Firstly all California's colorful landscapes had to fit into one of these six zones. Where did the coast redwoods fit in? Where should I place the oak grasslands in the Central Valley? And there was the irritating fact that most of California's life zones had foreign designations. My knowledge of Canada and Mexico was almost non-existent, and yet I was being induced, for example, to see the Sierra pines and firs as somehow related to Canadian natural history. The same thing was true of the lower life zones with their Mexican referents. Finally, I found the term "Transition" less than satisfying. While there was an obvious logic in it–the transition between Canadian and Mexican zones–weren't nearly all the zones transitions from one to another? What made this zone a special type of transition worthy of its name?

Of course, I was not alone in being dissatisfied with this overly simple scheme, which, it seemed to me distracted the student away from examining the unique features of the landscape to a preoccupation with geographical typologies on a continental scale. Ecologists had begun to work out the idea of natural, or biotic, communities long before our visits to Yosemite, but their work had not yet impinged on the guides for tourists in the national parks and elsewhere. In these places in the 1950s the life zone classification was still holy writ.

In 1959 Philip Z. Munz and David D. Keck published their *California Flora*, with later editions, which described not six life zones, but twenty-nine natural communities in the state. Following their footsteps, Jaeger and Smith's *Natural History of Southern California*, (1966) lists twenty seven natural communities in the southern end of the state alone, while Bakker's *An Island Called California* (1971, 1984) identifies in Southern California nine major natural communities with twenty subdivisions. *The Terrestrial Vegetation of California* (1977, 1988) identifies fifty-four natural communities in our state. The latest survey, Allan A. Schoenherr's *A Natural History of California* (1992), returns to Munz and Keck's twenty-nine natural communities, but considerably refines their characteristics. (I have relied heavily on his book for this essay.)

Not only have such investigations established the concept of natural communities and gone far in identifying their traits and so recognizing the diversity in the state's landscapes, they have abandoned any comparisons between native scenes and distant regions. Excursions to Canada and Mexico are no longer necessary. Ecologists now assign the name of the dominant vegetation to the community, in most cases, for example, Blue oak-digger pine forest, Valley oak savanna, or Coastal sagebrush. What is more, they emphasize the concept of natural *community*, which includes not only the flora but also the region's fauna, down to the smallest invertebrate, as well as all the relationships on the land, encompassing, for example, geology, soil chemistry, climate, and slope gradient and aspect.

This preamble leads me to the middle elevations of North Peak and its natural communities. For my purposes, the heart of the community is an area of two and a half acres (by coincidence this is about the same as the ecologists' favorite measurement of land surface, the hectare), the land we own. Located at approximately 4300 feet above sea level, it is at 33 degrees north and 116 degrees 37' 30" west. The soil is woodland humus overlying a dense iron-stained red soil which is the product of weathering gabbro underlying the region. At places this rock reaches the surface as outcrops measuring up to ten square yards in area. Studding the surface are numerous boulders which have washed down from steeper ridges above. The slope is modest, perhaps ten degrees, at most.

Several features complicate the pattern of vegetation on the site, the first being that since the plot is on the rounded shoulder of the mountain it faces west through northwest and the angle of the sun on the land varies; as a consequence the west slopes are hottest, northwest coolest. Secondly, a shallow ravine cuts the site where a temporary stream flows late in winter after the heaviest rains have fallen. This shallow draw is both shadier and moister than the remainder of the site and this is reflected in the vegetation which grows there. Thirdly, a gravel road borders the lower edge of the property, allowing sunlight to penetrate the tree canopy. The roadside bank provides a scant few yards of raw earth suitable for the invasion of new plants and sun-seeking annuals.

The commonest tree on the plot is the deciduous Kellogg oak, or black oak, the same as we admired in Yosemite valley. Here rise more than thirty trees of at least six inches girth, as well as an abundance of saplings and seedlings everywhere but in the heaviest shade. Dominating the plot, Kellogg oaks are distributed fairly evenly over the area, but they are thickest on the shadier slopes; I have the impression that they are competing quite successfully with the other plants on the site.

Two other species of oak trees grow on the plot, both within the shallow ravine, On its shadier west slope, the coolest area on the site, grow three canyon live oaks, also called gold-cup oaks.

One of these is a confused cluster of six sturdy trunks which may have sprouted from the burned out trunk of an older tree dating from the last fire which swept this area, perhaps a hundred years ago. The other two trees are much smaller, about a foot in diameter, and perhaps they are the offspring of the larger tree. In addition, at a sunny spot in the mouth of the ravine stands a solitary coast live oak, its dusty curled grayish leaves contrasting with the laurel-like leaves of the canyon live oak. Both these oaks appear to have successfully cast their acorns, for under them in broken shade grow seedlings of both sorts which emerge through the heavy duff on the floor of the ravine.

In addition to the three tree oaks on the plot—Kellogg oak, canyon live oak, and coast live oak—there is yet another handsome native tree oak growing nearby on this westward slope of the mountain, but just outside our plot.

Five minutes' brisk walk westward down the lane will take me to a grove of small globular oaks with distinctive oval dark-green leaves. These are Engelmann oaks, growing both within a shallow ravine and on open west-facing slopes. Usually Engelmann oaks are described as savanna oaks, occurring on open grasslands, but here they are in the midst of a mixed forest with some chaparral as well. The distribution pattern of Engelmann oaks is something of a puzzle. Common in areas of the county, particularly towards the north, here they appear as scattered specimens in an area with many other species of trees.

In addition to the three tree oak species growing on the plot, and the Engelmann oaks nearby, there is a prominent conifer common all across the plot. Within its boundaries grow twelve mature Coulter pines. With a couple of exceptions these trees are all about thirty inches in diameter and about fifty feet tall. Impressive, these pines are grouped in cooler sites at the north end of the plot, although a few of them venture out onto sunnier slopes as well. They are replacing themselves on the plot on a modest scale; perhaps a half-dozen saplings grow nearby with some seedlings as well. These young trees grow in locations where the canopy has been broken to allow the sun to reach the ground, such as on the fringes of the meadow we have made or in small ephemeral clearings in the woods.

Although there are none on the central plot we have been scrutinizing, in the immediate vicinity, within a few hundred yards, grow scattered incense, or western cedars. Near the lowest altitude in their range, on sunny slopes they are nearly as wide as they are tall, almost squat, but on more northerly slopes they are respectable forest trees. Nowhere do they dominate any of the slopes, occurring always as an occasional tree in the midst, particularly, of groves of Kellogg oaks. Under the older trees have sprung up crowded thickets of seedlings and saplings in locations where sunlight warms the soil.

As the gravel lane passes our plot it swings towards the east so that almost imperceptibly the roadside slope faces due north. While most people would hardly notice this small shift in the aspect of the slope, it has an effect on the vegetation and the atmosphere. The plants' leaves become a more intense green, the air moister, the shadows a softer azure. Here at a location about a thousand feet from our plot grows a solitary white fir, well below its usual haunt with Jeffrey pines and other northern conifers up the mountain. True, its tip is a little bedraggled and its topmost needles somewhat wan, a consequence, no doubt of dry air and harsh wind, but still it holds numerous stout cones upright. How it came to grow at this isolated place I do not know, but perhaps it sprang from a seed blown down from the upper slopes by an exceptionally powerful gust of the east wind, or it passed through the gut of a Steller's jay fleeing a snow storm on the summit .

In her book, *An Island Called California,* Elna Bakker notes that there is a consistent difference in the countryside in northern and southern California: in the north the forest dominates the chaparral, while in the south the reverse is true, trees standing isolated above the chaparral. This principle rules our tract, for with the exception of the shadowed ravine there is an almost unbroken under-story of brushy vegetation beneath Kellogg oaks and Coulter pines. This chaparral is of of two sorts: manzanita claims the sunnier slopes, a plant whose striking maroon bark and complementary delicate light green leaves flaunt a color scheme worthy of a La Jolla interior deco- rator, an effect heightened by shell-pink flowers in January and February. ("What are those beautiful little trees?" our trans-Sierran visitors ask.) Often, chamise, an attenuated green and brown chapar- ral plant which occurs from sea level to five thousand feet, accompa- nies the manzanita, and under them both grows the strange California peony, the color of its flowers matching the colors of the chamise.

On the other hand, if the slope inclines to the north, and so is a bit cooler, scrub oak replaces the manzanita and chamise. This is the botanists' *Quercus berberidifolia,* a tough dark green bush which produces great quantities of acorns that animals of the chaparral rel- ish. Accompanying it are white-flowered ceanothus, snowberry, and poison oak. In this environment it disguises itself as a vine draped over the scrub and up into the trees, particularly the Coulter pines,on whose rough gray trunks it resembles diminutive Virginia creeper.

When we first purchased the land on North Peak I was puzzled by the fact that some of the scrub oak appeared to grow more vigor- ously than others, forming clumps that were perhaps thirty feet tall, but as isolated shrubs rather than in pure stands. Only after some reading did I discover that this is the southern variant of interior live oak. South of a line through Ventura county, this impressive oak of the north becomes an outsized shrub with perhaps a dozen small trunks and considerable bulk, bearing a scientific name that is nearly as large as the shrub itself, *Quercus wislizenii,* variety *frutescens.*

Given the heavy mantle of tree and scrub, little sun reaches the ground on our plot. So dense is the shade under the coast live oaks and canyon live oaks that the chaparral cannot survive there; this is virtually the only place where no brush grows. Only along the road where sunlight reaches the ground will you find sun-loving annuals. The year's most spectacular floral display is on a large sprawling shrub, summer bush penstemon, with its sprays of tubular orange flowers. In semi-shade, often where broken rock emerges from the forest soil, grows wood fern, sounding its pleasant cooling note in the midst of the hottest summer day.

If the floral display is modest, the rich bird life offers a kind of compensation. Undoubtedly the most prominent denizens of the woodland sky are the acorn woodpeckers that cry and cackle without pause from snags or swoop into clearings to catch insects on the wing. Nearly as startling are the the voluble scrub jays, their blue backs and wings flashing as they glide from tree to tree, always alert for the main chance.

As befits a site with both trees and chaparral, bird life flourishes at two levels: close to the ground and in the trees. Visitors will recognize the wrentit's bouncing ball song in the brush, a bird often heard but almost never seen. Rufous-sided towhees scratch briskly in the oak leaves and clouds of bushtits call to each other softly as they sift through the manzanita. If you are fortunate, you may catch a glimpse of a California thrasher in the lowest chaparral. In spring, families of mountain quail, not the California quail of the lowlands, patter through the dry leaves, returning in the fall in flocks of up to a hundred birds. I hear reliable accounts of wild turkeys nearby, recently introduced to the lower oak woodlands. Perhaps they will find their uphill to our place; they would be welcome.

In the trees above the chaparral a different guild of birds, some of them vagrants from the higher coniferous forest, make their appearance, ignoring the residents downstairs. Mountain Chickadees call in the trees. Seemingly defying gravity, white-breasted nuthatches circle the branches. Western bluebirds nest in abandoned woodpecker holes in the oaks. Neatly groomed ash-throated flycatchers make forays after moths in the clearings between the trees. You become aware that all the birds have fallen silent, and then through the branches darts the commonest predator of the woodland's song birds, a Cooper's hawk, gone almost before you mark its presence.

Mule deer bed down in the clearings, a wary eye open for mountain lions that my neighbors have seen in the woods. Through the oak groves gray squirrels leap from branch to branch, thoroughly at home. Gray foxes leave their scat full of manzanita seeds along the roadsides; I've heard their rusty coughs. Bobcats hunt for dusky-footed wood rats and deer mice. On sunny patches on the lane bask king snakes and gopher snakes. Neighbors report they have seen western rattlesnakes but for the sake of the dogs I am happy to report that they are not common. On rocks and logs in the sun fence lizards abound, the speed of their movements directly related to the temperature. Alligator lizards frequent the duff under the chaparral in search for food.

Once, overturning a boulder, I disturbed an indignant ensatina, the large-blotched mountain salamander. Western toads find cover under logs where they can survive the long dry summers. Tree frogs make their appearance in season.

All in all, animal life is surprisingly rich here in this land of chaparral and emergent oaks and pines, especially when you recall that the nearest permanent source of water is perhaps a half a mile away in neglected water-storage ponds or far down the hill in Cedar Creek. Creatures on this land must be mobile enough to reach distant water or tough enough to survive months of a hot sun and no precipitation.

After this brief summary of the flora and fauna on the western slope of North Peak at 4300 feet, the question arises: to what natural community should I assign this site? A reasonable answer, it seems to me, is to see it as a point at which two communities meet and merge. These two communities are the Upper Chaparral, advancing from below, and the Southern Mixed Forest descending from above. The double classification is appropriate because the tract displays features of both communities. Technically such a mixed community is called an ecotone, a meeting place between two communities that shares the characteristics of both.

For example, the dominant tree on the plot is Kellogg oak, a typical tree of the Southern Mixed Forest, as are the nearby incense cedars. The white fir growing a short distance away is also a representative tree of the community. However, on the plot the second commonest tree is Coulter pine, which Schoenherr identifies as a tree of the north facing slopes of the Upper Chaparral community that quite accurately describes the land under question. Other characteristic Upper Chaparral plants on the site are manzanita, scrub oak, and interior live oak in its scrub form. This sort of chaparral is adapted to a relatively rigorous climate with regular snowfall and temperatures well below freezing.

On the site grow at least one coast live oak and several canyon live oaks, but they are thriving within a shaded ravine which guarantees them additional soil moisture and damper air during the trying heat of summer. They grow in a narrow strip in the ravine entirely enclosed on two sides by other species of trees that outnumber them overwhelmingly.

The essentially mixed nature of the woodland is apparent if you pause to look across it at your leisure. The over-all appearance is billowing greenery at several levels. Within a small acreage you will see tall Coulter pines and a few incense cedars, then somewhat lower, Kellogg oaks, then globular interior live oaks to thirty feet, perhaps, then at the lowest level, scrub oak and manzanita to about fifteen feet. At some locations you may see coast live oaks or canyon live oaks, but as isolated trees in shadier locations, and rarely Engelmann oaks above sunny chaparral.

This multi-level woodland seen at some remove has no counterpart that I am familiar with in Southern California, perhaps in the entire state. For me it is one of the most distinctive and attractive features of the genial countryside on the middle elevations of North Peak. What's more, because this is where two natural communities meet, the place supports an unusual variety of plant and animal life.

From above come Kellogg oaks and incense cedars and band-tailed pigeons. From below manzanita, globe lilies and towhees have made their way. We are favored to have the best of two worlds, it seems, and a richer world than either of the natural communities above or below us.

february

February

This February delivers beach weather and today I almost forget I'm in the mountains at more than four thousand foot elevation. Earlier, the thermometer rose to 76 degrees. The weather is so mild, the air so balmy, the zephyr so gentle, that I half expect to see girls in bikinis and surfers with sunburned noses somewhere in the neighborhood. While I'm not in swim trunks, I'm wearing a short-sleeved shirt and I'm more than comfortable. When I arrived from the city I donned a Pendleton jacket, appropriate for a mountain day, but I soon cast it off.

Maybe I think it's summer because the day is sensibly longer than it was only six weeks or so in the past. Then, at the winter solstice, the sun set by five in the evening, while now it doesn't descend below the clouded horizon until much later, adding more than an hour to the day's sunshine allotment.

Recently on television I watched an interview with a Holocaust survivor. "Now," he said, "Every day is a gift from God." That's the way I feel as we advance into the longer days after winter's longest night. What, I thought then, in a fit of winter despair, if the days don't lengthen after December 21, but continue to fade until we have only total darkness? Totally irrational, of course... By now in February I'm confident that everything is in order. The days are lengthening and spring and summer and warmth and new life will come shortly.

One creature in the neighborhood shares my enthusiasm for the lengthening days. On a brushy hillside not far away I heard a sweet rippling bird song resounding over the manzanita and chamise. At the top of a tall scrub oak I found a California thrasher, teetering in full view, his head thrown back, declaring to the world that he was a fine fellow and this patch of brush was all his and the best place in all the world.

I've seen these foot-long birds before in the chaparral, but always more or less skulking in the brush or swinging their scimitar beaks through the dry leaves on the ground. They are drab, like so many of the chaparral birds, like brown towhees or wren-tits. This coloration is an adaptation to their environment, their nondescript tint rendering them inconspicuous in their pastel world. A notable exception is perhaps the commonest chaparral bird, the rufous-sided towhee, but perhaps if he doesn't make the mistake of flying to reveal his white tail spots he is also inconspicuous in his way, red eyes, white breast, and all.

Somewhere I read that the chaparral birds' pale colors create a problem for them during the mating season because their inconspicuousness makes it difficult for them to find others of their kind, male and female. Therefore, some of them, including California thrashers, have exceptional songs to attract mates.

There was something dashing and foolhardy about the way he was displaying himself. Here he perched, a large bird, taking a proud place and singing out his heart to the world, no matter that he might attract the attention of predators for a mile around. "Look," he seemed to say, "Here I am, ready for love, and I'll take my chances. Life is good! Life is good! Life is good!"

Mild weather in February deceives some of the orchard trees and they bud and flower. These are European fruit trees, plums and apricots, not tropical mangos and avocados. However, their Old World origins did not prepare them for deceitful California mild spells; they assume it's spring and they bud and flower, only to have cold weather punish them for their foolishness.

One of my trees is a Green Gage plum, bred long ago in France where it is called "Reine Claude" in honor of the wife of Francis I (1494-1547). Sir Thomas Gage, hence its common English name, took it to Great Britain in the 18th century. It is a hardy tree that thrives in the miserable cold wet springs of northern Europe, bearing delicious amber summer fruit. But nothing has armed it against California springs that beguile it into bloom, then blast it with killing frosts.

One of the most melancholy sights in my mountain orchard's brief history was the Green Gage in full leaf in early April, with countless immature frozen green plums carpeting the ground under it. The tree mistakenly bloomed in February, set fruit, and then seven degrees of frost took the entire crop. This is why in the long run the orchard will become mostly apple trees–something makes them indifferent to a warm spell's siren song. They flower later in the spring, ignoring February.

In the meantime, I'll continue to enjoy the second month's mild weather in my shirt sleeves, savoring the sunlight, listening to an inner voice, like the thrasher's song, that declares a welcome affirmation of life.

First Man into the Country

There's little doubt who he was—morteros and pottery shards nearby show that native Americans were the first people to live on the west face of North Peak. When they arrived is still a matter of debate, but no doubt it was thousands of years ago that people hunting and harvesting berries and acorns first passed this way.

After Europeans settled along the coast, perhaps occasional vaqueros from the ranchos rode this range, but not in any great numbers. The terrain is too rugged here for any heavily traveled trails. While parties such as the one that Pedro Fages led wrote records of their visits to the Cuyamacas, they avoided our district between Middle and North Peaks. To the south the entry trail led from Viejas to the Sweetwater Valley and over into the desert, while to the north the main traveled route wound from San Pasqual through the Santa Maria Valley to Santa Ysabel and Warner's Ranch. True, a faint, rarely used trail, later known as the Eagle Peak Road, ascended the San Diego river valley and then crossed lots to Santa Ysabel, but it was too rugged to be popular. No one attempted to follow the river and thence up Boulder Creek between Middle and North Peaks (the shortest route into the mountains as the crow flies), for the ascent was too abrupt and the riverside vegetation too thick even for a horseman. To this day the race of the creek from the reservoir at its head to the Cuyamaca foothills remains virtual *terra incognita*.

What brought many white men to this quiet place was the discovery of gold in Julian, first known to the world in February 1870. No doubt prospectors followed the course of Boulder Creek and its tributary Azalea Creek with a sharp eye open for color in the omnipresent gabbro and the rare outcrops of Julian schist. Apparently, they found nothing. The mines of lower Boulder Creek opened only in the 1890s and it was also in that decade that the Gold King Mining Co. laid claim to land not far from our property—but more about that later.

In July 1870 a group of surveyors may have found their way from the Laguna Seca (the site of today's reservoir) around the shoulder of North Peak and down to Cedar Creek. Charles J. Fox led this party. He had been hired by the Julian mine owners to survey the district in order to establish beyond a doubt the north boundary of the Cuyamaca Rancho, for a consortium of out-of-town lawyers who had purchased the Rancho now claimed that its lands included all of the Julian gold deposits. Fox's party spent only two weeks making their survey, but its findings were crucial in settling the dispute in favor of the mine owners. Their sojourn was too brief to examine the district in any systematic way, nor did they leave any written description of what they saw, to the best of my knowledge.

The distinction of leaving the earliest written description of the west side of the Cuyamacas belongs to one of the most respected men in early San Diego history, Judge Benjamin Hayes, born in Maryland in 1815 who came to California in 1850 and settled early in Los Angeles. As a lawyer practicing in San Diego, he, along with Fox, was hired to defend the mines against the Rancho claims. So he also took to the trail in July, 1870, to explore the mountains, in his hand a copy of the 1845 diseño that defined the Rancho's boundaries. With him were a companion, Samuel Ames, who had farmed in Green Valley, and Chono, an Indian guide.

Hayes had a lively interest in the mountain Indians and he left perceptive notes on their way of life as he observed it, especially their practice of cremating their dead that seemed to have fascinated him. He also left a description of the Cuyamaca Indian settlements that is invaluable today. Later, in 1874, he listed those camps along with the name of their "Capitans." The only settlement on the west side of the mountains he named was "Anahuac," today's Inaja, but he said nothing about Cosmit, indicating that the settlement there was small and impermanent.

It's not clear whether Hayes visited the west side of the range or depended on the testimony of his companions for information. He interviewed Samuel Ames, Carlos Escrich, another Green Valley settler, and Chono, all of whom had visited the district, no doubt rounding North Peak and so on through the Cosmit.

According to Hayes, Anahuac was a few miles away on the western base or side of the third Cuyamaca Peak; here had settled the Indians who had formerly lived at Iguai on the east side of North Peak. Perhaps they were fleeing the prospectors who were flooding this area. Hayes found, if he was not reporting his companions' observations, that other white men had preceded them to Inaja: "Prospectors for gold have been here too, as two piles of earth hard by indicate." Ames told him that the settlement had about thirty inhabitants, with peach and other fruit trees, and gardens as well.

Escrich confirmed Ames's report.

Chono contributed information about the region's natural history. Particularly common hereabouts were the "aiglons," that is, California condors or golden eagles, birds of great size that made their homes in the Cañon of Coscar, the defile by which Boulder Creek passes through the mountains. The Indians favored the black feathers for their ceremonial headdresses.

This is not much, but still, it is a beginning. The isolated district west of the mountains had now entered written history and something was known and set down about its inhabitants and its wild creatures.

The controversy over the ownership of the Julian mines and the official boundaries of the Cuyamaca Rancho was not settled until December 1874. Now that the rancho's boundaries were uncontested, surveyors and settlers moved into the district. Within one year, by December 1875, homesteaders had claimed the best land at Cosmit and Inaja, and President Ulysses S. Grant had established pocket Indian reservations at both places. A new era, an American era, had begun, but that subject demands another essay, "The History of Two and a Half Acres," which follows in good time.

Two Blue Jays

When I'm in the Cuyamaca mountains I know that every day I will see a blue jay. Raucous, restless, conspicuous, and numerous, they scream for attention. However, I'm never quite sure which of two blue jays I will see: will it be a scrub jay or a Steller's jay? Both species flourish in the Cuyamacas.

Not that the two are difficult to distinguish. Scrub jays are light blue with a brownish saddle, and a somewhat lighter blue breast. Most obviously, they lack a crest; this is the source of their scientific name, *Aphelocoma coelerescens*, the genus name from Greek roots meaning "smooth" and "hair," that is, "crestless." The species name means "azure blue." Steller's jays, on the other hand, have a prominent crest, and their blues are much darker. The blue head is so dark it is almost black, the body is a medium blue while the wings are a brilliant sky blue. Its unimaginative scientific name is *Cyanocitta steller,* "dark blue jay." The species bears the name of Georg Wilhelm Steller (1709-1746), German naturalist in the North Pacific.

I can make one generalization about where I expect to see them in the mountains, but this has exceptions, as we will see: scrub jays are lowland birds and Steller's jays are denizens of higher altitudes. As I drive through Cuyamaca Rancho State Park past Green Valley Campground in the midst of coast live oaks, Coulter pines, and sunny slope chaparral at four thousand feet, I see scrub jays mostly. As I drive further on the highway to 4,800 feet at Paso Picacho Campground among canyon live oaks, Kellogg oaks, and incense cedars, I see Steller's jays. Chaparral is rare here. Somewhere between these two altitudes stretches a loose wavering line that separates the homes and haunts of the two birds.

Our cabin is located in the zone where the two jays meet. At 4300 feet on the west slope in chaparral and Coulter pines, it correctly is in scrub jay country; I have never seen Steller's jays on the property. But two hundred yards away my neighbor, Dick Storekeeper, reports that both Steller's jays and scrub jays visit his bird feeder, with a preponderance of scrub jays. What's more, he gets more Steller's jays in the winter, probably because they drift down the mountain seeking food; occasionally they even appear in winter back yards in San Diego. Perhaps the presence of Steller's jays on his property may be related to the fact that he maintains a year round pool of open water.

Another neighbor, whose house with a bird feeder is about a quarter mile away but three hundred feet higher than ours, reports that the jays at his feeder are divided about equally between the two species. If I were forced to draw a line dividing the territory of the two birds–and it would be an artificial line–I suppose I would draw it at about the 4500 foot level, the altitude of his house.

In our location the two jays move freely between four thousand and five thousand feet. However, when I visited a house in a valley shaded by dense coast live oaks at 3800 feet altitude in August, I was surprised to see several Steller's jays, well below the four thousand foot level. Perhaps the Steller's jays were at home there because a nearby stock pond offers a permanent supply of drinking water.

On the mountain we have two jays because it is where two worlds meet: hot lowland chaparral and cool mountain conifer forest, each with its own jay. The origins of the two birds also lie in two worlds. Steller's jays are members of a family of birds that originated in the cool Northern Hemisphere. Its sibling (taxonomists, forgive me) is the eastern blue jay, *C. cristata,* the crested jay. Where their ranges overlap in Colorado the two species sometimes hybridize. The European common jay is the Steller's jay's cousin.

True to their homeland, Steller's jays are happy in cool wooded country with conifers, usually, from coastal Alaska east to the Rockies and south into Central America. In these conditions they thrive from sea level to about nine thousand feet altitude. At this height Clark's nutcrackers replace them, but because we have no mountains this high in San Diego County this bird is unknown here except for very rare erratics.

As befits a bird happy in the heat, scrub jays originated in tropical Central America and then diffused north into cooler territory. None of them live at much higher elevations than our Cuyamaca birds, but they have spread as far north as Washington and Idaho. Another population survives as an island in Florida, far from any other scrub jays. Biologists have devoted much attention to these birds because they often share nests, a very rare trait in birds of the temperate world, but common enough in the tropics. Acorn woodpeckers do something similar, as I point out in another essay.

Scrub jays have three close relatives, all living further south in Mexico or southern Arizona. They bear the same uninspired scientific names as our birds: *A. ultramarina,* Mexican jay (Why not ultramarine jay?), and *A. unicolor,* the unicolored jay.

Although there is much that is similar in the lives of the two jays, living in two worlds the two evolved in different ways. Most obviously, the colors of their plumage are appropriate to either a sunny world of sparse vegetation or one enjoying heavy cover. The light blue, tan, and creams of the scrub jay's feathers blend convincingly with thin chaparral foliage and bright broken shadows under scattered trees. A predator would have difficulty picking out scrub jays in this light-spattered, thinly shadowed world. Scrub jays are equipped very well for an open world of tempered light. They are birds of the sun.

Steller's jays are birds of the shade. Their darker colors conceal them in heavy shadows cast by conifers they favor. Their intense blue feathers make them almost invisible, say, against a shadowed mossy fir or the shutter-green foliage of incense cedars. If I could paint a Steller's jay, I would do so against green sprays of incense cedar, the perfect complement to its saturated blue plumage. A Cooper's hawk, a major predator of both jays, on one of its raids through the trees must have difficulty seeing either of them as it passes, a scrub jay in chaparral or a Steller's jay in the conifers it is so fond of. The light and dark colors of the scrub jay and the Steller's jay are very advantageous adaptations to their environments.

According to Allan A. Schoenherr in his *Natural History of California,* scrub jays have another adaptation that must be invaluable in their arid world: they need never drink, but derive all the water they require from their food. This frees them from dependence on surface water and allows them to thrive virtually anywhere in their chosen environment, even many miles from water. This helps me understand why they are so numerous—one authority calculates the density of scrub jays in one favored area in central California as one for every five and a half acres, a remarkably high figure, it seems to me. By extreme contrast, Cooper's hawks, at least in the nesting season, occur as one bird per half square mile.

Schoenherr also points out that scrub jays are keenly efficient at dissipating heat from the unfeathered portion of their legs. During the hottest hours of the day they can sit out the sun until the coolness of evening, more comfortable than most.

Steller's jays need to drink at certain intervals. However, this is not a problem so long as they remain at higher altitudes where flowing water, if only in the smallest rivulets or seeps, is available. Absence of standing water in most of the chaparral surely discourages their descent into such areas far from their mountain homes.

Still, the two blue jays have things in common. They both build a single nest every year, but scrub jay nests are close to the ground, while Steller's jay nests are higher, sometimes very high in trees. Both birds lay an average of four eggs. Both jays hop, not walk. Their food habits are similar: a wide variety of fruits and nuts, including acorns and pine nuts, just about every imaginable insect, small mammals, lizards, and small snakes. In the springtime I have watched scrub jays hop silently from branch to branch in search of bird eggs and nestlings; in the springtime in San Diego I see cracked and empty mourning dove egg shells on our street under telephone lines where scrub jays have brought them for a quiet meal.

One food related habit has earned universal praise for these birds from all commentators. This is their custom of burying acorns and pine nuts with the intention of returning to eat them at a later date. Inevitably, they forget some of them and these sprout to begin new groves. Since acorns or pine nuts fall close to the parent tree and roll in only one direction–downhill–jays play an important part in dispersing tree seeds, sometimes to a considerable distance from the parent tree, over the ridge and down the valley.

Both birds are noisy and often forage for food in family bands. Both are weak flyers whose characteristic flight pattern is flap-flap-glide, flap-flap-glide, so that it sometimes seems doubtful whether they will make it to the next tree–but they do Both add a welcome note of color and cry to chaparral and woods, even if their repertoire of calls is not to everyone's taste. They also serve as watchmen of the forest, first to give alarm if a predator appears. I have seen scrub jays mob a gopher snake, doing it no real harm, but informing every creature for half a mile that an unwelcome presence stalks the countryside.

Steller's jays made a remarkable contribution to the history of exploration. In 1741, Vitus Bering, he of Bering Strait, led his second expedition to establish the relationship between Siberia and the lands to the east we know now as Alaska. On board Bering's ship

70

was the naturalist Steller, whose name is also on Steller's sea eagle; Steller's eider; Steller's sea cow, an extinct sea mammal; and Steller's sea lion. On July 31 they sighted a fifteen mile island (today's Kayak Island), beyond which appeared to be the mainland with great mountains. Steller begged to go ashore.

When he stepped on the island he became the first European to touch the soil of Alaska, although no one was certain where they were and whether they were truly in North America.

After Steller's return to the ship that evening, a hunter gave him the carcass of an unknown dark blue jay that he had shot. Years earlier in St. Petersburg, Steller had seen a copy of Mark Catesby's *Natural History of Carolina, Florida,* etc., published in 1731, with a depiction of the eastern blue jay. The bird in Steller's hand, while it differed in color from Catesby's jay, had a similar form, complete with crest. Recognizing the similarities between his jay and the eastern blue jay, Steller concluded, as he entrusted to his journal, that "this bird proved to me that we were really in America."

The rest of the crew accepted his argument. Together they drank a cup of chocolate to celebrate the attainment of one of the major goals of their expedition: to reach North America. Steller's jay had made its contribution towards closing the ring of European exploration around the globe in the northern hemisphere—no small contribution.

Note: I wrote this essay in the winter of 1995-1996. That spring I saw a pair of Steller's jays skulking near the cabin, probably preparing to take up housekeeping. Later I saw them in the same neighborhood frequently; in June I saw a fledgling not far away. These Steller's jays probably took up residence at this relatively low altitude because our neighbor provides them with reliable drinking water. Apparently they had no difficulty displacing the numerous brush jays from what is normally their territory.

Call of the Wild

I can't say when we first began to talk about acquiring some land, perhaps on which to build a cabin, in the mountains. Nor can I say with any certainty why our thoughts drifted in this direction. It seems to have been something almost instinctive, a new and fresh idea, a bent that crept silently into our lives and became a preoccupation and a common subject for conversation.

Perhaps it was the result of the noise which increasingly bedeviled our urban lives. Thanks to California's benign climate, her people tend to live outdoors, to relax, engage in sports, and to entertain in back yards, on balconies, on driveways, or if indoors, it's with all the windows open, so that everyone within earshot can share the occasion. Perhaps it is because of their fondness for outdoor amusement that Californians have gained their erroneous reputation for endless pleasure-seeking; but no, Californians don't necessarily devote more of their time to amusement than other citizens do–they just do so more conspicuously. I have heard the ghetto blasters of Manhattan, outsize portable radios carried with swinging step along the sidewalks of upper Broadway; the California equivalent is a new car with the tape-deck at maximum volume and all the windows open cruising Any Boulevard, the sound rising boundlessly into the balmy California night.

Perhaps it was the too close proximity of people, particularly on our postage-stamp plots of land; not that we would not prefer the Midwest's spacious green fenceless lots, or the graciously sited Colonials of suburban Boston. But land costs are so high in coastal California that only the rich can afford expensive elbow room. Perhaps it was the roar of freeway traffic with five lanes of cars speeding a few feet apart in both directions, so that a miscalculation in changing lanes causes a fender-bender, or worse, forcing young fathers with incipient stomach ulcers to arrive home when the children are already asleep. Perhaps it was the police helicopters overhead pursuing malefactors day and night. Perhaps it was the fire trucks and ambulances howling and burping without end, or so it seems.

Perhaps our thoughts turned to mountain solitude because of the growing difficulty of finding space in the parks in the county. Reservations are needed for overnight camping, even if you hike in three miles to your campsite, and there are limits on the number of people and cars where you put up your tent. During the fairest time of the year the campgrounds are full. Trails are crowded with hikers and horsemen and no dogs are allowed. Yet I don't feel any animosity towards the park managers who create and enforce these regulations, because within an hour's drive from the mountain parks live two and a half million people, enough to overwhelm any park without strict controls. Of course, the thought of the white granite of the Sierras is enticing, but separating us from it are four hundred miles and the troll under the bridge, Los Angeles and its traffic.

Opportunities for outdoor solitude are limited in San Diego County because its mountain ranges are narrow and barely exceed six thousand feet in elevation and there are no lakeside tracts worthy of mention. The desert beckons, but the punishing heat limits activity to only part of the year and privacy, except for isolated regions, all too often is minimal.

We felt a lemming-like urge to leave the city behind and seek a piece of land that offered relatively unspoiled contact with nature. Perhaps we might yet find an expansive view over hill and lee, a show of seasons exceeding what we know in San Diego, and a place of contemplation with the opportunity to hear the wind and see the stars without the roar of the city.

We began to peruse the want adds under "Rural land–San Diego County" and spent our weekends on long country drives. We discovered that the county has a wealth of backcountry with isolated houses or small settlements, some of them of astonishing beauty in oak-filled valleys or on heights with views over misted hills extending to the mesas of Baja California. What was lacking was the protective forest cover we longed for, a cooler climate than what we knew near the coast, and the sweeping landscape present at higher altitudes.

Our spirits rose, however, as we toured the highlands around North Peak and the Julian area northeast of San Diego. Here were forests of mixed conifers and oaks, rough terrain of ravine and ridge, glimpses of distant landmarks, and perhaps a view of the sea; we sensed that nature still dominated this landscape. Man was here only a sometime thing, and he had not yet altered the wildness, even if it was not really wilderness. Probably this was because most of the land was national forest and state park. We voiced a wordless prayer of thanks that this region so close to two large cities had not become another Big Bear, an Idylwild, or a Pinetop, Arizona.

Glimpsing a For Sale sign on a plot alongside a winding wooded road, I paused to write down the realtor's name when I saw a familiar figure, a man who had come onto the road in pursuit of a straying dog. Now semi-retired, he had worked with me for years. He told me he lived in a house below the road. Why yes, there was in fact abundant land for sale hereabouts, he said. Twenty years earlier a developer had cut a tract of land into small parcels of two to five acres and put them on the market; this when the public was not as yet opposed to the idea of selling forest land in small plots to private parties. He recommended a realtor in Julian, who was pleased to show us land available for purchase on the front slope of North Peak.

The tract extended across the rounded shoulder of North Peak at an altitude between 3800 and 4800 feet, generally facing west, northwest, and rarely, south, and therefore no two plots had the same exposure, slope, views, and accessibility. They ranged along a network of unpaved lanes laid out on a level contour whenever possible. Two certain principles were that the higher the elevation the better the view and the closer to the county paved road the more accessible the site. Some of the lots we inspected were small and close to their neighbors. Some were so long and narrow that they offered limited building sites, given the steepness of the terrain, while others were so close to the county road that we rejected them out of hand; if we wanted noise and dust and the threat of thieves and vandals we could easily find them in the city.

But there was one lot for sale that caught our eye. It was a mile from Engineers Road so it was quiet. It was above the lane so no one passing by could look down at us from their cars. Most important of all, it had a variety of terrains with a ravine which promised a rain brook during the winter. In this swale grew oaks and the largest Coulter pine we had seen on the mountain. The lot sloped gently upward, and the skirt of the hill was perhaps flat enough for a house site. From this point there was a view through trees towards Mount Woodson and Starvation Mountain half way to the coast. Later I was to discover on a wondrous day free of the haze almost perpetually hanging over the Pacific beaches that we could indeed see the ocean like beaten brass when the afternoon sun was low in the sky. But when we were considering the purchase of the property the possibility of an ocean view was still questionable. A tiny shack stood on the property that could serve as a temporary camp site and tool shed. A

74

local water district delivered excellent water to the plot; we were relieved of the worry and expense of digging a well–this was perhaps $10,000 saved. Since the soil was the richest humus, at least for the top foot or so, and the slope was moderate, it looked as though a small vineyard and an orchard might thrive. I knew that Julian, not far away, is famed for its apples, and I had noted an abandoned but flourishing grape vine on a roadside fence nearby which hinted that this might be a land of the vine, a fact we later found to be true.

Oddly, the fertility of the soil was also a source of some concern, for the land faced northwest so that it retained moisture unlike the baking west and south slopes, and it had such rich soil that on it grew an unbroken mantle of pine, brush, and oaks. If we wanted to build on this site we would need to hire a bulldozer to clear the fallen trees and flatten the luxuriant underbrush. If we wanted an orchard we would have to carve it out of a wooded hillside.

After some discussion of the merits and limitations of the land, we found ourselves in the realtor's office at the point of making an offer to buy two and a half acres of mountain wilderness. But sitting with my wife across from the realtor, who hung on our every word, I was suddenly taken by doubts about buying the place: the lane would become a bog in heavy rain and was there really a house site under that pile of rotting vegetation?

Sensing my hesitation, my wife leaned over to me and said in a stage whisper: "Buy it!" And so I bit of the apple the temptress offered. But we were not fleeing from paradise, but entering into an Eden with dusty roads, fiercely vital brush, and perhaps a view of the Pacific Ocean. I've never regretted it. Well, hardly ever.

Two Longs and One Short

I don't know how many people live in the Cuyamaca mountains. What's more, I don't know why they have chosen to live here.

Some, especially along the Highway 8 corridor, are not really mountain people because they commute to work in San Diego, find their friends there, and pass their leisure time in the city. They are suburbanites who happen to live in the mountains. Others live in the Cuyamacas because they are natives. This is where they passed their childhood and this is where their forefathers lie in mountain cemeteries where they too will be buried.

Yet others choose to live in the Cuyamacas, although they have the option to live elsewhere. As adults they abandoned familiar places and sank roots in the mountain soil because this is where they want to live.

Felix De Rooy, a native of Great Falls, Montana, after serving as an infantry officer in World War II, graduated from Montana State University. With a degree in Mechanical Engineering in hand, he found employment with U. S. Gypsum; he would work for this company until retirement. In accordance with the management theories of the day, the company assigned him to a dizzying round of assignments, at first supervising part of the operation of a plant, and finally as plant superintendent. As a result, his growing family–by now he had a wife, Margaret, and three children–lived in Lewistown, Montana; Sigurd, Utah; Empire, Nevada; Midland, California; and two times at Plaster City, California, in Imperial County. For two years he worked at U. S. Gypsum's headquarters in Chicago.

While employed at Plaster City, he and his wife began to think of mountain retirement. They had become acquainted with the Cuyamacas when they attended church camps or dined at a well-known mountain restaurant. In 1970 they bought three acres off Engineers Road and began the weekend construction of their comfortable home; it has a typical retirement floor plan–two thousand feet of floor space with two bedrooms. Not far from the house is a work shop for pursuing hobbies and projects. They built the house themselves with the exception of some of the plumbing and the roof which a contractor put on. Engineers tend to be proficient house builders. This is understandable–anyone who can run a wallboard plant can read a blueprint, run a power saw, and toenail a 2 x 4. The house finished, the De Rooys retired for good in the mountains in 1980.

Why did they choose to live in the Cuyamacas? Open space was important. Native of sparsely-populated Montana and having spent most of his working years in small western towns, for De Rooy city life with close neighbors and confining quarters had no appeal. Pine trees are important too, and the breath of mountain air and a view over an expanse of hills and forest. In all of Southern California it would be hard to find mountains like these. In winter snow falls, although in twenty five years the deepest accumulation he remembers is about two feet—just starters for a Montana winter. The change of seasons only adds spice to life.

But it is more than mountain scenery which gives meaning to their lives. This is their home and this is where they choose to live as part of their community. Felix has been a member of the Cuyamaca Sponsor Group (a citizen planning group) for the last eight years. He has been on the board of the Julian-Cuyamaca Fire Protection District for nine years. He was on the board of the North Peak Mutual Water District for twenty-two years, and he has been chairman of the Cuyamaca Property Owners' Association for more years than he can remember.

He also operates the road grader owned by the home owners' association, maintaining private roads in the area. Before that, because he owned a tractor, everyone called him when someone was stuck in mountain mud. He pulled them out, free of charge. To anyone who lives off Engineers Road he is the man to turn to if you have a leak in your water line, if you need an electrician, or someone to repair the roof. He is our walking Yellow Pages.

What are his concerns about living in the mountains, I asked him. He paused a moment and answered: mountain people need better communications, better telephone service. There is always the possibility of a medical emergency and everyone fears the outbreak of wildfire, when help is needed, and now. When cellular phones were first available he didn't hesitate to pay $1700 for a telephone. Now they are almost free, although the service is not. But still the line is not always open and sometimes it goes dead. What the mountains need, he opines, is reliable low-cost telephones.

Perhaps the most telling answer he gave to questions I put to him about his renewed life in the mountains was the response to the question: who are his friends? Without hesitating he answered they were his neighbors. Among a group of people from a variety of backgrounds he has found individuals who are most important to him in the world anywhere, besides his family. The mountains have given him something which is rare in the city–close neighbors who are close friends. I can't think of a better definition of community.

Relying on his engineer's training, so that he and his circle can stay in touch, he installed a surplus army field telephone. He rigged it up to connect the neighborhood, stretching the wires from tree to tree and from house to house. If you're fortunate enough to be one of the fourteen home-owners who are part of the system, you know that to call the De Rooys, just to chat or in an emergency, you crank the handle on your telephone two longs and one short. Somebody will answer.

March

March

At the age of twelve when I discovered that girls were not the same as boys, I sometimes played spin the bottle with other children my age. The idea was to sit on the floor in a circle and spin a bottle, preferably a milk bottle. When the bottle stopped, pointing at a member of the opposite sex, you had to kiss her. The girl might be a Shirley Temple look-alike, or something less. You took your chances.

In the mountains March is spin the bottle month. The bottle spins, but who knows where it will stop? It might show blissful mild days or an Iditarod wind, swelling moist soil or mire, temperatures in the seventies or in the twenties, a foot of snow over mud like chocolate pudding or peach blossoms, or daffodils proudly in bloom or nailed to the ground by wet snow. March is unpredictable, uncertain, chancy, t-shirts or down jackets, dry roads or chains, a doze in the sun or trying to find some place where the wind is not blowing. March in the mountains is fickle, a Jezebel, the kind of a lady who goes out on the town when her sailor husband is in the Western Pacific.

Not that I'm complaining. Anyone who thinks that our weather is grim and demands more from the soul than it can deliver should read one of the tall stack of books New Englanders have written about country life. He will cease complaining, instantly. For example, the coldest temperature *ever* recorded in San Diego County is four degrees below zero. Some New Englanders have weather much colder than that in March when we're nearly sure it's spring.

Daffodils begin to open in the sunniest places at our land about March 1 and the peak of bloom is about March 15. David Grayson, whose real name was Ray Stannard Baker, wrote in his 1936 book *Countryman's Year* that at his house in Amherst, Massachusetts, the daffodils "were coming into glowing bloom" on April 22, about six weeks later than ours. Our winters are real, but laid back, not New England gnarly, as they might say in Mission Beach.

But still March weather is unpredictable, more so than any other month. First the good news about the weather. As noted, daffodils are at their most magnificent this month. We admire them under the oaks and pines in all their splendor. I have planted nearly two thousand bulbs on our acres; they thrive without care, multiply like brush rabbits, require no water or fertilizer, and best of all, neither deer nor the curse of the mountain gardener, gophers, eat them. Everyone loves them and they keep well as cut flowers–what more can anyone ask of a flower?

The color of daffodils is hypnotic, penetrating in the shade, fluorescent, a color that glows against any background, but especially the siennas and umbers of early spring. Unable to describe the essence of daffodil yellow in words, I turned to *Webster's Third International Dictionary,* where I found the most wondrous definition, as follows: "A variable color averaging a brilliant yellow that is greener, lighter, and stronger than lemon yellow and greener, stronger, and slightly darker than butter yellow." Next time that someone asks me what color is daffodil yellow, really? I'm going to spring that one on them. But one thing is clear: everyone recognizes and loves daffodils in the mountains.

In March our few lilac bushes bloom, usually towards the end of the month. For comparison, in Moscow they bloom in May. We have in fact very few lilacs that bloom, because the gophers that will not eat our daffodils compensate by eating our lilacs. The history of my attempts to grow the variety of Persian and French lilacs I remember from my childhood does not make pretty reading

I suppose that everyone knows that lilacs are rare in coastal California. Only recently has Descanso Gardens produced a variety that blooms in spite of the region's mild winters. My neighbor, born and bred in the Southland, admitted he'd never seen a lilac and asked me to describe one. Taken aback, I had to struggle to describe a plant that in much of North America and Europe is almost as common as daisies.

Notable wildlife makes its appearance in March. I have seen a western bluebird on March 16; later that day as the sun set I saw bats. This is good evidence for the mildness of the month because neither of these creatures would have appeared had the weather not been temperate enough to hatch the insects on which they feed. But the creatures did not stay with us, because a few days later the weather was beastly, or should I say in this context non-beastly?

During the month of March my little weather station has recorded temperatures of 75 and 79 degrees, very mild indeed. However, there's a downside to the month. For example, 7.7" of rain fell in three March days last year. In the last two years we have had March snows that measured more than a foot in depth; my neighbors could not make their way out their driveways to civilization and their mail boxes. March 1995 showed the worst the month can deliver: one day at the end of the month the temperature was 74 degrees. Then snow fell and a few days later the thermometer dropped to 25 degrees. While we may not live in Vermont, this was a winter experience to remember.

March is the month that rightly belongs to a twelve-year-old— every day is full of surprises and some nasty tricks too. But mostly it's a month of hope for the future, as yet only dimly perceived.

North Peak Trail

In 1975 the State of California purchased 2,003 acres of land on North Peak that it appended to the northern end of Cuyamaca Rancho State Park. This panhandle on the park cost $1,362,000, which pencils out to less than $7,000 an acre, an outstanding bargain today when mountain land may fetch $20,000 an acre.

The swathe of new state land crosses the high slopes of North Peak at an altitude from about 4,500 feet to 5,500 feet. Excluded is the peak's summit at 5,993 feet and the many private homes surrounding the crest that are emerging as the community of Cuyamaca. Mostly sloping westward, this is a beautiful secluded segment of the State Park. Recently, my wife and I spent a half-day visiting these nearly unknown Cuyamaca woods.

We met no one else on the trail. I doubt that this corner of the park will ever become as popular for hiking and riding as the southern and more genial sections of the park with their gracious circling trails, springs, and sunny picnic sites with views to the Laguna Mountains or the distant metropolis. This extension is long and narrow and only this solitary trail, the North Peak Trail that begins above Kelly Ditch and ends at William Heise County Park on Cedar Creek about five miles north, threads this northern projection on the park. Friends dropped us off at Engineers Road where the trail begins; we were to follow the trail north to the County Park where our own vehicle waited.

After saying good-bye to our friends we followed the signs to an old dirt road dating from the time when lumbermen harvested trees hereabouts. Today no one is cutting lumber anywhere on the mountain; summer home owners and park rangers rule this kingdom. According to the files of the *San Diego Union* a saw mill existed on North Peak as early as 1869; if this is correct then the Cuyamaca lumber industry began the same year as gold mining. Later records show a new mill was built in 1897 on the mountain; it burned down and was replaced in 1902. According to a 1933 map an "Old Sawmill" stood somewhere along the road we were walking, directly north of North Peak. The sawmill was probably small, since a contemporary newspaper article states that the mill mostly manufactured

84

apple boxes needed at the Wynola orchards. However, no doubt many of the downed trees were dragged off the mountain to be milled elsewhere–as we shall see.

What species of trees did the lumberjacks cut on North Peak? While ponderosa (or Jeffrey) pine and sugar pine are the most desirable Western lumber trees, I've never seen either of them on the front of North Peak. The conifers I've seen are Coulter pine, whose wood is so light and brittle that it is good only for firewood and mine timbers; white fir, sometimes of quite large dimension; and incense cedar. I imagine the woodmen mostly put their axes and saws to these last two–white fir and especially incense cedar. Although it is light, it is also strong and readily accepts nails without splitting. Resistant to rot, it is well suited for placing in water or soil. In 1951 when the developer Ed Fletcher took well-publicized legal action to end logging on land he had sold on North Peak with the stipulation that it could never be timbered, the article in the *Union* says that the timber being cut was destined for the "Mission Bay project," perhaps as pilings. According to the article "The tract is the largest timbered area remaining in private ownership in San Diego County."

Further along the trail we found confirmation of sorts for the theory that the lumbermen cut primarily cedar: here stand three mossy cedar stumps, obviously hand cut, conspicuous relics of the North Peak lumber boom of the early 20th century. And finally, we asked ourselves, what kind of trees should we expect to see growing near Cedar Creek?

There's something very pleasing about the early stretches of the trail. In breadth it is more than ample. Fallen oak leaves litter and soften the road. Deer tracks stitch every dried puddle with their uncial v's. Foxes have left little twisted brown calling cards for anyone to read. The breast of the mountain has a wonderful swelling rise, just as you'd expect a mountain to have. Through the trees you can see Palomar Mountain and its pimple observatory. Below, the hills between North Peak and Ramona lie a rumpled carpet of oaks and chaparral, with pine trees, a newer and richer green after the winter rains, puncturing the carpet here and there. Dirt roads loop over the landscape below, like strands of spaghetti, coming, going, rising, falling. The early spring sun warms the air in the open, but it's cool in the shade.

Not only conifers grow on the mountain. Here, nearly a mile

high, scattered canyon live oaks are sturdy, sometimes stout. They hold fast to their dark green leaves, and spatter the ground below them with their generous acorns. In places Kellogg oaks grow, now leafless, although in the more protected locations they reveal their shocking new buds, something like ripening peach or fuchsia, some have written, or baby blanket pink.

These sunny open groves of Kellogg oaks provide some of the most agreeable scenes in the California mountain landscape. For five months or so of the year they are leafless, and under them prospers an under-story of snowberry and wild rose that is so low–thigh high–that a walker can stride through it easily anywhere he wishes to go. Under the understory grows an under-understory of herbs, especially wild strawberry, whose fresh green leaves are opening just now.

In the sunnier places at this altitude bracken fern grows everywhere. Now it is only bedraggled brown strands from last year littering the meadows, but soon its fiddleheads will spring open and the land here will be high in bracken. Bracken flourishes all over the northern hemisphere; I've seen it under Russian birches and firs. In Russian folklore they tell many stories about bracken. On midsummer night the peasants believed it flowered secretly deep in the woods. With the help of its flower a lucky man could find buried treasure or work spells. In time of famine peasants ate stinging nettle greens, bread made from a weed, crows foot, and boiled bracken roots.

We had the foresight to bring a picnic lunch with us and this is the place we chose to eat it. The sky is expansive still and vistas open towards the lowlands at the mountain's foot. Pines and oaks dot the landscape, nicely spaced, offering pleasant shade and vantage points across miniature meadows into rolling woods, open patches of rank grass, and chaparral oaks and manzanita here and there. This is where Azalea Creek has its origins, in these open meadows; there must be azaleas (*Rhododendron occidentale*) along its course, but I have not seen them. Most of the year Azalea Creek lives as a stream a foot wide and six inches deep, but one that wildlife in the region deeply appreciate; the best place to see wild turkeys this year is where Azalea Creek flows under Engineers Road. Almost a straight line on the maps, its brief tumultuous course ends at Boulder Creek, a mile from these mountain meadows and a thousand feet lower.

The old timber road curves around the shoulder of North Peak until a rusting barbed-wire fence and a sign reading "No Hunting or Trespassing" block it. Our map shows that the road continues east to circle the mountain. From here on we followed a trail that is narrow, shaded, recent, and man-made. Crews from the California Conservation Corps, the West Fork Honor Camp, Boy Scouts, and 4-H Club volunteers built this trail early in the 1980s; it was opened to public use on June 1, 1985.

Walking the trail reminded me that New York is a great city for monuments. Everywhere stand statues to the great men of the past–politicians, writers, thinkers, and others. The most imposing is Grant's Tomb, above the Hudson, now sadly neglected and graffiti-ridden in a run-down section of the city.

However, after spending a summer in Manhattan, I decided that what the city sorely lacked was a monument to the men who keep it operating from day to day: elevator repairmen. Virtually everyone in the city rides elevators every day, and all too often these require the services of the unknown men whose voices you can hear echoing in those awe-inspiring elevator shafts. I once lived on the sixteenth floor of a building in Manhattan; when the building's elevators ceased to function I might have as well been on a desert island, not in the world capital. Few can walk up sixteen flights of stairs. All hail the nameless unseen workmen who keep those entirely essential elevators rising and falling–the elevator repairmen! And where is the monument dedicated to these modest individuals who make life possible in the city?

In the mountain west a memorial is needed to a similar group of humble unknown men who have made access possible into the mountains–the trail builders. I have walked thousands of miles of trails in the Rockies, the Uintas, the coast ranges of Washington and California, the Sierras, the southwest desert ranges, very rarely knowing who built the trails I trod that added so much to my life. Who were these faceless men? Why are they forgotten today? Forest Service summer employees, enthusiastic volunteers, honor camp prisoners, the CCC boys of the 1930s–thousands of unknown men (and some women) opened up the mountains of the west.

Somewhere in the west there should be an imposing monument depicting the trail blazers, perhaps in the high boots of the 1920s with their shovels and picks and pack mules with canvas tents and wooden boxes of dynamite, laboring on some granite face to open a trail into remote canyons, glacial cirques, or over a trackless pass. This small army of workers deserves the endless thanks of the western mountain lover. Let's take up a collection and build them a fitting tribute. Without them the western wilderness would never have become the treasure it is today for millions of walking and riding Americans.

We began our descent into the canyon cut by Cedar Creek. Without the trail this country would be entirely inaccessible. Oak and manzanita chaparral, dark thickets of cedar saplings, tangles of wild rose and gooseberry, festoons of poison oak, rotting logs–the accumulation of perhaps eighty years of unchecked vigorous plant growth–mantle the cool northern slope leading down to the stream. Anyone who wished to pass here before the trail was built would have had to crawl on his hands and knees much of the time. Through this tangle the trail makes progress easy and rapid, open, and touched with sunshine.

This slope has not burned for many decades. True, some old trees, snags and multiple-trunk trees that the lumbermen elected not to cut, display fire scars, blackened healed wounds at ground level. At our cabin a few miles away I can't find any of these charcoaled brands, evidence that this part of the mountain burned more recently than our neighborhood. Perhaps the lumberjacks set fires to burn off the slash, making it easier to drag trees off the hill. Since the last fire, an accumulation of dead brush and rampant new growth has piled up, the most impenetrable being cedar thickets that choke much of this cool slope. Any passing fire would have decimated these youngsters, leaving park-like glades less likely to produce a holocaust today. The proximity of many houses, especially those in Pine Hills that are visible from the trail, makes preventive burning by park authorities unlikely.

On the last stretch of the trail, a new sound imperceptibly crept into my awareness, a persistent, sweet, fresh murmur, the sweetest sound in the west–water running over stones, music especially haunting on this mostly waterless mountain. Other signs declared that water was not far away: willows flashed their incomparable spring green, bare-twigged alders rose above the willows like disapproving older brothers, dusty coast live oaks, here at their highest range, extended far enough up the slope that if they could hear the stream at all it would sound like little girls whispering and giggling to each other in bed after lights were out.

We crossed the brook on mossy boulders, enjoying the flash of light off the water's surface. and cooled by the sight of plants swaying in the current. Someone had planted a bench above the stream, and so we paused to rest, our legs trembling after the swift drop down the last mile of trail. Later in the year the sun will be so hot in this hidden place that no one will sit on the bench during the day, but at twilight it must be pleasant to rest here and listen to the water and watch swallows and then bats fluttering over this vale, not of tears, but of cool mountain air made yet cooler by the stream.

As the trail climbs up and out of the valley it falls into a curious feature on the landscape, a deeply sunken ascending road, reminding me of the roads in the Brady photographs of the Gettysburg battlefield, but without the corpses. This is a skid road where teams dragged logs off North Peak to the road in Pine Hills, each one gouging out soft woodland soil until they cut a yard-deep trench across the landscape. Once the skid road must have been ugly, muddy and raw, but now it is a placid lane under oaks that have closed ranks above it. Only a few hikers plod by, but once it was busy with horses and mules and cursing teamsters.

Through the trees we saw our truck waiting for us by the roadside. Three hours earlier our friends let us out at Engineers Road. Two hours we walked and one hour we sat at our picnic under an old Coulter pine where there were not too many ants. After lunch we both napped under a mild springtime sun.

I Design a House

*Building a house for yourself is exciting, because of the feeling
of possibility that a new house carries, and because creating shelter
is a basic human urge, whether or not you are an architect. It is the
same urge that makes children erect playhouses out of blankets and
cardboard boxes, and build sand castles at the beach...*

Witold Rybczynski

During my lifetime I have seen the Pope in immaculate white
emerge from St. Peter's balcony at Easter to bless the multitude. I
have crossed the Atlantic on a troop ship from whose deck I saw the
white cliffs of Dover in the moonlight. I have studied with a teacher
who received the Nobel Prize as we all applauded. I have circumam-
bulated the Kremlin and toasted the American ambassador and his
lady at Spaso House on the fourth of July. I have seen the astilbes
bloom in Kew Garden. From the terraces of Topkapi Palace I have
watched a rusted tramp steamer sail up the Bosporus. In the Louvre I
have contemplated the most beautiful painting in the world, Leonar-
do's *Virgin of the Rocks.* And in these later days I have designed a
house.

Not a very large house, mind you, and one that wouldn't merit
much more than a glance from a professional architect, but to design
it produced the greatest exhilaration, combining irresolution, vision-
ary dreams, cold calculation, and pure pleasure. When I had completed it I not only felt satisfaction as the exhilaration faded, but also
a puzzling gratitude that I had been awarded this joyful, disquieting
experience. We pass much of our lives in our shelters, but few of us
have the opportunity to plan and build our domiciles; we must take
what others grant us. The privilege of designing a house was now,
unexpectedly, mine.

When I pondered the surprising emotion that gripped me in the
process of designing this simple house, I realized that there was, perhaps, an explanation for my heightened feelings: all these years I
dimly yearned, subconsciously yearned, to be an architect, but for
some reason this had never come about. Or perhaps my desire to
design was simply an expression of a basic human urge to build, as
Mr. Rybczynski describes it. Whatever the reason, I had the opportunity and I would take advantage of it, with long-buried, little-

understood enthusiasm.

My subconscious interest in building, perhaps, was because in my childhood I often had the opportunity to see architects at work. An uncle and three cousins were partners in an architectural firm that designed some of the prominent, if undistinguished, buildings in our city. Sometimes my father and I visited their office where I was given a pencil and paper and told to amuse myself; only an architect would think of this as a suitable pastime for a twelve year old. When I recall those visits it occurs to me that my uncle's attentions had a hidden motive–if I had demonstrated any aptitude for drawing or design he would have noted it. After all, I was a member of the family, and besides, it's my observation that architects are unusually sympathetic to talent. But in this case I must admit that I had no special aptitude for the skills required of a future architect. So my uncle's office door never opened for me.

Often architects visited our home to leave work for my father. Many architects are unsure about their ability to engineer the elements of load and stress in the buildings they design; this was a branch of the profession in which my father excelled. So they would bring their blueprints which he spread out on our dining room table and a few days later he would have all the specifications ready for the architect. At this time in my life, if you asked me to describe an architect I would have answered that he was a young man in glasses who needed a haircut for his thinning hair, always in a hurry, carrying an armload of blueprints, and who, unlike my father, could not design girders and trusses.

Years after I left the city of my birth I discovered that in my childhood I was unknowingly familiar with the work of one of America's great builders. Who knows, maybe his exceptional structure somehow, some way, encouraged in me an interest in building design I was hardly aware of, and at an early age.

In the late 1930s my father rented an office in a business block downtown. I remember the building's expansive lobby and stairs, the massive cornice that topped it, and the large, handsome Romanesque windows that adorned its facade. It was constructed of a distinctive red sandstone quarried from a site in view of the city. Chicago's Louis Sullivan, America's most influential architect and Frank Lloyd Wright's mentor, designed this building, the only structure in the city to which he turned his hand, and in it my father had his office.

Unfortunately, the building was later razed and a shiny orange, white, and blue "motor hotel," eminently forgettable, unlike Sullivan's building, now stands in its place.

Before I began designing the house I perused a dozen books, perhaps, on domestic architecture and house building. Some of them were so discouraging that I thought of abandoning my project, but some were inspiring. Of them, two books were especially engaging, although they were very different in their approaches. *A Field Guide to American Houses* by Virginia and Lee McAlester contains hundreds of photographs of houses in America built during the last three hundred years. It became my favorite evening reading and a source of some ideas that I later claimed as my own–the highest praise, I think.

I was also taken by Cathy Johnson's *A Naturalist's Cabin. Constructing a Dream,* in which she enthusiastically describes how she built a small place in the woods in northwest Missouri, a combination part-time residence and artist's studio. Her cabin, like the one I hoped to build, rises at an isolated site out of the reach of her neighbors and close to trees and wildlife.

Almost from the first page I discovered that she constructed her cabin under a set of rules very different from ours in urbanized Southern California. To build her cabin she hired a skilled and trusted carpenter who worked without plans, relying on her instructions and his abilities. From random sources she bought old windows and doors and accessories that the carpenter installed here and there. She and the carpenter set up the posts supporting the cabin/studio in a few days. The result, judging from her sketches, is a whimsical structure bursting with originality and idiosyncrasies that meets all her expectations for a cabin in the woods.

On the other hand, before beginning construction on our cabin we had to submit five copies of our plans prepared by a state licensed architect to the County Planning Commission. Clerks in the office inspected them, as well as a civil engineer who did not always like what he found.

We also operated under the strictures of the Universal Building Code, the planner's bible. The UBC sometimes ran rough-shod over our fondest ideas, for it has all the power of the Code of Hammurabi over the ancient Babylonians.

For example, the Planning Commission and the UBC strongly

influenced the size and placement of windows in the house. The front wall of the house catches the southwestern sun and so I saw it as virtually one great window. Not so fast, the engineer pointed out. This is a shear wall, that is, a wall intended to prevent rack across the width of the house. You must maintain at least four feet of the wall in stud and siding. As a consequence, we abandoned the idea of one giant window and placed three large windows at one end of the wall and left the other end solid. Since this wall possesses the best view, I thought we would extend the windows from floor to ceiling. Not so fast, once more the UBC decreed. No windows can extend more than eighteen inches from the floor or else a tipsy guest might mistake a window for an open door and try to walk through it. The windows were raised well above the floor.

Another example will show why Cathy Johnson could never have built her dream cabin on North Peak. Since the bedrooms face the full power of the cold Santa Ana winds it seemed reasonable to make these windows small. Hold up, the UBC said, every room must have at least one generous window at a certain height from the floor so that in case of emergency it could serve as an exit. So we revised the windows in the bedrooms.

These restrictions make good sense and I have no quarrel with them. I don't want the wind pushing over the house, or a guest slicing an artery on a window pane, or a fire trapping a visitor in his bedroom, but they add a new set of limitations on the builder of a house in our region. And because the planning bureaucracy must support itself with fees imposed on the builder, I spent more money at the Cashier's window of County Planning even before we began construction than Cathy Johnson did for the total cost of her little studio cabin.

Another question presented itself: should the house be innovative, an original shaping of space, to use the jargon, or, on the other hand, should I look to the past for models, and if so, to what aspects of the past? While the first option at first had powerful appeal–the idea that not only could I design a house for the first time in my life, but that I could create something which would be innovative and original–I was afraid that I lacked the talent to design a convincing and attractive structure. I was afraid that with all my efforts and enthusiasm I would succeed in designing a house that was ugly. And we would have to live in it.

No, I would make the the more cautious choice and turn to the architecture of the past as my inspiration. I was comfortable with this course of action. I wasn't searching for history in the narrow sense; I had no desire to built a Cotswold Cottage or a Saltbox or a Prairie House. In existing houses I would look for the elements to which I responded in a positive and pleasurable way. In a word, I would be eclectic, picking, choosing, adapting, modifying, and expanding what I found worthwhile, as the spirit moved. I hoped to design a house which pleased my eye and also functioned satisfactorily.

Of course, this declaration contains the seeds of a contradiction. Not to my surprise, often in the design of the house I had to decide between an attractive aspect of the house's design and its functioning. Nowhere was this more apparent than when I had to choose a design for the cabin roof.

From the first I was determined that the house would be crowned by a hip roof with as low a profile as possible to repeat the rounded outlines of the surrounding hills. But a hip roof would provide very limited headroom in the loft, since of course the ceiling would slope down in every direction. Obviously, a shed roof or open gables or dormer windows would greatly increase the space available on the second floor. The conflict between two concepts was clear–aesthetics or utility. I pondered this question many times. Ultimately, I decided to retain the hip roof in spite of the fact that it was at the expense of living space. Now that the house is standing, I'm confident I made the right decision.

This conflict between appearance and function arose often in the design of the house. I found that I nearly always felt (it was hardly a rational decision) that form over-rode questions of function. Puzzled at first by what seemed to be almost an instinctive bias, I decided that my approach to the design of the house was primarily aesthetic. Considerations of appearance, in the widest sense of outline, material, and texture, came foremost. I wasn't just designing a house to be lived in, but something I hoped to admire. So overwhelming was this impulse that I finally surrendered to it completely. For better or worse, this house would reflect my sensibilities.

Early on, we accepted some limitations shaping both the appearance and functioning of the cabin in radical ways. Of these, the most important was the decision that the house would not exceed one thousand square feet, since I was determined that it would remain a cabin intended for weekends or vacations and not duplicate our urban residence. I came very close to my goal since the cabin measures only 1008 square feet. It must have a screen porch so we could sit in the fresh air in June and July when the air swarms with gnats, deer-flies, and mosquitoes, and so it does. Because the climate is so benign, the cabin was to encourage easy movement between indoors and outdoors. I can stroll entirely around the house under three foot eaves and an expansive deck fronts the house; the thousand foot interior is matched by six hundred square feet of walkways and decks. To enhance the bond between house and field, there would be no concrete walks, steps, or retaining walls, but we gave priority to ramps and gravelled paths that would not be edged, the grass and wildflowers invading the walkways at will.

Inside, I chose to find as much space as possible for a large living room, and the bedrooms were to be small. As a consequence, the living room is twenty-four by eighteen feet, and the two bedrooms have space for a bed, a chair, a dresser, and precious little else. The kitchen and bathroom are minimal; this is no place to prepare a banquet or luxuriate in tile and vapors. There is a loft for the children (with not much headroom), but they have to climb a ladder to reach it, for I found no place for a staircase. I specified ample windows and two skylights to lighten dark corners. The largest windows face south and west–the sources of sunlight.

We chose board and batten for the exterior walls that were to be stained a soft tan, like a faded oak leaf; board and batten is the favored surface for cabins in gold country, the battens repeating the vertical lines of the pines. After much discussion, we decided to paint the interior off-white to enhance sunlight within the house.

The house is now nearly completed. I have the pleasure of standing back to see it profiled against the pines and oaks. Gratified, I know that I have created a dwelling where nothing was before. I like to think what I have done is attractive to look at and welcoming to visitors who find its door. Designing a house was a pleasure I would not have missed for all the world.

Topographic Maps

When I was fifteen years old I fell in love with maps. Not the ordinary maps of the states or even the world, but topographic maps published as the United States Geological Survey Quadrangles at 1:24000 scale with forty-foot contour intervals. I'll never forget how we first met on the third floor of the post office building in a noisy room with tall cabinets equipped with pull-out drawers so that the maps lay in thick rich piles, their edges sensuously curled. For a song, a fifteen year old boy could purchase one of these wonderfully detailed maps, and the mountains he knew only sketchily and casually became solid, with ridges, lakes, passes, trails, mines, roads improved and unimproved, all shown in many colors and many names.

The first quadrangle I bought had a wonderful name: "Dromedary Peak." I wanted it because I knew the mountains there a little and because it had family connections. It was in Mineral Fork on this map that my father had owned a mine, nameless, but once rich in dreams of wealth, if not high-grade ore. Flush with money earned by taking contracts to construct highway bridges in the road-building frenzy of the 1920s and in the face of my mother's violent opposition, my father believed that his mine would at last make him rich, richer than his brothers. After two years of nearly fruitless labor and high expenditures my father had to admit that while the ore was there (isn't it always?) it was so lean that it would not pay for its own extraction, let alone make a profit for the owner. So he threw in the towel, not for the last time, leaving only family memories of "Father's mine," now so insignificant a scar on a talus slope that it is not even recorded as a prospect on the Dromedary Peak quadrangle.

With the sweat-stained map in my backpack, I crossed and re-crossed the trails along the ridges above the mine, exploring my miniature *terra incognita*. The map was an essential aid in avoiding disaster in a rugged landscape where a thousand foot cliff is common. Later in the year when snow made it impossible for me to leave the house, I found pleasure tracing the features of the map, struggling to visualize the slopes from the map's contour lines that curl like a dozen night crawlers in a can for sale for fifty cents according to the hand-written sign on the front lawn.

Another pleasure came from reading the names of the mines on the map, a wonderful record of name-giving, full of the whimsy and zest of human life. Above my father's hole in the ground was the Regulator Johnson Mine. I do not know who Regulator Johnson was. A Baby McKee Mine was there, as well as a Tar Baby Mine. Had a Taffy named the rich and productive Cardiff Mine? The Sampson Mine had a favorite name, and also, its syllables singing to the ear, had the Reed and Benson Mine on Reed and Benson Ridge. On the map are the Eclipse Mine and the Flagstaff Mine. Every one of these names had a story and a history. Doubtless every one of its owners hoped that a shaft dug into solid quartzite on an inhospitable slope at 10,200 foot elevation was going to buy him a mansion and a gaudy wife in Salt Lake or Denver or even New York City.

So, like all good western boys at an early age I learned that mountains mean USGS maps, the two going together like a prospector and his burro. Now, most of the Cuyamaca range fits onto two topographic maps, the Cuyamaca Peak quadrangle and the Julian quadrangle. To the west are the Tule Springs (before I die I'd like to see Tule springs) and the Santa Isabel quadrangles. My favorite is the Julian quadrangle, of course, because it details the front of North Peak, my neighborhood.

Like the maps I loved when I was a boy, it is on the scale of 1:24000, so it covers the terrain from Lake Cuyamaca to Arkansas Canyon and from Boulder Creek to the Cigarette Hills. But unlike the land over which I rambled long ago, much of the Cuyamacas is inaccessible, thanks to almost impenetrable chaparral and woods mantling its slopes. Then, too, the map does not show the No Trespass signs that discourage entry into much of the back country. The map utilizes the same forty-foot contour lines as the maps of my youth, so that reading the map, while still difficult, at least presents a familiar challenge.

The map tells me that our cabin is at the 4250 foot level and that Sandy Creek where it crosses our lane is at 4060 feet, which helps me understand why sycamores grow there. From the map I learn that rain falling on our land flows to the west and ultimately joins Cedar Creek. The Tule Springs quadrangle shows that Cedar Creek merges with the San Diego River until El Capitan Dam detains it. Raindrops falling on our land ultimately emerge from someone's tap in the city of San Diego.

The topographic map is especially good at showing improvements to the land. So far as I can judge, it indicates every unpaved road in the region, including some of which are only bulldozer tracks through the chaparral. Every older house is a brown rectangle, including my neighbors' places, and the map also indicates rare clearings, guacamole in the avocado of the woodlands. This precision is the result of modern technology, for a note at the foot of the map states that the map was revised on the basis of aerial photographs in 1980. No longer must surveyors spend exhausting days dragging their instruments through the poison oak to revise the map; a pilot and a draftsman revised it. Perhaps even the pilot was not needed, thanks to the work of earth satellites and their unmanned cameras. The next revision of the Julian quadrangle will no doubt show our house, too. Then I will be able to say I have made my mark on the world.

The map shows that the nearest standing water is three farm ponds along nearby Sandy Creek, but perhaps they don't qualify, for they are cross-hatched to indicate that they are questionable bodies of water. If they don't qualify, then the nearest open water is a pond in the county park about a mile and a half from our place. The map also indicates that our land faces northwest and as you climb up the slope it becomes steeper; the contour lines become closer on the map as you ascend the hill.

As to mines, our immediate neighborhood has none, but they are common in the eastern half of the map. Here I find the King Mine and its consort, the Queen Mine, as well as the Golden Ella, the Lucky Strike, the Cincinnati Bette Mine, the Warlock Mine, and the Lucky Pardner Mine. To end this brief essay about the indispensable USGS topographic maps on a gustatory note, perhaps adolescent note, here I also find the Golden Sugar Mine and the Cold Beef Mine. I think I would have liked those names especially when I was fifteen years old.

April

April

Sometimes we don't see familiar things until we look hard at them. This obvious idea occurred today to me when for the first time I really looked at the new spring growth on North Peak's Kellogg oaks.

Circumstances gave me a half day's leisure in the mountains and so I settled down to see what was going on around me, listening to the insistent three note song of a plain titmouse in an oak near the cabin–if you want to see this nondescript crested bird look in an oak.

I surveyed the hillside before me where Kellogg oaks were budding out delicately, in stark contrast to the darkly green Coulter pines and incense cedars. I realized for the first time that these oaks displayed at least four major colors, forming not a modern monotone wall to wall carpet, but a Turkish kilim of shades including twig black, pinks that have no name, an exotic North Sea amber, and finally new leaf green. I'd always assumed that, well, deciduous Kellogg oaks simply unfolded buds that became green leaves. Something else was going on here.

Kellogg oaks are opening their buds very late this year, perhaps because we have had a dry winter, with only about ten inches of precipitation, one-third of average. Perhaps the trees delayed opening their buds until the very end of the rainy season because it was now or never. Hard on winter's heels warm dry summer weather will march in, and it will be too late then.

I could see that the location of the oak determined its stage of growth. If a tree grew on a windy point, the buds on its branches had barely begun to swell. In one large oak on a knoll I could plainly see clumps of mistletoe against the blue spring sky because the trees had budded so sparsely that their leaves did not yet hide the harsh green parasites the tree nurtured. Other oaks in protected sites, swales and draws, displayed tender powder-green leaves; one of these trees in leaf might crouch only a hundred feet from a hilltop tree that still held up charcoal gray branches to the sweeping south wind.

Most of the oaks, though, were shades of pink, or more accurately, to my mind, rose. As they open, the new leaves are faintly green but tipped with a unique dusty-reddish tint that defies naming. Other writers, as I said elsewhere, resort to fuchsia and ripening peach to describe this color. I wrote that baby blanket pink might do. I don't believe that anyone has yet found the right word to capture this shade; therefore I'm going to call it "Kellogg oak spring rose," a clumsy phrase, but one at least that expresses the uniqueness of the color. Of course, as the buds open this color alters, the original rose fading as more and more verdure unfolds. As a result, no two oaks possess exactly the same shade, since every tree has its own combination of rose and green. And every tree every day changes color.

Why were some of the trees amber in color, almost orange? Intrigued, I walked to one of these trees to find the answer. As the buds open they show not only new leaves, but also male catkins, finger-length pendant chains that cast pollen into the air indiscriminately. After a short time the catkins dry up, their work done. The color of these dessicating catkins is a tint that I see as amber, somewhere between orange and yellow. From a distance these trees look as though they are flaunting exotic flowers in this rare color, almost as though the tree belonged on some tropical island, say, Sumatra or St. Kitts. Soon the catkins drop to the ground and the amber bloom disappears; not a lengthy stage in the trees' spring unfolding, it is a surprising sight. I must admit I had never noticed it before, although I have seen budding Kellogg oaks many times.

The catkins fallen, new leaves capture the tree. Lime green with the dusty under-surfaces flashing as the wind blows, they have six months or so to nurture the tree by carrying on photosynthesis until autumn's shortening days destroy the chlorophyll and the tree strips down for winter cold and snow's burden. When the leaves turn from summer's business-like green to a soft buttery yellow (in a good year), Ansel Adams emulators will be out in force in Yosemite Valley to capture on film the meadows, the streamside Kellogg oaks, and the soaring granite canyon walls, the perfect fore-, middle-, and background for a prize-winning photograph. Perhaps they will wait for a daytime moon over Half Dome to complete the composition.

I ask myself, has anyone ever captured the subtle range of finely gradated shades that Kellogg oaks display in the middle of April? I'm not sure, but it would be a great challenge. As a matter of fact, there was one painter who succeeded in mastering this muted play of sky and glorious tints in a landscape. I have in mind the eighteenth century French painter Jean Honoré Fragonard, the great exponent of misty garden scenes with aristocratic mademoiselles in billowing gowns and attentive cavaliers in wigs, knee-breeches, and silken hose posturing against an idealized setting where the shrubs, trees, and statuary fade from ornament into unreal insubstantiality. Jean Honoré Fragonard would be the perfect artist, if anyone, to paint oaks in springtime, and particularly to put on canvas Kellogg oak spring rose.

Deeply Graven Rock

I have never expected to discover Indian morteros on our land. This is because it is heavily overgrown with trees and chaparral and the nearest water is a mile away, except in winter when a rain brook chatters down the ravine. I know that Indians lived in the district, just as they lived in all the Southern California hills. They wandered from favored site to favored site, often where oaks grow best, or they made their seasonal migrations to the sea, to the hills, and to the desert. Somewhere, if not on our land, in our district I knew I would find their morteros.

I had seen a place down the mountain that looked promising. One day I walked the road for half an hour to gentler terrain where a small stream, Sandy Creek, flows most of the year. At this place the hills retreat and a plot of alluvium has accumulated where a nameless tributary joins the creek. Here someone has planted an apple orchard of three or four acres. The trees appeared to be Golden Delicious and on this November day the fruit hung heavy among leaves that were still green. Windfalls covered the ground under the trees. I think they were Golden Delicious, but I couldn't verify this at closer range because a five-foot deer fence stood between me and the orchard. Not that a five-foot fence would stop a hungry deer, but it was enough to stop me now.

Past the orchard the dirt road climbed through open meadows, mostly cheat grass and wild oats that long ago usurped the rightful place of the native bunchgrasses. The oaks were magnificent here where I could see them at some remove. Most were the dense dusty blue-green mounds of coast live oak, the commonest oak in Southern California. Scattered among them rose deciduous Kellogg oaks, their leaves now touched with yellow and russet; this year their tints were subdued, perhaps because of the dry summer or the absence of frost this warm autumn. On the margin of the meadows stood an occasional Engelmann oak, with its striped gray bark and spare branches. It looked as though a tree-pruning service had thinned every single Engelmann oak to best display its character, as the garden books say.

Climbing further up the sunny slope, I knew I was not far from a place where I would find morteros. The gracious incline, the oak

104

copses, the sunny meadows, the sense of water nearby, if not in streams then perhaps at a spring, made me confident I would find what I was seeking. On a low knoll I saw the only essential element that was lacking: a massive rounded rock outcrop among the oaks that crowned the hill. Sure enough, walking closer, in the bedrock I counted twenty-two morteros clustered in one small area, and there were probably more that fallen leaves concealed.

For practical reasons the women chose solid rock for their morteros, never cracked or fractured stone, preferring ancient granitic or metamorphic bedrock. These morteros have been here for uncounted hundreds or even thousands of years. I stood near the morteros and felt through the soles of my feet the absolute firmness and permanence of the rock into which they are worn, and the great unknown age of the morteros.

No two of them are identical in size and shape, because each is differently related to the surface of the bedrock into which the women ground them, each in its own fashion; some are deeper than others, some wider. In our modern age when uniform and interchangeable objects are the ideal, the uniqueness of every mortero, like all the work of human hands made with simple tools, asserts the maker's individuality, "You see," each one seems to say, "I wasn't made by a machine, but by human hands, and muscle, and brain."

Probably the Indians collected most of their acorns under Kellogg oaks, their favorites, yielding large and sweet nuts, but they also gathered coast live oak acorns, or in time of need, even scrub oak acorns; all are palatable. The women cracked every acorn, winnowed the papery cover from the cotyledons, then carried the acorns, now free of their husks, to the morteros. Here the women gathered in groups, close together, to crush and grind them into meal, perhaps singing as they did their light work, a rounded stone in their hands serving as a pestle. Later, they would make the meal into mush or a hard bread.

I have seen these morteros in many places in California; they remind me that acorns were the basic provender for the state's large Indian population. They are always in beautiful sites such as this near Sandy Creek. Often situated on hillocks, the morteros, in bedrock, are on flat surfaces where the women could sit comfortably and there was space enough for a small group to work. Overhead arched oaks, or they grew not far away. The women preferred sites where

105

they could look across meadows into the country around them. Perhaps they did so because such vistas are so attractive–to look from the shade into the sun is always gratifying–but they were also probably concerned for safety. California Indians were not war-like, but sometimes they fought over territory, possessions, or women. Better to have an open view into meadows.

Morteros are a living reminder of the Indians' presence in the woods and evidence of people's ceaseless measures to survive and to work with the earth. For me, morteros are much the most impressive monuments, graven in stone, to man's shared life with nature in the mountain woodlands. I think this is why I seek them out when I can and why I am always pleased to find them.

Men and Mountains Meet

Great things are done when Men and Mountains Meet;
This is not done by Jostling in the Street.
William Blake

Long ago and far away in my student days I read that all situations in human life and therefore all themes in literature could be reduced to three: man struggles against his society, he wars within himself, and he combats nature. These are such broad categories that they are in fact not very helpful in understanding what life or literature is all about. But for anyone who has ever undertaken the building of a mountain cabin there is no doubt that one of the three–man's struggle with inimical nature–is very much alive and kicking.

This is what I thought as I struggled to dig sixteen wide and deep holes to provide a foothold for the poles that were to support our cabin. But first I should explain how I became involved in this humble and exhausting labor, a task that made me wish I was almost anywhere else, such as at the beach, in front of television watching the Padres, or stretched out on a chaise longue with a book in my lap and my glasses tipped onto my nose.

When we began to discuss designing a possible mountain cabin, the Builder was, for him, unusually outspoken: "We ought to build a pole house," he said, explaining that if the cabin rested on a framework of poles anchored in the ground, it would not be necessary to grade the site–scarring the gentle slope and scalping the meadow grasses. Furthermore, this design would allow the cabin to float above the hill, ethereal, feather-like, schooner-like. This effect would be enhanced by the fact that the building would be cantilevered well beyond its supporting poles. With these words he convinced us that pole construction was the only suitable design for the mountain site. What's more, it would be cheaper than a conventional foundation of stone and mortar. That was an argument not to be ignored. Pole construction it would be.

I found an excellent popular manual on residential pole construction, and in a fit of extravagance bought three copies, for me, for the Builder, and for the architect who drew up the plans. This manual answered some of my questions, since, like nearly everyone I have met, I had no idea of the details of the method. I learned that the poles were nothing more than the familiar telephone poles chemically treated to resist decay and insect attack. The poles were planted usually three to six feet in the ground, depending on the slope and the nature of the soil. I learned that pole construction is especially popular in beach areas where the holes can be easily excavated in sand and an unobstructed ground floor allows flood water to pass harmlessly under the dwelling itself. Much of Malibu Colony is built on poles, I discovered.

Calculating that sixteen poles planted twelve feet apart should be sufficient, I turned my sketches over to the architect who established on the basis of a formula which only he understood that the poles needed to be planted at depths of three to six feet and that they could be backfilled with spoil from the holes.

For the time being, the question was how we would excavate sixteen holes. On a beach the answer is simplicity itself: the contractor hires a large auger mounted on a truck that in a few hours drills the holes as needed. But our site was a sloping meadow difficult of access. Worse yet, the soil is rich in boulders, the infamous "floaters" that over the years have weathered free from the underlying stratum or rolled down the mountain. Unfortunately, a truck-mounted auger balks at rocks, since they foul its cutting edge, reducing even the largest auger to impotence. No, if we wanted sixteen holes dug on our mountain site, someone would have to dig them by hand.

"What! You dug all those holes by hand!" This is how friends react to the information that resting places for the poles supporting the cabin were hewn from the soil and rock with hand tools and muscle. They register shock, even indignation, that at the end of the 20th century men still perform such labors, assuming wrongly that the machine has relieved modern America from such primitive, third-world tasks. But given the rocky sloping site, if we wanted to build a house on a pole foundation someone would have to loosen, lift, and remove the rock and soil to make a settled home for sixteen massive poles. And it looked increasingly that the one fated to perform this unenviable task was me.

Why was I doomed to emulate for a time the workmen who built the Great Wall of China, the pyramids of Egypt, or the Hanging Gardens of Babylon? Because I was the only adult involved in the project who had the time to expend on such a lengthy chore and, unfortunate but true, it was I alone who had no skills which qualified me to work elsewhere on the cabin. By silent acclamation the crowd designated me as the individual to take responsibility for this stage of the project. I had all the qualifications for the role of supreme hole-digger. I was the perfect marriage of time and incompetence.

Those around me looked on with silent approval, their faces saying, in effect, it's all yours and don't expect me to help. This is how I was chosen to join in almost single combat with the forces of nature, otherwise known as the mountain.

My weapons in this encounter were a shovel, useful until the hole was about two feet deep, a digging bar four feet long which I replaced by a six foot bar as the holes grew deeper, and, most importantly, a supremely frustrating tool called a clamshell post-hole digger. This is two shallow facing shovels mounted on long handles that when brought together and driven with force hopefully penetrate into the ground to capture a large handful of earth. Then I spread the handles to tighten the tool's grasp on the soil and lift the entire load from the hole. It is hard to imagine a tool more inefficient than the clamshell post-hole digger; apparently the best minds of the industrial age have never turned to the improvement of this instrument. It remains essentially as it was when Irish navvies dug the first post holes for the transcontinental telegraph in the last century. The Cognoscenti refer to this tool as "the idiot sticks."

Naturally, as the hole grows deeper the soil tends to become denser and I soon learned that if I filled the hole with water and left it a few minutes the digger would penetrate more easily. However, if too much water rested too long in the hole it reduced the soil to gruel that the digger could not lift to the surface; not enough water and the soil remained impenetrable. Of course, I could always loosen the soil with the help of a steel bar, and this I did many, many times on many days.

However, it was not the dense red soil of the mountain that gave me the greatest difficulties. It was rocks of unpredictable size and location that brought me close to despair. Some were the size of my fist, some the size of footballs or medicine balls.

Some had the dimensions of an end table. One behemoth, nearly three feet across and deep, was concealed precisely at the center of a hole; it took two of us to prize it out of its bed because it was too heavy to lift. Many of them remain today of an unknown size

109

because I had to work around them, excavating a hole that resembled a corkscrew, but much larger. In one case I dug a hole almost five feet across in a futile attempt to find a channel through a heap of boulders which lay just below the surface.

After spending many weeks at such sweaty labor I had to admit I did not have the strength to lift the digger out of the ground when the hole passed five feet in depth. I hired an assistant, a robust young man who saw the digging of these holes as an opportunity to enlarge his "pecs" or pectoral muscles, if you will, but of course I also paid him for his labor. When a hole passed the five foot mark I assigned it to him and his muscles, but I like to think that while he surpassed me in raw power I was more skilled in outwitting the rocks which blocked the way, being more experienced in deviousness and more aware of hidden malice than he was.

The Builder thought we might be able to break up some of the most troublesome boulders with pneumatic equipment, and so we hauled a compressor and drill to the site. Into a hole he clambered, placed the drill bit against a boulder, and began his work. At the end of three hours, black from head to toe from the dust on his body and clothes which had turned to mud when it combined with the sweat produced from man-handling a ninety-pound drill, he had to admit that while he had succeeded in drilling holes in the boulders, they would not shatter. They were the toughest granitic stone. Chagrined, we towed away the pneumatic equipment like a tail between our legs, tacitly admitting that in this conflict the rock had defeated us. Score this round to the mountain.

After three months of this part-time labor I foolishly concluded that a generous building inspector, undoubtedly impressed by the efforts we had made and the purity of our intentions, would, out of pity, judge our holes as meeting the specifications of the County Planning Department, in spirit if not in letter. Of course I was mistaken; the inspector refused to pass our work, saying that some of the holes were neither deep nor wide enough.

Upon recovering from the shock of rejection, I phoned my young assistant and we undertook to improve on our efforts. But after two more months of part-time labor, it was clear to me that because of the rocks I could not complete the holes to the satisfaction of the inspector. Score another round, perhaps the last, to the mountain.

Under the circumstances I did the only thing possible: I phoned the inspector and told him we could not bring the holes up to standard. What could we do? Hire a licensed engineer, he said, who could visit the site and recommend a solution to our problem.

And so we began a new stage in the project, which did not involve a struggle with nature, but a struggle with society, that is, how to find a licensed engineer who would devote his time and knowledge (for a considerable fee) to aid a little man who wanted to build a little cabin. One civil engineer said he would work on the project, but he would do nothing until he received a preliminary report from a licensed soils engineer. On inquiry, a soils engineer told me frankly that he would not spend his time on such a small project. Another engineer told me that from what I had said the situation was hopeless and it was a waste of his time to go to the mountains. Yet another engineer told me that yes, he had actually worked on a pole house in the past, but that he recommended such heavy footings for the poles that the builder had abandoned the project.

I never called him back. It seemed to me that even at a distance of forty miles I could hear the mountain laughing. Just at this moment of despair, the Builder, utilizing his incomparable circle of acquaintances, informed me that he had found a licensed engineer who would work with us to get the holes through inspection. In fact, Mr. Cliff La Monte met me as promised at the cabin site, took soil samples, and inspected our efforts. Shortly afterwards he supplied us with a formal report on the state of our project to be submitted to the County Planning Commission. Employing a formula even more arcane than that of the architect, he concluded the holes were in fact adequate, but for insurance he recommended that we backfill the holes with concrete. Armed with his report, I once more called the County Planning Office and requested a second inspection for the holes. But the mountain was not yet ready to throw in the towel.

A few days before the scheduled inspection we had a heavy rain; when I visited the site several of the holes were filled to the brim with rain water. Knowing that no inspector would pass holes when he could not see into them, I phoned the Builder and the two of us hurried to the site to repair the damage. The portable pump we brought with us refused to transport the water because gravel and debris had washed into the holes. And so the Builder and I nailed sticks to coffee cans and began to bail out them out. Once more we had to abandon modern technology for the simplest kind of hand

111

tool, a can attached to a stick.

Even now the mountain played a nasty little joke on us, for several of the holes held drowned wood rats in a state of advanced decay. To this day I can see the Builder lying on his stomach bailing out a six foot hole with his scoop, his nose delicately averted from the stench.

And yes, the inspector was satisfied with our holes. Eight months had elapsed from the day that I, full of confidence and good cheer, dug the first shovel-full of earth until the day I saw the inspector's initials on the fateful planning document. It was a long and at times desperate struggle with the mountain, but I could triumphantly claim that I had won hands down–for now.

Four and a Half Fine Trees

In the first chapter of an excellent recent book, *Oaks of California,* the author tells us that while the Latin name for oak is Quercus, and hence the scientific name, this is not a Latin word. The Romans borrowed it from Celtic "quer" and "cuez" meaning "tree" and "fine." And oaks are certainly fine trees. Growing abundantly in the northern hemisphere and some tropic locations, but apparently not in Australia, they render supreme service to mankind as lumber, food for livestock, and shade; they are also among the most beautiful of trees.

Oaks are a conspicuous feature of the California landscape. If you had been in California at the time of the Gold Rush nearly everywhere you could have seen oak trees, although agriculture and urbanization have decimated them since. Only in the southeast deserts would they be lacking, but even there they grow in some of the mountain ranges. Sixteen species of oaks grow in the state from sea level to nine thousand feet. Of these, eleven grow only in the California Floristic Province, stretching from southern Oregon to northern Baja, and nowhere else in the world. We have many oaks in the state and most of them are travel-shy natives.

Our small plot on North Peak reflects this oak abundance and variety. On it grow four and a half tree oaks and an omnipresent low-growing scrub oak, technically *Quercus berberidifolia.* Oaks grow everywhere on the slope, but two species stick close to the best source of water, a ravine where a rain brook flows for a few weeks each year.

The most abundant oaks on the property are perhaps the most beautiful, especially in the eyes of anyone who thinks of oaks in terms of eastern hardwood forests or European oaks, for they are deciduous, with an oak's characteristic large lobed leaves. These are Kellogg oaks, sometimes called black oaks because of their dark gray bark, and they grow just about everywhere on the plot except at the hottest sites. They come in all sizes, from seedlings to trees two feet in diameter, so they are prospering; their only real rival is dense chaparral because their acorns cannot germinate under its thick cover. Nicely spaced, their branches just touching, they cast delicate gracious shadows on the ground below.

In April they put out their pendulous male catkins from bare branches. The subdued female flowers hide within the tree's inner

113

twigs. Intensely green lustrous leaves appear later that turn yellow or russet in October. Reflecting the mildness of California's maritime climate, the beautiful trees are bare-twigged for only about five months of the year.

Shedding leaves in fall is a response to the threat of snow because naked branches hold a lighter load. Since the trees seem to be inclined to decay in crotches along the trunk, snow might cause great damage to Kellogg oaks if they were evergreen.

The deciduous habit suggests, rightly, that this is a tree of higher elevations, two thousand to six thousand feet, where snow may fall. However, it is not the highest growing California tree oak; this distinction belongs to canyon live oak which also grows on our tract. Kellogg oaks pay a price for losing their leaves in the fall; this reduces the time for photosynthesis, as contrasted to evergreen oaks, capable of utilizing sun and air the year round.

Many observers have noted that Kellogg oaks always associate with conifers such as ponderosa pines, incense cedars, or white fir. On our property this is true, but the conifer is Coulter pine, with incense cedars not so far away. This mating of Kellogg oak and conifers is an attractive habit, since the two kinds of trees complement each other wonderfully, creating an enticing attractive landscape. If folk poetry was part of our tradition, as it is in Russia, for example, there would be many songs about the maiden (Kellogg oak) and her stalwart lover (a Coulter pine or perhaps an incense cedar).

Kellogg oaks grow from central Oregon to northern Baja, forming a ring around the Central Valley in the lower Sierras and coast ranges. They flourish most luxuriantly at medium elevations on both sides of the Sacramento River Valley. A small lumber industry utilizing Kellogg oak is centered in Oroville in this district. With proper milling and drying Kellogg oak makes attractive stock for doors, flooring, and furniture. In the same region in Placer County grows the largest known Kellogg oak, a mighty tree 9.4 feet in diameter.

Possessing large sweet acorns, Kellogg oaks provided favorite food for Indians. If available, they were the acorn of choice–it would be interesting to see if there was any correlation between density of Indian population and the distribution of Kellogg oaks.

While Kellogg oaks flourish on all our two and a half acres, coast live oaks grow only in the cool shady ravine that divides our property in two. Here rises one large specimen, perhaps two feet in diameter and forty feet tall, as well as several saplings nearby.

For most Californians, this is the oak they know best. This is because its range is mostly along the coast but beyond the tang of salt water, the most densely populated region in California. From north to south it grows from the Bay Area into northern Baja.

Probably it is no coincidence that this range includes the sites of all the California missions. This is because the padres, advancing northward, claiming the most favored land with sea access, mild climate and fertile soil, occupied the coast oak's home territory. Creating the image of a typical mission, you would sketch a dusty adobe church with coast live oaks enclosing it and growing on the swales and hills in the background. Coast live have also left their names on the land in the mission belt, for example, Encinitas, Encino, and others. Many movie goers, especially in the pre-television era, acquired their first impressions of the California landscape from seeing westerns filmed in the San Fernando valley, the white-hatted hero pursuing the black-hatted villain against a background of rounded granite boulders and coast live oaks.

Because it grows abundantly in the first region Europeans settled in California, coast live oak, along with valley oak, was the earliest to attract scientific notice. After the Spanish Malaspina expedition in 1791 collected it near Monterey, the expedition's botanist, Luis Nee, named it *Quercus agrifolia*, "scabby-leaved oak," because of the rough spots on its leaves.

Since they are evergreen and the wood is not especially tenacious, these trees are susceptible to snow damage. As a result, coast live oaks shading our land are near their maximum altitude, 4200 feet. But our trees are thriving, their small convex leaves almost dusty to my eye, almost resigned, drouth resistant, but grateful for rain, and seemingly prepared for all eventualities, including fire. Like all California oaks, they have no special defense against wildfire, except thick bark. If not totally consumed, they send out new shoots at the bases of fire-scarred stumps and try again.

Leaves deep within the tree testify to its adaptability. Shaded and in a light-starved world, they are brighter green, larger, and less drouth-resistant than external leaves.

They have a special friend in the animal world: not far from coast live oaks often dwell wood rats, but a host of other animals take refuge in their branches or in the sere litter in their shade, feeding on their acorns.

A hundred feet away from the coast live oaks in the ravine grows a ring of six oaks surrounding what was probably the burned out core of a much older tree. Nearby grow several other sturdy examples of the same species. These are canyon live oaks, which some prefer to call simply canyon oaks, others gold-cup oaks, because of the gold cups that hold the acorns. Because the wood is so dense (fifty-three pounds per cubic foot by dry weight) and obdurate, settlers called it maul oak and iron oak and hickory oak. Its scientific name is *Quercus chrysolepis,* "gold-scale oak," this referring to the small scales on the acorn cup.

It is a remarkable tree. Evergreen, it nonetheless has an impressive vertical range, growing from sea-level to nine thousand feet altitude, a home territory matched by few other trees. Apparently it can sustain the heaviest snow load and montane winds because its tough wood resists breakage. Over its range it takes an extraordinary variety of forms. On exposed slopes it becomes a tattered shrub, in thick stands such as the 4800 foot level on North Peak it is a slender handsome tree, while in the most favored locations it is a very impressive sprawling giant. *Oaks of California* reveals that the largest known canyon live oak grows "within a shady canyon" in Cleveland National Forest in San Diego County (On Palomar Mountain?–the peak is known for its huge canyon live oaks). Not far from our property on a gentle north-facing slope grows an unremarkable giant that is 6'8" in diameter. The tree seems to have a special fondness for steep rocky canyons; this has given it its common name.

The tree is at home throughout much of California, in southern Oregon, in Baja, and in central Arizona. It scratches out a hard living in the Providence and New York Mountains in the Mojave desert, convincing evidence for its exceptional durability and adaptability.

Canyon live oaks have the disconcerting habit of displaying leaves of two shapes on the same tree, some lightly spined and others smooth-margined. However, even an amateur naturalist can identify it with certainty by locating its squat acorns under the tree, the largest of any North American oak.

Not alone am I an admirer of the canyon live oak. John Muir said this about the tree, having in mind the largest specimens that thrive in the best locations:

116

The Mountain Live Oak is a tough rugged mountaineer of a tree, growing bravely and attaining noble dimensions on the roughest earthquake taluses in deep canyons and Yosemite valleys. The trunk is usually short, dividing near the ground into great wide-spreading limbs, and these again into a multitude of slender sprays, many of them cord-like and drooping to the ground.... The top of the tree where there is plenty of space is broad and bossy, with a dense covering of shining leaves, making delightful canopies, the complicated system of gray, interlacing, arching branches as seen from beneath being exceedingly rich and picturesque.

Coast redwood is of course the California state tree. But I think a case could be made to have canyon live oak take its place, at least among people who love the California hill country. Hardy and adaptable, thriving from the seashore almost to alpine heights, widely found throughout the state, majestic in fertile well-watered canyons and slopes, always green, in many places in the world it would be illustrious and venerated. Perhaps only in California where even more spectacular trees overshadow it, does it fail to receive the recognition it deserves, at least in the opinion of some.

Five minutes walk down the lane from our cabin delivers me to a grove of small open-branched Engelmann oaks. Looking down the hill to the open meadows along Sandy Creek a half mile away, I see more of these trees mixed with coast live oaks, their silver-green foliage contrasting nicely with the dusty bluish leaves on the coast live oaks. The Boston botanist Benjamin Daniel Greene named the species for George Engelmann, who from his residence in St. Louis collected and dispersed western American botanical specimens to plant taxonomists in the U. S. and Europe. His name is also on the sweeping Engelmann spruce from the Rocky Mountains.

Currently Engelmann oaks, sometimes called Mesa oaks, are the center of attention in California conservation circles, because some experts consider them endangered, thanks to the manner in which their range has shrunk in the last two centuries. Native to Southern California coast ranges up to 4200 feet, formerly common in the northern foothills of the Los Angeles basin where they were known as Pasadena oaks, the heart of their range is now San Diego County where 90% of the trees survive. Although they are most numerous on

117

the Santa Rosa Plateau west of Elsinore and around Black Mountain north of Escondido, as an amateur observer I have seen them growing, in addition to the sites near our cabin, along the front of the Cuyamaca range, in the hills above Jamul, and even in the foothills alongside the freeway leading east out of San Diego.

These are unique and interesting trees in many way. First of all most people assume that oaks are either evergreen or deciduous, but Engelmann oaks belong to a third category: usually evergreen, if stressed by drouth, they drop their leaves.

Their closest relatives are Arizona white oaks and Mexican blue oaks, not other California oaks. The obvious conclusion is that their point of origin is the Mexican Sierra Madre, a region with numerous oak species today. At an earlier time with a much milder rainier climate Engelmann oaks grew in an unbroken swathe across all of Southern California. As the climate became dryer, emergence of the low deserts cut off Engelmann oaks from their homeland, leaving them on a Southern California island.

The plants whose origins lie in the Sierra Madre are called Madrean or Madro-Tertiary, and include such well known broad leaved plants as Madrone (its nearest representatives grow on Palomar Mountain), manzanita, laurel, and some of the other oaks such as valley oaks and our scrub oak. One explanation for the complexity and richness of California vegetation is that it results from a mix of two ancient plant communities, the Madro-Tertiary from the southeast, and the Arcto-Tertiary geoflora from the north and east, including all the pines, for example. Today plants from these two geofloras live side by side, manzanita under sugar pine.

Paleo-botanists, who identify the immediate origin of Engelmann oaks as Madro-Tertiary, trace its ultimate homeland far beyond Mexico. Peter H. Raven and D. I. Axelrod (*Origins and Relationships of the California Flora,* 1978) assert that Engelmann oaks, among others, are in fact "Madrean-Tethyan," the latter term referring to the Sea of Tethys, the ancient ocean separating Eurasia and North America, then one land mass dubbed Laurasia, from Africa to the south. In other words, Engelmann oaks are ultimately related to the oaks of the Middle East. The authors include another conspicuous southwestern tree, that in fact grows along Sandy creek not far from our cabin, in the Madrean-Tethyan geoflora as well: western sycamores are closely related to the plane trees of Europe and the Middle East.

118

Having seen London plane trees and the mighty plane trees shading cemeteries in Istanbul, I, for one, was astonished to discover they are near relatives to sycamores growing in the desert water courses of the southwest.

Engelmann oaks jutting from the rocky hill below our property are not typical in one respect: they appear to emerge from chaparral, particularly manzanita. Usually they are savanna trees, clustered in loose scattered groves across a grassy landscape. This proclivity for open country may be the result of a susceptibility to fire damage. Fire-sensitive trees growing in open grasslands are much more likely to survive intense but brief grass fires than higher hotter chaparral blazes.

In 1844 Fremont, riding down through the Sierra foothills into the Sacramento Valley noted the presence of many evergreen oaks new to him. In 1851 Dr. F. A. Wislizenius, friend of Engelmann, collected foliage and acorns from the trees; the Swiss botanist, A. De Candolle, evidence in hand, named interior live oak in honor of the doctor, *Quercus wislizenii*, in 1864. Very widely distributed along the Sierra foothills and northern Coast Range, it is a large impressive tree.

George Engelmann, however, first described the variety of interior live oak occurring south of Ventura County. This variety Engelmann named "*frutescens*," meaning in Latin "shrubby" or "bushy," an apt description.

On our property a common tree, interior live oak is a large shrub about one half the height of its northern brother. Forming a clump of five to fifteen trunks, the thickest about a foot in diameter, it rises to less than forty feet. Its foliage thin and grayish, its bark an attractive cream color, it contrasts markedly with the lustrous foliage of scrub oak half its height with its tangled nondescript branches.

It bears heavy crops of long pointed acorns that are indistinguishable from the northern variety's fruit. Growing on hot slopes, it seems quite content to remain a prominent member of the chaparral community. For us, it has one undeniable advantage: cut into one-foot lengths the modest trunks of this shrub make excellent fuel, just right to fit into a wood-burning stove.

This is not the right way to end an essay on our local oaks. California oaks do much more than provide firewood. The California landscape would be incomparable poorer without these fine trees, for

119

shade, and for food for animals domesticated and wild, from raccoons to mice, and from jays to woodpeckers. Their trunks, lithe and strong, sometimes massive, their leaves evergreen or deciduous, are a delight to the eye. California would not be California without its oaks.

Certainly our plot on North Peak would be incomparably less attractive without its quota of four and a half fine trees and the scrub oak that persists under them. The loss of the oaks would not only change the landscape beyond recognition, it would alter the community of plants and animals on the mountain in the most fundamental way.

May

May

This is the misty and blustery time of the year, a difficult time of the year for anyone trying to capture in words the play between mountains and sky, between woods and clouds.

Late in the afternoon I walk out onto the mountain meadow and look to the west. Driven by steady wind, low clouds endlessly sweep over my head in a steady flood from the Pacific's hidden horizon towards the continent that stands behind me. The cloud's fabric parts for a moment to grant me a glimpse of the blue springtime sky, but then mist quickly closes the gap and once more I can see only an unbroken seething shift and swirl of advancing clouds. I can sense the huge power of this cloud river flowing who knows where into the space behind my back, but I can't put what I see into words–even if I could plausibly describe what I see for a moment, I would fail in a larger way, because the slaty mass of clouds ceaselessly alters its face, fading from the color of a junco's wing to the purest white, and back, billowing and retreating, throwing out plumes and breaking mist, but always hurrying onward.

Two crows appear from nowhere, struggling to stay their course, flapping low above the trees to escape the west wind's breath. Gusts of wind buffet them up and down and around, their pinion feathers spread like fingers clutching at the unsteady air. Sunlight filtered through the mist reflects on their plumage, black as damp shadows under the manzanitas. The birds careen against a background of dark green oaks and pines whose foliage is rich with six months of winter rain. In their disarray, they look like a pair of soaring Rorschach ink blots, but before I can decipher their meaning they veer and swoop and take a different shape, a different significance.

I'm told there's a simple explanation for this misty blustery weather which dominates the month of May on the west slopes of the mountains. As spring advances, the land over the west's interior begins to heat up–in Las Vegas it's 96 degrees and in Phoenix it's 102. The warm air rises, like heated air up a fireplace chimney. The foggy air that lurks off the Pacific coast slides in to take its place, like cold air from under the bedroom doors moving towards the fireplace. The saturated sea air crosses the coastal plain and ascends the mountain slopes. This is the source of the endless fogs and clouds I can see from the cabin as they climb up the hills and sail by overhead.

Ten miles to the east these springtime clouds will die a sudden death. Seen from an airplane these gray invaders take the form of an immense blanket stretching forever into the Pacific ocean. But at the eastern escarpment of the Cuyamaca and Laguna mountains it looks as though a giant has cut the blanket clean. This is where the clouds have completed their journey over the mountains and drop into the desert's warm dry air. The billowing blanket disappears, as though the clouds were plunging over a cliff, like lemmings into the water. The clouds don't emerge from the base of the falls because the dry desert air has absorbed them completely.

Sometimes, and this is one of the most glorious sights of the weather year, in May the air's flight from the ocean is not strong enough to lift the clouds over the summit and they pool against the face of the range below the cabin. When I look towards the west I can see at my feet a cloud ocean which silently touches the hills. This gray shifting surface hugs every intricacy on the slope. It fills in all the empty spaces, so that I see Norwegian fjords and Mendocino promontories where it meets the ridges. In this sea, rise islands and reefs and stacks, darkly wooded or grassy green and bright in the spring sun. Cloud fingers, some slender and sinuous, others blunt and broad, feel out every recess in the hills.

The level of this sea rises and falls ponderously. As I watch, it advances up the slope until it nears the cabin, and then it retreats, almost as though it has lost heart. It is a magnificent sight, this sea of clouds crashing softly against the hills, one which never loses its fascination, like the play of water or fire. It is ours to enjoy mostly in late springtime. Only then, when the mountain wall hems in the western clouds, can I observe this stand-off between the invading sea air and the barrier of the hills.

The moist air, which an hour ago rested on the cold waters of the California Current and is now streaming over the ridge, is still cool, but not as cold as it was over the water. The touch of the land has warmed it. Still, it is unbelievably fresh and brisk. The west wind is not yet capturing automobile exhaust and industrial pollution; that will happen with gentler breezes and warmer air. I don't yet see our infamous coastal smog, but it will hover over the coast in August and September, as surely as there are automobiles in Los Angeles and San Diego.

But sometimes the sea clouds neither race past overhead nor rest

124

along the front of the range. This is when mists lie low on the face of the mountain, sighing through the oaks and across the meadows in their death march to the east and extinction. Everything–sky, trees, land–floats in an icy windy fog. Drops fall from the eaves of the cabin and the dust of the footpaths becomes shallow slippery mud. On exposed points the wind roars and I can lean into it and I expect it to sweep away all the mist, but it cannot, because all of the cool air of the Pacific littoral is flowing over the heights. When the fog thickens, a drizzle commences which the wind catches and throws almost horizontally against trees and into the face of anyone unfortunate enough to be caught out in this difficult weather.

Now is when I put another chunk of oak on the fire, watch the icy rain peppering the west-facing windows, and feel misguided pity for the animals that thrive in these conditions so uncomfortable for us humans. Two weeks ago I saw a pair of western bluebirds fluttering in the meadow. Where are they now? Perhaps enjoying the golf courses at Palm Springs, after descending to the mild desert air. And where are the tree swallows I recently saw? Certainly gone, for their food, flying insects, cannot survive this watery bluster. Even the acorn woodpeckers are absent, having dropped down to a more congenial altitude. Rodents are comfortable in this weather; it's all the same to them. Bobcats and foxes go about their business as usual.

Higher up on the mountain, in yet sterner weather, a cougar is stalking the doe I saw yesterday near the roadside. For it this cold windy weather presents no difficulties; cougars thrive in the Absarokas and the Medicine Bows, as well as in California's benign climate. Here the worst a mountain lion must face is a foot of new snow or the horizontal rains of May. Undeterred by the mists, it fixes its eyes on the feeding doe, ears down, inching forward behind the cover of logs and shrubs. It takes a soaring leap, seizes the doe by the neck, and makes its kill. Life and its inseparable comrade, death, find their way in the worst of weathers.

Our Very Own Mining District

Those of us who live on the western front of the Cuyamaca mountains don't have a lot to brag about. True, we have wonderful views toward the coastal lowlands, splendid sunsets, a gracious countryside of pines and oaks, but other districts have these or similar attributes. However, our neighborhood does have something that sets us apart from most–we have our very own mining district.

Sometimes I choose to return to the city from North Peak by taking the slow but scenic gravel road that runs along the western foot of the range. For most of the route it is called Boulder Creek Road. As I drive south below Cuyamaca Peak I pass through the Inaja Indian Reservation and cross the headwaters of Kelly Creek. As the road continues its dusty way south I overtake a shallow draw with a sandy dry bed marking its course; this is Johnson Creek. Within a half a mile, the road drops lower yet until it fords Boulder Creek itself. This stream exits from Cuyamaca Reservoir and eventually merges with the San Diego River five miles further west.

When I park the truck up the hill beyond the creek I have an excellent view of the mineralized area north of Boulder Creek through which I have just passed. Here where the erosive power of Boulder Creek exposes it, lies the gold bearing igneous rock and the schist which caps it. And here, for a mile and a half alongside Boulder Creek, from Mineral Hill to Johnson Creek, miners made the Boulder Creek Mining District. In the course of fifty years it was born, flourished, and died, probably never to be born again.

In spite of the fact that mineralization seems obvious, prospectors did not find gold here until about 1885, fifteen years after the Julian strikes. From the first, prospectors did not find ore as rich as in the Julian district, but still for about ten years many claims were registered in the district: the Ella, the Old Trail, the Crown Point, the Waterloo. Many of the owners named their mines for home towns in the east, so there was the Omaha, the Council Bluffs, the Philadelphia, the Detroit, the Cleveland, and the Toledo.

126

At the same time a lively commerce in the buying and selling of claims sprang up, as reported in the *San Diego Union*. No doubt some of them were not much more than a hole in the ground, if that. Speculation was the result of western experience: if you want to get rich quick, don't prospect or work in a mine, sell mining claims and mining stock–that's where the bonanza lies hidden.

As time passed, a disquieting feature of the district's deposits became increasingly obvious: there was not enough high-grade ore to attract major outside capital to sink shafts and adits, to erect tramways and construct mills. Mining was fated to remain a hardscrabble operation in the Boulder Creek District.

By 1902 the district had nearly faded away. That year when the *San Diego Union* published its New Year Edition extolling the county's mineral wealth, it praised the potential richness of deposits in Julian and Banner, even Escondido and Mesa Grande, but said not a word about the Boulder Creek Mining District.

But one man had high hopes for the district; for more than thirty years George Moyer sought wealth alongside Boulder Creek. As early as 1890 he bought claims in the district and in 1900 with his partners in Phoenix he organized the Boulder Creek Mining and Milling Company with capital stock of $1 million. He named his biggest mine between Boulder Creek and Johnson Creek the Little Giant and perhaps with capital from the stock offering he built a ten-ton roller mill, a flume and water wheel to generate electricity, settling tanks for cyanide processing, an assay office, a blacksmith's forge, and residences. Eventually, his miners excavated several thousand feet of tunnels and drifts in the Little Giant. In later years he also claimed prospects as far east as Mineral Hill and toward the headwaters of Kelly Creek to the north.

The other significant producer in the district was the Last Chance mine, also north of the creek. In 1925 a report issued by the California Mining Bureau stated that the mine, owned by the International Gold Mines Co. of San Diego, had reached a depth of 110 feet. Nearby were a small mill and a blacksmith shop. This mine, with its appropriate name, had the distinction of being the last to close in the district–that was in 1941.

Moyer worked the Little Giant until 1928 when he sold out and retired to La Mesa. Unfortunately, his buyer failed in 1929 and Moyer found himself in the mining business once again. For four more years he worked in the hills, but limited himself mostly to exploiting placer deposits along Johnson Creek, rather than in the hardrock Little Giant. In 1934 he sold his holdings, leaving Boulder Creek for an easier life in the lowlands. No one worked the Little Giant or the Johnson Creek placers after this date.

In March 1975 Gerard S. Petrone published an excellent article with photographs on the history of the Boulder Creek Mining District (in *The Wrangler,* vol. 8, no. 1). At that time he interviewed Moyer's daughter, Mrs. Audrey Moyer Crane, of El Cajon. She provided a rapt description of a child's life at Boulder Creek, particularly in the years 1930-1934, describing a western idyll close to the hills, self-reliant, with abundant fresh air and the friendly presence of the district's miner and ranch families.

Moyer built a row of four one-room houses near the Little Giant, one cabin serving as a living room-dining room, while the others were bedrooms. While the Moyers bought their staples in El Cajon, they maintained a garden and kept a few goats and a milch cow. Trout, planted in Boulder Creek by the County, came to the table more or less the year round; I suspect that venison was also part of the diet throughout the year, true to the western tradition of poaching at mines and ranches. The lower levels of the Little Giant served as a refrigerator for perishables.

Because the Moyers had such confined living quarters, social life in the district centered at the large house of Bud Birdsell, well-known in the mountains as a rancher and saw-mill operator. His house stood to the north above the Last Chance mine. Here during the summer everyone met for square dances, the floor slicked down with corn starch. As the evening wore on, the children were put to sleep "stacked like cordwood" in the bedrooms, while their elders continued the festivities into the small hours.

All of this is gone now. All that remains is a few faint foundations and fallen stone walls. Even the Last Chance, last mine in the district, Petrone reported, by 1972 had collapsed and suffered the ignominious fate of becoming the neighborhood garbage dump.

Next month, if I have the time, I'll take the slow drive across the front of the range. As I ride along this open road I'll glory in the spacious views toward the west and Eagle Peak, El Cajon Mountain, even Point Loma, if it's a clear day. As I ford Boulder Creek, I'll nod my head in memory of the miners and their families who lived and worked here not so long ago. This was not San Diego County's richest mining district, but perhaps it is the most attractive in the county. Here grow prospering live oaks in open meadows and hillsides and the sun shines bright in the western sky. I'll pause to get out of the truck and listen for a moment to the pleasant murmur of Boulder Creek, cutting its bed ever deeper into the rock in its way toward the sea.

Selective Annihilation

Perhaps the mammal that mountain visitors see most often is a gray squirrel, nearly always within hailing distance of a Kellogg oak, source of food, refuge in hour of need, and site of nests and resting places.

Often, though, when visitors see the squirrel it is dead on the road. I often wondered why they perish so frequently on the asphalt, legs sprawling and upright, bloody unmentionables pasted to the pavement, eyes forever fixed in horror. Recently I was pleased to discover that at least one expert, the late biologist Lloyd G. Ingles, shared my impression that squirrels suffer from a high rate of road mortality. He wrote, when discussing the squirrels' predators, "Although no factual data are available, in the opinion of the writer it is doubtful if all predators take more than a small percentage of the number of squirrels that are annually killed by automobiles on the highways. They seem to have no ability to recognize the danger of an approaching car. " (*Ecology and Life History of the California Gray Squirrel,* 1947.)

In the greater scheme of things, the evolution of gray squirrels seems to have had a flaw that is certainly fatal for the road-killed dead. Why is this not true for all mammals? Why are some endowed with an innate aversion to automobiles when others don't know better? Dead foxes and bobcats, for example, are very rare on roadways, it seems to me. Skunks, accustomed to having everything defer to them, including vehicles, die by the thousands every year on California roads, but that is understandable. What, we may well ask, is responsible for this oversight in squirrel evolution?

I can't answer that question, and I'm not sure anyone can. But I have a practical suggestion for a way in which squirrel road deaths might contribute to the advance of science by providing an irrefutable example of natural selection at work.

Someone should keep careful records of squirrel road-kills on a given stretch of highway for a lengthy period of time. If I understand evolution correctly, the rare squirrel that innately has "an ability to recognize the danger of an approaching car" might transmit this trait to its offspring, resulting in an automobile-averse race of squirrels, road survivors.

Or perhaps sometime in the future there will be a mutation occasioned by a passing gamma-ray and somewhere in a hollow in some Kellogg oak a super-squirrel will be born that is organically car-shy. His descendants will thrive. At any rate, a decline in road kills over a long period of time (I leave the experts to deal with questions of squirrel birth rates, disease, and other variables) would demonstrate the principle of Darwinian natural selection in a conclusive way. The best-adapted will survive, and more of them, at least when crossing the road–and so will their descendants.

But I have another question for biologists. Would the evolution of this squirrel super-race have any effect on the raven population grown fat and prosperous on tire-tenderized road-killed squirrels?

Uninhabited and Uninhabitable

The name Cosmit, sometimes spelled Kosmit, remains an enigma. According to Alfred L. Kroeber, it is a Diegueño word whose meaning is unknown (*California Place names of Indian Origin*). On the Julian topographical map it appears on two features: Cosmit Peak (elevation 4575 feet), the culmination of a ridge running southwest off North Peak; and the Cosmit Indian Reservation, situated north of Sandy Creek in Section 25. The word may be related to the word Coscar in the expression "Paseo de Coscar" with which it shares a syllable, cos-, probably with a common element of meaning. This name for the Boulder Creek defile through the mountains appears on the Cuyamaca Rancho diseño of 1845 and a few other sources. Charles F. Sawday, grandson of Frederick R. Sawday, tells me that ranchers pronounced the word with the accent on the second syllable, Cosmít, reflecting the original Indian pronunciation; the Kumeyaay language always accents the last syllable of the word. Sometimes a definite article is placed before the word, as "in the Cosmit," referring to the Sandy Creek valley.

From the deck of our cabin, if I look to the northwest, I can see a rolling tract of heavily wooded land. Unless I look at the map I have no way of knowing that this is the Cosmit Indian Reservation whose boundaries are unmarked. It is an eighty acre parcel of land on a low ridge north of Sandy Creek. South of it are meadows and coast live oaks and Engelmann oaks and sometime water. The reservation's north side drops towards Cedar Creek, but never reaches the stream.

The reservation is minuscule, arid, and choked with an unbroken cover of chaparral and Coulter pines, standing and down. No one lives on it today; to the best of my knowledge no one has ever lived on it. It is uninhabited and uninhabitable.

I often used to ask myself the question: why was this tiny reservation created, so worthless and barren it is? To answer this question I turned to books about the local Indians and visited the San Diego County Recorder's Office and the Archives of the San Diego Historical Society. Using these resources, I found the answer to the question of how white authorities created the reservation towards the end of the 19th century, its purpose, and the reasons for its inutility.

Two current books sketch the history of the San Diego County Indians and their reservations. Both books have titles with the same message: exile of the Indians from their best land. They are Richard L. Carrico's *Strangers in a Stolen Land* and Florence Shipek's *Pushed into the Rocks*, each describing the manner in which white men dispossessed the Indians in order to claim the region's riches for themselves.

Both these books describe how in the mid-19th century some local and national politicians became sincerely concerned over the manner in which Indians were being driven from the land. They also feared that the harassed Indians might rise in rebellion with loss of life and property unless measures were taken to conciliate them. They became convinced that the Indians should be given reservations.

Ultimately, President U.S. Grant signed an executive order in December 1875, creating nine reservations in San Diego County with a total of 52,400 acres. Among them were the Inaja Reservation over the hill from us in the distant west, and the Cosmit Reservation that I see from our cabin. The Inaja Reservation was enlarged slightly in the 1890s, but the Cosmit Reservation remains the same size as when President Grant established it 120 years ago: Township 13, Range 3 East, N 1/2 of NE 1/4 of Section 25, San Bernardino Base Meridian.

Nearly all of the headwaters of Sandy Creek lie in Section 25 (there are 640 acres in a Section), the level well-watered meadows I described in an earlier essay, "Deeply Graven Rock." This is fertile country. At an altitude of four thousand feet, protected from high winds, on the Julian topographic map it is designated as Mountain Meadows. Judging from the numerous morteros and the pottery shards littering the area, it offered an attractive home for Indians for centuries.

Why was the Cosmit Reservation not sited here in the midst of oak-rimmed meadows, but on the hillside chaparral to the north? The answer is that when President Grant's Executive Order established the reservation white settlers already occupied the best land in the Cosmit.

In 1875 (month unknown, but probably well before December), after the Cuyamaca Rancho boundaries were firm, an English immigrant, Frederick R. Sawday, established a sheep and bee-keeping ranch in the best part of Section 25 south of the future reservation. Sawday came from Devon to California in 1874, established his ranch in 1875, and settled down to make his fortune. That year he retrieved his wife, whom he had married in England, in San Francisco; they began housekeeping in a small residence on his land about one mile west of the Cosmit not far from today's Pine Hills Fire Station. The foundation, cellar hole, and a few ancient apple trees still mark the site. Here to them three children were born.

What is more, in 1877 after the reservation was established, Herbert and Martha Crouch, warm friends of the Sawdays–their daughter, Bess, married George, the Sawdays' oldest son in 1904–homesteaded 320 acres of land in Sections 25, 30, and 19, surrounding the reservation to the east and south. I find it difficult to believe that the Crouches ever lived on this land; they ran their sheep along the coast near Oceanside and in the Laguna Mountains. Probably they homesteaded this land as an act of friendship for the Sawdays and to prevent anyone else from claiming it.

Florence Shipek knows the Cosmit well, has visited it, and has discussed its status with local Indians who remember its history. In *Pushed into the Rocks* she writes that "Another reservation, Cosmit, was located within band territory but it was an uninhabited and uninhabitable waterless rock hilltop rather than in the diagonally adjacent section where the people were living near a spring." In this passage she means "area" or "district" not a legal Section.

Later in the book she writes: "It has already been mentioned that Cosmit was mislocated on a dry, rocky hill on which no Indians lived. The land was unusable except for the occasional grazing of cattle and as a source of a small amount of firewood and a few minor usable plants."

Unfortunately, the word "mislocated," suggesting some sort of error, is misleading. The authorities intentionally placed the reservation where it is today because settlers already had homesteaded the choice Cosmit meadow land with water. The surveyors knew that the reservation land was barren; settlers held the best land and their holdings had to be respected.

We might ask why the surveyors did not give the Indians possession of the settlers' land. Simply stated, in the last half of the 19th century, the white authorities did not believe it was right and just to award any land legally belonging to white settlers to Indians. In San

134

Diego County at the time such a transfer would have met violent opposition.

The *San Diego Union* repeatedly stated its editorial opposition to giving Indians "white man's land." Carrico quotes an editorial in that paper for September 7, 1873: "The land is for the people who can cultivate it and become producers, adding to the prosperity of the commonwealth, and the Indians must go." When discussing the possibility of granting a reservation at San Pasqual where white settlers already had farms, the editorial went on to say that a proposed reservation at San Pasqual "...would be a failure. It would be resisted by the Indians, and it would be a gross outrage upon the farmers of that section."

The editorial concluded that not only should the Indians be kept off land already occupied by whites but that Indians should be forbidden from any land "likely to be occupied by whites within the next twenty years." Under these conditions, taking white man's land to give to Indians as a reservation was out of the question.

The authorities granted reservations to Indians in San Diego County out of good intentions or to salve a guilty conscience or to prevent an Indian rebellion. There was yet another reason the Cosmit Indians got their barren patch of chaparral–to provide a source of labor. In an interview recorded at the San Diego Historical Society, speaking of the tiny Cosmit Reservation, Shipek theorizes convincingly that the authorities created it to provide a residence for Indians who were to work for white settlers who claimed, quite legally, the best land and water in the district. The Cosmit Reservation was conveniently close to Sandy Creek Valley; here, living on their eighty acres, the Indians could find work as day laborers on the land that for centuries had been home for themselves and their ancestors. Now I understood why the reservation was tiny–because it was meant only to house the Indians. It was barren because they were meant to find their livelihood elsewhere.

Shipek also identifies another serious liability of the Cosmit Reservation, as well as three other San Diego reservations that President Grant established in 1875: none of them have any road access. Today, if for any reason Indians wished to utilize the Cosmit Reservation they would have to obtain permission to cross white man's land to reach it. And if I know my neighbors, I'm sure some of them would never grant permission for anyone to cross their land.

June

June

This has been a good year for rain lovers in the mountains. According to the local paper more than fifty inches of rain mixed with a little snow has fallen since last July. The rain began later than usual in November, but then early in the year it came down often and persistently.

Now it's June and the second season has begun: a long rainless summer with only stray northern storms and rare tropical downpours marching north up the tepid waters of the Gulf of Cortez. Alternating rainy winters and dry summers tell the plants on the mountain when it is time to grow vigorously and then subside into dormancy in expectation of the cooling fruitful rains of autumn.

The shrubs which make up the chaparral are among the first to show the invigorating effect of the winter rains as they hurry into bloom. In January the manzanitas open their petite waxy pink bells which mantle the little trees and then carpet the ground in their shade. The fallen flowers resist decay, as though they were made of real wax. Blue ceanothus shrubs are not far behind, beginning to bloom in February near sea level, and then advancing up the slopes with the passing of time. At our four thousand foot altitude, their flowers don't open until about April or even May, but they are worth the waiting. The flowers on no two plants have exactly the same shade of blue. Some are so dark I'm tempted to call them sapphire or even purple, and others are so light they look like tattered levis bleached by the sun. Not surprisingly, these spectacular flowering shrubs have attracted the attention of plant breeders and my garden manual lists ceanothus available from nurseries under such imaginative names as "Dark Star," "Frosty Blue," and "Gentian Plume." I understand they're not easy to grow, despising summer water, and like the young men in A. E. Housman's poetry, they die an early death under the best of circumstances. It's better to admire ceanothus in the wild where it is one of the glories of the California springtime.

We don't have much of the blue ceanothus on our land. However, we do have an abundance of Palmer's ceanothus, which opens its thick creamy flower trusses in May. Unfortunately, it must live forever in the shadow of its flamboyant cerulean cousin. But it has its admirers in the mountains, especially when a spring shower enlivens its muted white flowers contrasting with nearby pine needles and

137

new oak leaves made darker by the rain.

Just as the chaparral shrubs are displaying their early spring blossoms, I see patches of brilliant violet-red color high in the brush. These are the flowers of the chaparral sweet pea, a vigorous vine that climbs quickly through the dwarf forest, flaunting its flowers in the sun to catch the attention of bees and other pollenizers. Here I am! Here I am! its startling colors cry.

At the same time that the sweet pea displays its colors the strangest plant of the chaparral springs to life and blossoms. Under the chaparral where duff is deepest grows the unmistakable California peony, an ascetic brother of its robust eastern garden relatives. In the dry season its leaves wilt and wither away; the rains bring fresh shoots from its underground tubers. I must look close to find its faintly pendulous flowers, because they are a subdued reddish bronze with maroon overtones blending well with the duff. The California peony, I must admit, looks like a plant that strayed from its proper home to find a place in the sun and acquired a deep California tan.

In fact, the geographical distribution of the Peony family (*Paeoniaceae*) is a puzzle. The Greeks knew peonies very well around the Mediterranean sea. They named it for Paeon, the physician of the gods, because they believed its roots had medicinal properties. Peonies also thrive from Central Asia into the Orient where they have long been a beloved garden plant. However, in addition to this range across Eurasia, two species of the genus occur along the Pacific coast from Baja California to British Columbia. It is unknown in the rest of the world.

David Douglas discovered *Paeonia browni* in Oregon in 1823, although he could have seen it growing at higher altitudes anywhere from Tuolomne County north into Canada. Our southern species, now called *Paeonia Californica*, grows from San Diego County north to Monterey and frequents chaparral and the hottest sites.

How can we explain peonies' distribution on three continents? Botanists interpret the distribution of some plants found in Eurasia and the New World by conjecturing they originated in Laurasia, the ancient continent which included both North America and Eurasia . Perhaps peonies had the same history, resulting in their distribution in America and Eurasia. Why they have such a limited distribution in North America is yet another question.

138

But these chaparral shrubs and their companions, sweet pea, California peony, and others, strike only the opening chords in an outburst of flowers which comes into its own in June. In June the ground's moisture reaches three feet and more. In June the temperatures climb unmistakably into the summer range; the damp mists and winds of late spring subside for four hot months.

On our hillside of broken shrubs and trees the first spring flowers, other than the chaparral plants, blossom in small meadows or along roadsides. The earliest of these is blue-eyed grass, a foot-tall mound of sparkling blue flowers; the plant's leaves are so sparse that at a glance it appears to be all flowers. In spite of its common name, it is not a grass at all, but a member of the iris family, sprouting from tubers and closely related to blue flags which grow in mountain marshes. Not far away from this false grass may flower one of the many bright blue lupines. It is probably guard lupine, a perennial which likes forest openings, with roots so long and tough the plant survives the driest summer.

Years ago on a sunny June morning we discovered that with our mountain property we had purchased a wild flower garden. In a small patch of sunny roadside, well-watered from the moisture which seeps out of the cut, a carpet of brightly colored blossoms emerges every June. First to appear are the tall purple balls of blue dicks. Right after them open the sprawling flat delicate pink blossoms of checkerbloom, the size of a Susan B. Anthony dollar, another sturdy perennial found throughout these hills. Wild strawberry and a small wild blackberry blossom modestly nearby. Wild animals harvest their fruit long before I do. Creeping over the ground, as though asking for support, are the feeble vines of vetch, its flowers a magnificent cobalt blue, fading to purple.

But the queen among these courtiers is the delicate and charming globe lily. The scientific name for this plant is *Calochortus albus,* which might be translated as "White beautiful grass," a fittingly graceful name which acknowledges the sparseness of its basal leaves. Its popular names are less fortunate and certainly inadequate. I choose to call it globe lily, but some call it fairy lanterns (disagreeably precious, to my mind), others call it snow-drops, Indian bells, and also satin bells, the last capturing the texture of its white petals. But the flowers are not bell-like in shape, but rather they are little globes, heavenly ping-pong balls, if this description is

139

not too absurd for words.

Members of the lily family, in spite of their scientific name, they are closely related to mariposa lilies which are common enough in the dry meadows on the mountain. But while mariposa lilies turn their faces to the sun, globe lilies, as many as twelve blossoms on a plant, have deeply pendulous blooms. What's more, if you carefully open the flower, you will see that delicate hairs line the pure cream of the petals. They are almost too fine to touch. This is one of the wildflowers which deserves the adjective "exquisite." These blossoms belong in a formal garden with contemporary bronze sculptures, precise boxwood hedges cut low, and tall slender women with bowed heads as beautiful as the globe lilies themselves.

Later in the month as the globe lilies fade, in sunnier places appears foothill penstemon, showing cheerful up-standing stalks of violet flowers that fade to a winning bright blue. It is as brash, ebullient and assertive as the globe lilies are retiring. Flourishing in open meadows and along the country roads, it is probably the most conspicuous of all the June flowers.

I have to look harder to find the small purple flower clusters of the chaparral nightshade, instantly recognizable because of the bright yellow cone formed by its stamens. It prefers the edges of meadows in light shade. Not only is it a rather rare plant, but it insists on growing almost horizontally through grasses and herbs. The purity of its deep purple petals and egg-yolk centers makes the search worthwhile. This June plant bears the scientific name of *Solanum xanti,* indicating it is a member of the nightshade family, while its species name is the eponym of Janos Xantus.

When I discovered the scientific name in Beauchamp's *A Flora of San Diego County, California,* it brought back a forgotten chapter of my childhood. When I was fourteen years old my parents gave me *The Book of Birds* published by the National Geographic Society. Quickly it became one of my favorites, not so much for the text, but to admire its handsome bird portraits, done by Allan Brooks and Louis Fuertes, and to provide food for teen-age dreaming. For me, growing up in a small inland city, its most exotic bird was Xantus's murrelet (*Endomychura hypoleuca (Xantus)*), a resident of California's and Baja California's offshore islands. What's more, I found its name intriguing: I'd never seen a surname beginning with the letter x, and I've seen none since. I used to ask myself: who was Xantus and what was he doing in California?

Janos Xantus was a Hungarian with a Greek name born in 1825. An adventurer and a colossal liar, he managed to get official support to collect natural history specimens as a soldier in the U. S. Army, having emigrated to America in 1851. In 1857-59 he was stationed at Fort Tejon north of Los Angeles and later he served as tidal observer at Cabo San Lucas, Mexico. While there, he collected the little ground-nesting sea bird which bears his name. At Fort Tejon he collected and dried the chaparral nightshade. In 1875 Professor Asa Gray of Harvard University officially named it in Xantus's honor. He died in his native land in 1894, far from California.

I will probably never see a Xantus's murrelet (few people have), but, taking a small liberty with botanical nomenclature, I have had the small satisfaction of seeing Xantus's chaparral nightshade among the June flowers on North Peak, a satisfaction undreamed of in my boyhood.

The Last Hippie Bus

Not many people know that I am an authority on Hippie busses, but I am. I have not only seen the most famous Hippie bus in America, I have also seen perhaps the last Hippie bus in the country. I even know where it is buried, sort of. Let me add that I know Hippie busses from the outside, not the inside. During the 1960s when the Movement crested, I was too busy raising a family and completing my education to go around barefoot, smoke grass, hang out in the Haight, or crash in a Hippie bus.

At the end of that decade we spent a summer house-sitting in Larkspur, California. Larkspur, a midwestern town that somehow got lost in Marin county, is home to lawyers, accountants, and other professionals who commute to San Francisco. When we lived there they still held dances every Saturday night at the town's outdoor dance floor. This is indeed a community that works hard to maintain its traditions.

On one of our walks in Larkspur we observed a school bus with window curtains parked in front of a craftsman cottage. Someone told us that this was the house of the novelist Ken Kesey (he wrote *One Flew over the Cuckoo's Nest* and *Sometimes a Great Notion,* among other books), and this was not just any 1939 school bus, but the bus that Tom Wolfe immortalized in his *Electric Kool-Aid Acid Test.*

As Wolfe tells it, the bus was once owned by a man with a large family who fitted it out as a mobile residence complete with bedrooms and kitchen. Hence the window curtains. Under Kesey's auspices it became a rolling Hippie pad. In his loaded bus Kesey and his loaded friends toured the country, provoking consternation and arrests wherever they went.

Not long ago I got out Wolfe's book and tried to re-read it, but I found it hard going. Not only is his breathless style dated, but I don't find his jolly descriptions of drug taking, particularly LSD, amusing or even something I can read without discomfort and unease. Drug use, as publicized by Wolfe, Hunter Thompson, Timothy Leary and others, has done too many monstrous things to too many people for me to find reading about it a pleasant pastime.

But as a historical phenomenon the Hippie bus was colorful and original, one of the flowers of the 1960s. Whether that flower was a fair rose or the deadly poppy is still subject to debate. And I have seen the most famous Hippie bus of them all. There it was–parked in front of Ken Kesey's house in Larkspur, CA.

When we bought mountain property in 1988, twenty years after Wolfe published his classic, we discovered that not far away from the cabin site was perhaps the last Hippie bus in America. Walking to the end of the lane, I found a bus's outsized engine, two still inflated giant tires, and a steering wheel half buried in mountain soil and oak leaves. Beyond these relics projected two steel beams that once supported the chassis, terminating in a rusted wheel-less axle. On the beams rose a house.

A neighbor told me how this bus-house found a resting place on a hillside amidst the oaks in San Diego County. As is the case of so many historical events, the details are uncertain, but the most important facts are firm, like the bus on its hillside.

A little more than ten years ago, about 1982 or 1983, someone drove a Hippie bus to Valley Center, or was it to the Wild Animal Park? Because the bus's engine was near collapse, the owner of the mountain property bought the bus cheap. Deciding to park it on his land, he drove it to the mountains where its engine, overcome by the long grade, turned over for the last time. What's more, the disabled bus slid partially down the hillside. Its owner, with the help of the neighbors, propped up the rear axle until the bus was level. For a time, the owner and his family lived in the bus on weekends. There's no evidence, by the way, that they obtained the approval of the San Diego County Planning Commission for the creation of this unconventional residence.

Since he now had a more or less permanent vacation home, the owner thought that a deck surrounding the bus would be desirable. After he completed it, he built a roof over the bus to protect the rusting chassis. Then, no longer satisfied with the cramped quarters inside the bus, the owner decided to remodel–he cut off the chassis and built a house on the bus's frame. This was as I first saw it, a bus converted to a house, but still preserving its original Hippie bus incarnation. To my eye it was one of the most unusual objects I have ever seen. Was it a bus? A house? Neither? Both? Was it the archetypal expression of a society preoccupied with mobility, combining as it did the fixed and the peripatetic? Was it an icon of a rootless society lacking history and the permanence of authentic traditions?

I'm not sure–it looked like a house on a Hippie bus to me, something so outside the ordinary that I didn't know how to classify it.

At this time the owner sold the property. The buyer erected a large residence precisely at the site where the bus and its additions stood on the hillside. Recently, when I was preparing to write this backhanded off-beat homage to the Hippie bus, I asked about its fate. What had happened to it when they built the house? Was it razed and the remains disposed of in a nearby ravine? What happened to its outsize tires and that magnificent steering wheel? Do they lie forgotten in a remote bus graveyard?

Why no, it seems. As the new owner constructed his house he left the bus intact, but stripped of its wooden afterthoughts, and built directly over it. The bus is still there, the new house completely enclosing it, under the floorboards.

Somehow it seems right that the bus, a relic of the most tumultuous decade in the American century, was saved from destruction, even crowned by a sort of mausoleum. At times, though, I'm troubled by the possible consequences of this unexpected turn of events. What will archeologists in the year 5000 think if they discover the bus's bones under the ruins of a twentieth century house? Will they conclude the bus was concealed from its enemies (Did a new dynasty take power?) at this remote site? Will they ask why it was preserved and protected from the elements?

And will they even know what a Hippie bus was?

The Poet of Cuyamaca Peak

Traveling alone, a young midwestern lawyer, former judge and member of the Minnesota state legislature, arrived in San Diego in 1875. Photographs from the time leave no doubt why he had fled to the warm dry southwest. Painfully thin and stoop-shouldered, the young man patently suffered from the plague of his day, tuberculosis.

The invalid was Theodore Strong Van Dyke and he came from patrician stock. A Princeton graduate, his father was also a lawyer who sat in the U. S. House of Representatives for two terms 1847-1851 from the state of New Jersey. In 1868 the elder Van Dyke left the east with his family and settled in Wabasha, Minnesota. In addition to Theodore, the Van Dykes had another son, John, who was an academic and librarian and the author of many books on art and travel; today he is remembered as the author of a perennial classic, *The Desert,* devoted to Arizona and the southwest.

Doubtless Van Dyke's thoughts were not on his profession or family when he arrived in San Diego, but on how to restore his failing health as soon as possible. Probably he had come to San Diego in hopes of a cure because the city housed Dr. Peter C. Remondino, who had also moved from Wabasha a few years earlier to establish a practice in San Diego specializing in the treatment of consumptives.

Van Dyke had reason to be concerned. While something of a rarity today, especially among those of us who are well-fed and with good medical care, the disease ravaged young adults at the turn of the century, numbering among its victims Anton Chekhov, Robert Louis Stevenson (although it did not kill him), Stephen Crane, and later D. H. Lawrence and George Orwell, to name stricken writers only.

Van Dyke had original ideas on the best way to achieve a cure. Living in Minnesota, he had become an enthusiastic outdoorsman and hunter. In San Diego he intended to camp under the open sky, take moderate exercise, a horse carrying his gear, and explore the region's marshes, meadows, woods and chaparral, with an eye

145

cocked for water fowl, quail, or doves, in wilder places mule deer, and, surprisingly, antelope that still grazed the hills from Poway to Jamul. He also observed grizzly bear tracks in the northern part of the county, but apparently he never had the opportunity to stalk *Ursus horribilis.* So, in a successful search for health (he died at age eighty one) he began ten years of solitary wandering from Mexico to the San Gabriels, sometimes on the coastal belt in pursuit of game birds, but most often in the mountains hunting deer. He also packed a fishing pole, finding the best angling in the streams flowing off Smith's Mountain (today's Palomar) and in the foothills of the San Gabriels.

What's more, he intended to earn a living from his hiking and hunting: he would write about the country he met and especially about hunting and fishing, because he knew a market existed for articles and books among outdoorsmen who were curious about the little-known southwest and its game. Later on, after passing the California bar in 1880, Van Dyke also turned his attention to water development, becoming one of the founders of the San Diego Flume Co. that constructed the dam at Laguna Seca, today's Cuyamaca Dam, but that is another story.

For twenty-five years Van Dyke lived in San Diego, publishing five books in addition to many magazine and newspaper articles. The pieces fall mostly into two categories: hunting and fishing accounts, and promotional books devoted to San Diego County's geography and its economic potential, especially for agriculture. Van Dyke based his writings on a knowledge of the San Diego backcountry that was unprecedented. Unquestionably he understood this district better than any other man, thanks to his excursions, emerging as the acknowledged expert on the remote nearly roadless regions where he hiked and hunted. One book, *Millionaires of a Day,* he devoted to San Diego's real estate boom and bust of the 1880s; it is far and away the liveliest and most readable of all his books.

In two of his books Van Dyke described the view from the summit of Cuyamaca Peak. In his earliest book, *Flirtation Camp; or The Rifle, Rod and Gun in California. A Sporting Romance,* published in New York by Fords, Howard and Hulbert in 1881, he leads two fictional characters to the crest where he abandons them in order to describe the view. Forgoing his usual terse narrative style, the novice author employs conventional "literary" prose to create a static set piece, apparently convinced that the sublime view required sublime language. As a consequence, his writing is wordy, sometimes convoluted, stilted, and unconvincing. A small sample will make this clear: "A vast sea lies far below on the west, with tumbling waves of snowy white rolling like great masses of carded wool; with long shafts of golden light, touching, as they are shot through the eastern mountain-gorges from Apollo's fiery bow, the crests of these billows; with its hundred islands of different heights looming up here and there, some in a full blaze of light, others just tipped with gilded spires, others standing dark and somber in the shade of greater peaks."

Van Dyke meant well, but on this occasion the literary conventions of his day led him into almost impenetrable thickets of verbiage and cliché. Happily, about five years later, Van Dyke, now a more experienced writer, wrote a second description of the view from Cuyamaca Peak. Appearing in *Southern California*, also published in New York by Fords, Howard and Hulbert, it deserves to be quoted in its entirety:

"The summit of Mt. Cuyamaca is six thousand five hundred feet above the sea; and though the view is not so extensive as that from the higher mountains, it has a fuller and nearer combination of all the natural features of the land. But it is not this alone that makes the view attractive. It is not the great ocean lying beneath the afternoon sun like a long golden cloud on the western horizon; nor the great chasms that yawn thousands of feet deep just below one's feet, divided by high rolling ridges, ragged with rocks, smooth with grass, or green with trees; nor the great shimmering sea of sand on the east, with Yuma broiling on its eastern verge; nor the deep forests all around one, where the sugar-pine and the white cedar are standing in a dense mass of dark green through which one can hear the sigh of the breeze; while lower down the red oak, live-oak, and the mountain white oak fill up the vacant places. It is rather the rare combination of the old and the new, the rugged and the soft, the wild and the tame. A hundred miles away our former acquaintance, 'Old Gray Back' of the San Bernardino range, looms with snowy scalp two miles into the northern sky, with San Jacinto and Cucamonga but a trifle lower beside it, while between lies the long, high line of gray and blue mountains that separates the western part of San Diego County from the desert. On the south the lofty range continues dark with pine and other trees, broken by bright green valleys and deep-blue ravines, stretching far away into Mexico in range after range, clad in timber or bluish-green chaparral, or gray with ancient granite; a vast reach of primeval solitude. Almost beneath us on the north-east is a mining-belt where millions of gold [sic] yet lie concealed; and from the oak and pine clad knoll in the midst of green meadows where hundreds of cattle are feeding comes the thunder of iron stamps in the mill where the solid rock is being pulverized to reach the gold. [This is the Stonewall Mine near the peak of its production.] Below on the north-east lie rolling slopes golden-hued with ripened grass, and scattered over them thousands of oaks like vast orchards; and in the valleys between them are farms where the finest of fruits are growing and where grain crops never fail. Lower down are broad plains with thousands of acres golden with grain or stubbles, separated by high ranges of boulder-clad hills or deep canyons, filled with eternal shadow, or broad rolling table lands covered with chaparral. On all sides rise lofty mountains near by us; some like Volcan and Palomar, almost as lofty as Cuyamaca, crowned with forests, breaking away in long yellow ridges clad in grass along the backs and sides, with dark timber-filled gulches between them; others lower, like the great granite dome of El Cajon or Lyon's Peak. And the whole land is tumbling, tumbling, tumbling, on the north and on the south and on the west, tumbling in long alternations of hills and slopes and valleys away to the distant coast."

It still has the disadvantage of being a set literary piece with distinct promotional overtones, but Van Dyke condensed the earlier version by about one third and pruned it of its wooden descriptions and most of its excesses. Among other things, he introduces some variety by moving his point of view about and employing the contrast between "the old and the new, the rugged and the soft, the wild and the tame." The result is a description of the panorama he observed from the peak that can still engage the reader today, some hundred years after Van Dyke wrote it.

At times the passage rises to the level of poetry that is all the more unexpected in a book meant to boost the county as a place to make a profit and not impress the reader with its artistry. For example, see the lines; "And the whole land is tumbling, tumbling, tumbling, on the north and on the south and on the west, tumbling in long alternations of hills and slopes and valleys away to the distant coast." This sentence alone, that Van Dyke employs to finish off the best published description of the view from the summit I have read, justifies crowning him the poet of Cuyamaca Peak. But I must admit that so far he has few rivals for the honor–how many poets have made the three-mile hike up to the peak to contemplate the view and complete the demanding work of capturing what they see in the most elusive and insubstantial of nets, a net woven of words?

One Tough Tree

Although I don't think an Irishman has ever visited our cabin there has been an Irish presence on our land since 1831.

Let me explain. That year a native of Dundalk, Ireland, born in 1793 and an enthusiastic botanist, visited San Antonio Mission in the Santa Lucia Range not far from Monterey. Here he observed a medium sized pine bearing immense cones and needles in bundles of three that was new to science. He sent samples of its foliage and cones to Geneva and London; in 1837 David Don in the *Transactions* of the London Linnaean Society published the first description of the tree, naming it in honor of its discoverer, Thomas Coulter, *Pinus coulteri,* Coulter pine.

Coulter came to California by way of Dublin where he graduated from Trinity College; Geneva, where he studied with the famous botanist, August-Pyramus De Candolle; and Mexico, where he was "Medical Attendant" to the Real del Monte Mining Company. Henceforth, some would call him Dr. Coulter. An avid field botanist, he sought specimens in Mexico and then in 1831 sailed to Monterey looking for more unknown plants. Coulter spent several years in California, but little is known about his activities in the state. While in California he made a two-way journey from Monterey to the site of today's Yuma, becoming the first botanist to visit the future state of Arizona.

Coulter pines are indigenous to the Californias, growing from the northern slopes of Mt. Diablo in Contra Costa County to northern Baja. They find their niche mostly at three thousand to six thousand feet above sea level, usually dry, rocky, sunny slopes, but they also thrive where there is more moisture. The trees must be tough enough to survive five or six months of drouth every year. Characteristically, they are trees of the upper chaparral. Together with its relatives, gray or foothill pine (the former digger pine), which rings the Central valley, and Torrey pine of Del Mar and Santa Rosa Island, it makes up what botanists call the big-cone group of pines. Seemingly to confound plant geneticists, it sometimes hybridizes with Jeffrey pine.

Usually it's said that Coulter pine does not form pure forests, but grows with other pines. On North Peak at our land this is not quite true: it is the only conifer on our two and a half acres. With it consort

Kellogg oaks and coast live oaks and canyon live oaks. Nearby, though, grow incense cedars and a few white firs. As I move up the mountain, I see it with more and more canyon live oaks and soon white fir and cedars match it in numbers. At higher altitudes in the Cuyamacas Coulter pines fade away as Jeffrey pines and rare sugar pines take their place.

Coulter pines on our land are handsome trees with fissured gray bark. Their ponderous cones are unmistakable. Smeared with resin, flaunting fierce spines, they are as large as plump pineapples. They cling to the stiff branches for as long as five or six years, surrounded by tangled blue-green needles that persist three or four years on the trees. The oldest trees have a distinctive profile, since the lowest thickest branches, after they have grown well away from the trunk, abruptly turn upward. It's almost as though new saplings have sprouted at the ends of the tree's most massive branches.

Coulter pines adapt well to fire, as do virtually all California conifers. Old trees have thick bark which resists flame; I have seen thriving Coulter pines with blackened bark as dark as Cajun Chicken as the result of passing fires. Cones fall from trees late in the fall after fire danger has declined. Seeds germinate in sunlight and in open soil; this is the only place I can find young trees on our land.

Most conifers have cones that open over a period of time to release their seeds. A few "closed-cone" pines have sealed cones that must be singed to force the cones to release the seeds. Coulter pines have the best of both: they release their seeds gradually on the tree, but a few remain viable within the cones for long periods. If fire comes, these seeds can germinate after the fire has passed.

Seedlings and saplings are pretty things with open branches, their fresh foliage contrasting nicely with mostly evergreen chaparral plants. Even ten foot trees produce cones so outsized they look like young cowbirds in warblers' nests. This means that pines produce and scatter seeds when still quite young, yet another response to omnipresent wildfire.

Deer won't touch the seedlings because of an odor or taste we cannot sense, I assume. A few years ago I planted a Mediterranean Aleppo pine on the property, not knowing what else to do with a living Christmas tree outgrowing its container. With a month deer had gnawed it to a stump, while ignoring nearby Coulter pine seedlings. I conclude that Aleppo pines lack the chemical repellant which

151

Coulter pines possess. Are there no deer, then, in the Aleppo pines' native habitat? Or do their food habits differ from ours?

Coulter pines on our property are probably nearing their maximum size; the largest is almost three feet in diameter and perhaps sixty feet tall, offering a happy hunting ground for warblers, nuthatches, and brown creepers, and roosts for crows and woodpeckers. George B. Sudworth in his *Forest Trees of the Pacific Slope* gives as the maximum measurements for Coulter pines 42" diameter and "nearly 75' in height." He thinks their maximum age is two hundred years.

Taking a census of our Coulter pines, I found ten mature trees on our two and a half acres and perhaps a dozen seedlings and saplings; the low number of young pines simply means that tall trees shade most of our land, preventing germination of Coulter pine seeds. The mature trees fall into two classes: eight of them are about two feet in diameter and two larger trees are about thirty-three inches in diameter.

In 1953 Bruce Zobel published an article about Coulter pine distribution. Coring aging trees up and down the state, he concluded that trees in Southern California increase their girth by one-third of an inch each year. Utilizing his formula, I conclude that the two large trees are about one hundred years old and the group of smaller trees are about eighty years old. These estimates are approximate, since it is difficult to measure the pines accurately; nor is it safe to assume a steady growth rate always.

I surmise that in the 1890s a wildfire swept our property, destroying all the Coulter pines growing on it. This fire may also have burned out the large canyon live oak in the ravine that later sprouted to form a ring of trees. Many Coulter pine seeds germinated in the ashy sunny soil, producing a thick stand of saplings.

Twenty years later, say, about 1910, another fire destroyed all the young trees except two that became the large trees that survive on the property today. After this second fire, on the newly opened slopes numerous seedlings again competed for light; eventually today's eight mature trees won out, as well as others that died over the years, such as those the pine beetles killed about five years ago. These eight trees offer convincing evidence for dating the last fire on our land–it scorched the slopes about 1910, perhaps.

This conjectural history relies on Zobel's estimate for the growth rate of Coulter pines. A truly reliable history would require coring the trees to determine their precise age. While this might alter the dates I have suggested for the fires on the land, I don't think it would alter the sequence of events as I have reconstructed them. Unfortunately, I lack the knowledge and equipment to core the pines to determine their age. This would have to be done by the same experts who know if deer graze on Aleppo pines around the Mediterranean Sea.

When Coulter made his journey to the confluence of the Gila and the Colorado from Monterey he passed through Los Angeles, detoured to San Diego, returned to the San Luis Rey River, then went through Pala and the San Felipe Valley on his way to cross the desert; he returned by the same route. During his journey in Southern California at times he could clearly see the slope of North Peak where I am writing these lines about him and his pine 164 years after his passage.

He would probably have been astonished at this turn of events, but on second thought, perhaps this would not be so. He saw his big-cone pines growing along the route, and knowing he was probably the first to identify them for science, he might have assumed that a European closet botanist would give them his name. It was common practice at the time to name a plant for its discoverer, but there were exceptions. Perhaps he might have hoped that he would not be forgotten, as indeed he is not, at least not on our property under the Coulter pines.

July

July

July days are lazy days in the mountains. The sun rises in a cloudless sky and by noon it's too warm to work in the sun. I'd better retreat to the shade with a cold beer. The foliage on the oaks and pines is losing its luster, partly because a film of dust clings to leaf and tree; the last cleansing rain fell a month ago. At the end of the day the sun sinks into the fog bank over the ocean and the beach towns. Sunset is red, but not brilliant and the wisps of cloud above the fog bank look like the finest facial tissue, and on every cloud is a trace of lipstick.

June flowers are mostly gone now, but July has brought new blooms, not as varied as the spring flowers, but distinguished. In some places magnificent Humboldt lilies have opened. On stalks as tall as eight feet, these flowers with their recurved orange petals spotted with maroon look as though they have escaped from some fancy florist shop; they are too spectacular for their modest background of oak, pine, and dry hillside. As a matter of fact, they are too beautiful for their own good: a large clump of lilies I used to admire alongside Engineers Road is gone this summer. I'm afraid that someone dug it up to transplant to their own garden. A few years ago I saw a well-dressed woman in high heels in Cuyamaca Rancho State Park breaking off tall flower stalks of this splendid lily next to the highway; I thought traffic was too heavy for me to stop, but I regret to this day that I let her get away scot-free.

The most spectacular plant on our property is summer bush penstemon, a sprawling bush as tall as a Humboldt lily. Each trailing branch displays ranks of bright orange tubular flowers. I know that when this bush blooms in July I will find in its immediate proximity one or more Anna's hummingbirds.

This comparatively large and aggressive hummingbird, named for Anna, Duchess of Rivoli, whom Audubon described as "a beautiful woman...extremely graceful and polite," never leaves its pleasant home territory in coastal California, although the mountain birds must retreat down the slopes in the winter. Resident biologists have spent much time investigating the bird's habits. Howard Ensign Evans in his eminently readable *Pioneer Naturalists* says they have discovered that its oxygen consumption increases five times when it takes wing; at this instance it uses oxygen at the highest rate of any known animal. To sustain this fantastic energy output it visits a thousand flowers every day. This helps me understand why these birds congregate near summer bush penstemons that offer them hundreds of flowers on a warm July day. At night the birds conserve energy as their body temperature drops to about 70 degrees.

In July we sometimes see in the oaks the flashing white wing patches of a summer resident, phainopeplas. The scientific name of this bird is *Phainopepla nitens,* which in a fit of excess means "Shining (Latin) shining robe (Greek). Although bird-watchers prefer its Greek name, everyday folks call it silky flycatcher or black flycatcher. The only U.S. representative of a tropical family, its appearance is arresting. The male is an unusual glossy greenish-black. He has a prominent crest and flashing white wing patches, like a mockingbird. The female is a much more subdued grayish. Both sexes have bright red irises.

Whenever I see these birds in our woodlands I'm reminded of my boyhood neighbor, Mr. Smith. Mr. Smith drove a produce truck from my home town to Idaho Falls, Idaho, several times a week. Because the trip was so long, he had to spend the night there, and I was accustomed to seeing his big bulky truck absent from his driveway. I don't know how old I was when my mother told me confidentially that Mr. Smith, in addition to the family I knew, had a second family in Idaho Falls. I was old enough not to be too surprised, because I was growing up myself and understood that circumstances forced him to spend his time equally in two places. I don't know what his two families thought about this arrangement, or whether they knew about each other.

Like Mr. Smith, Phainopepelas are two-family birds. This is the only bird in North America which raises a brood in one location, its winter home in the low desert in March and April, and then in June and July migrates to coastal California where it builds a nest and raises a second family.

The regions where it raises its two families are very different. In the low hot desert it nests in mesquite and other scant vegetation. It is a very conspicuous bird in the desert's sparse cover–perhaps you've seen it there. It chiefly eats mistletoe berries, although it also feeds on flying insects. When it shifts its range to coastal California it nests mostly in oaks in the draws and feeds on chaparral redberry and gooseberries. In the lowlands it enjoys California pepper berries.

Ornithologists think that this divided range is probably the result of climate change. Once, the desert was cooler and moister than it is today and the phainopeplas nested in local trees. As the climate became dryer, the forest retreated to cooler coastal sites, like our mountains, and the phainopelas followed. Some of us might think that phainopeplas flee the desert to escape the ferocious summer heat, but there's no evidence this is true.

The curious reader may have a final question: does the male phainopepla travel with his desert mate from the mesquite to the pines? No, ornithologists have observed that the male phainopepla finds a new partner to establish a second family, like my childhood neighbor, Mr. Smith.

But, of course so does the female phainopepla.

Four Hundred Russians?

The greatest challenge in conducting research in my chosen discipline, cultural and literary history, is coping with the overwhelming volume of information that lies in libraries at my disposal. Everywhere around the world, it seems, students are publishing books and articles on every imaginable topic at a rate that daunts the researcher. In what we might call "mainstream" research in the Humanities, the scholar's challenge is to confront a flood of information, in that deluge identify what is significant, and put it into order for his readers.

On the other hand, research in local history, I discovered when I began to write about North Peak's human past, poses quite different problems. The challenge is finding any information at all, given the absence of adequate written records. The local historian, in search of truth, by the nature of things, must turn to unwritten records, that is, to the accounts of local people who are often his only source of information. As a consequence, he must deal with the obvious: memory can be faulty. Some of my witnesses to history were misinformed or their memories betrayed them. Alas, I concluded, just because someone says it is so, does not make it so. I learned to check my witnesses against a second informant, if at all possible. My interviewees were not deceiving me; they were misinformed or they were the victims of memory lapses, traits we as humans all share.

A second problem that confronted me is that local history, even when written down, is rarely documented. As a consequence, it can be vexing to identify the origin of some bit of information. It is difficult to verify what is true, if you don't know who wrote it, and where, and when.

An excellent example of both these problems is the mystery of the four hundred Russians who may have worked in the Cuyamacas.

Helen Ellsberg, in her popular *Mines of Julian* when she is describing the glory years of the Stonewall Mine, states that "A crew of four hundred Russians worked cutting wood for the sawmill [at the mine]." Later I read Charles R. LeMenager's *Julian City and Cuyamaca Country* to discover that "At one time a crew of forty Russians were imported from Baja California to cut the oak at two dollars a cord."

158

This was intriguing information, since he identifies the Russians as coming from Baja California. They had to be Russian sectarians, Molokans, whose history I know. What's more, I have visited the remains of their colony at Guadalupe and I am acquainted with some of the descendants of these Russians even as I write.

I phoned Mr. LeMenager to ask where he had obtained his information about the Russians. Unfortunately, as he acknowledged, his book is not rigorously documented and he could not recall the source of this factoid, but he was certain he had found it in one of the works in his bibliography. I neglected to ask how the number four hundred had become forty, but I suspect that he reduced it because he thought it unreasonably high, which it certainly is. Perhaps the discrepancy is the result of a typographical error.

Having read most of the items in his bibliography, I hastened to read the rest. In one of them, Gale Sheldon's M.A. thesis, "Julian Gold Mining Days," written at San Diego State University in 1959, I found this passage: "At one time a crew of 400 Russians were imported from a colony in Baja California to cut the oak at two dollars per cord." This was the source of Ellsberg's and LeMenager's Russians. Fortunately, Sheldon gave his source as the Ninth Annual Report of the San Diego County Division of Natural Resources, 1952. In this document I found the final link in the chain, for on page nine I read that "A crew of four hundred Russians were imported from the colony in Baja California to cut the wood, for which they received two dollars a cord." The author of the report gave no source for this information.

Where did he find this alleged fact? Perhaps it was in some written source unknown to me that he did not document. But, probably, he interviewed someone who remembered events at the mine fifty years in the past. This witness's memory provided that familiar mix of accuracy and error typical of the way we recall past experience.

Assuming there is a kernel of truth in the account, who were these Russians and what brought them to the Cuyamacas? Probably they were work parties that came to the mountains in search of gainful labor from their new homes in Guadalupe, some thirty miles east of Ensenada. They were sectarians, members of a group that split off from the official Russian Orthodox Church in the 18th century. The popular name for them is "Molokans," a name close to the Russian word for milk, "moloko." Usually it is said that this tag comes from the sect's practice of drinking milk during Lent when Orthodox believers do not. The origins of this sect and how they came to live in Baja California make an interesting story. What's more, the church survives and you might have the opportunity to meet Molokans today, particularly in east Los Angeles where most of their churches stand.

The founder of the sect, Simon Uklein, began preaching his beliefs in 1765 in Tambov, Russia. Stubbornly, he turned his face against some of the fundamental practices of the Russian Orthodox faith. The Russian Church has priests and monks; Uklein asserted that the congregation possesses final authority and no clerics are necessary. Russian orthodox churches are richly decorated; Molokan churches display only embroideries made by the women of the congregation. In addition, Molokans do not drink alcoholic beverages and they also observe some Hebrew dietary laws such as the prohibition against pork and shellfish. Uklein also preached that the members of the sect should practice communal ownership of land.

It is the nature of the services that the Molokans hold in their austere churches that give them the name of "Jumpers" or "Leapers." In their churches men assemble on one side, women on the other. Together they sing traditional hymns in rich harmonies at a heartbeat tempo of seventy-two accents per minute. One of the men "gets the spirit," and begins to leap and dance. Others join in. Everyone considers this proof that the Holy Spirit resides in the church and no service ends until this momentous event occurs.

This "divine dance" is not rare in Christianity. Among others, the 19th century Shakers danced wildly, and many Pentecostal sects today manifest the Holy Spirit by gesture and dance. After Molokans experience the ecstasy, the whole congregation eats together at tables set up in the church, the women preparing the food.

The Russian government persecuted the Molokans because they denied the Orthodox faith and because their young men resisted conscription. Police imprisoned Molokan leaders and exiled their congregations to remote regions, especially along the Turkish border. Under these painful circumstances, some of the Molokans, encouraged by the Russian writer, Leo Tolstoy, to whom they turned for advice, began to consider emigration. Some of them in fact came to the U.S. early in the 20th century, settling in Los Angeles. In part, they chose this city believing that the "angels" in the city's name

160

would protect them against their enemies.

Altogether about 3,500 Molokans abandoned Russia for Southern California; the great majority of the sect members, however, remained in Russia. Unhappy in Los Angeles, the emigrants purchased thirteen thousand acres of land as a group from President Diaz at Guadalupe in 1907 where they could do what they did best, farm. They built Russian style houses along a broad dusty street that still exists today off the Ensenada-Tecate highway. Here they grew wheat and raised large families of blond children.

Making new lives in Mexico, they encountered new problems. Early on, they became involved in the turbulence of the Mexican revolution. In the 1930s they had to deal with Mexican squatters who questioned their title to their land; eventually in the 1950s the Mexican army occupied Guadalupe to maintain order between the Russians and their Latin neighbors. (On my last visit to Guadalupe an elderly Russian woman, who still remembers clearing U.S. Customs in Galveston en route from Tsarist Russia to Mexico, asked me if I wanted to buy some of her land. Since it lay fallow, she feared Mexican squatters would seize it.)

As a consequence, most of the Molokans chose to leave for Southern California, where, except on Sundays, they can hardly be distinguished from their Anglo neighbors. Others intermarried with the Mexican population, giving rise to Spanish speaking families with Russian names in Ensenada and elsewhere. A few settled in San Diego County, especially around San Marcos. (Anyone interested in the Molokans must read Therese Adams Muranaka's *Spirit Jumpers,* published by San Diego's Museum of Man in 1988.)

Several aspects of the historians' descriptions of the Cuyamaca Russians left me uncomfortable. First of all, the number of Russians they placed in the mountains was impossibly high. Simply to transport four hundred men from Guadalupe and feed them would have been a huge task. Everyone agrees that the Stonewall Mine at its peak employed at best only several hundred workers; four hundred woodcutters were not needed to supply wood for a mine with two hundred employees. LeMenager's figure is probably much closer to the truth.

Then there is the problem of chronology. The mine's production peaked in the 1880s, while the Molokans began to arrive in America only in 1904, probably most coming around 1910. There were no

161

Molokans in the 1880s to work for the mine. I found my skepticism confirmed in a letter that R.W. Waterman, grandson of the one-time owner of the mine wrote in 1961 (in the San Diego Historical Society archives): "There were no Russians in lower Calif. until about 1910 or later. I clearly remember when they came there."

In spite of these doubts, were there really ever Cuyamaca Russians? The answer is a firm yes. They were Molokans who came to the mountains in cooperative work parties, an institution well known in Russia. They worked as wood cutters and perhaps on other projects as well, sending much of their earnings back to the colony in Mexico. But they never worked for the Stonewall Mine during its boom years and never in a group of four hundred.

Woodland Raptor

One mild Southern California winter morning as I was walking on a chaparral hill I saw a solitary mourning dove flying across the ravine at my feet. Out of nowhere a medium-sized hawk at blurring speed intersected its course and the two birds exploded in a feathery ball of predator and prey. Together they plunged to the ground on a grassy slope. I could see the hawk firmly clutching the dove, prepared to finish it off. But the dove had a resource: like all pigeons its feathers are loosely attached, and so it managed to wriggle out from under the hawk, shedding feathers all the while. It spurted into the sky and vaulted over a ridge with a speed that I could describe as like an arrow from the bow or an Indy car passing the checkered flag; the bird was fleeing for its dear life. The hawk collected itself, rested briefly, lifted into the air, and slowly flapped away in the opposite direction, its thoughts no doubt still on breakfast.

While the hawk was on the ground I could see its rounded tail and beautiful red-streaked breast. I didn't need to see these field marks, though, to identify it: the hawk's moderate size, its mode of attack, and its choice of avian prey, made me certain that I had witnessed a Cooper's hawk seeking its food in the air, as it usually does.

The cabin on North Peak is not a good place to observe hawks. The oaks and pines surrounding it restrict the view to only the sky overhead, obscuring the four horizons. Rarely I catch a brief glimpse of a soaring broad-winged hawk watching for an adventurous but foolhardy rodent. Rarely I hear the piercing "Kee-kee-kee!" of an unseen red-tail hawk announcing to females in the vicinity that it is available. When I see a hawk it is usually perched on the tip of a dead pine or telephone line near the lake, or sometimes flying rapidly across the cabin clearing or through the oaks. This land-loving, tree-loving, meadow-loving Cooper's hawk, although often described as "uncommon" or "rare" is the hawk I see most often on North Peak.

In 1828, Charles Lucien Bonaparte, Prince of Canino and Musignano, nephew to the emperor, named it in honor of the American ornithologist, William Cooper. Bonaparte also named the genus *Zenaida*, the doves, in honor of his wife, Zenaide. The hawk's would-be prey I saw that winter morning bears the scientific name of *Zenaida macroura*, the species name meaning "long tailed."

William Cooper had a son, James Graham Cooper, also an

ornithologist, and author of *Ornithology of California*. Long ago I was delighted to discover that the younger Cooper visited the Cuyamacas, publishing his observations in an article in 1874 in *American Naturalist*. My hope of finding an informative essay was soon dashed: Cooper made a flying visit to the mountains, only long enough to convince himself there were no new bird species or Mexican birds to be seen. In his article he also indited perhaps the most maddening sentence I have ever read in a work devoted to natural history, a small triumph of ambiguity: "The grizzly bear (or perhaps a different species called the cinnamon bear) is said to occur rarely."

Cooper's hawks prey mostly on birds, although in open country they also take lizards and small mammals. The victims are whatever birds are available, from English sparrows to robins to flickers and so on. Once I saw a Cooper's hawk resting on a manicured San Diego front lawn calmly plucking a domestic pigeon it had brought down.

In the eastern U. S. one of their commonest foods is the blue jay. I like to think that they prey on our abundant scrub jays; it would be gratifying to know these nest-robbers fear an enemy that feeds on them. In farm districts they take domestic fowl, thereby giving all hawks a bad name; for many farmers all hawks are "chicken hawks" and deserve to be shot on sight.

To the best of my knowledge no one has studied the food preferences of our local birds, but I suspect that many a mountain quail or band-tail pigeon ends up in their craws, as well as the young brush rabbits that seem to be everywhere in the springtime.

To catch their prey they employ two methods. Taking a position on a high point with a wide view of a clearing in the broken country they prefer, they watch for a bird to appear at its edge. Dropping close they stalk it through the trees and brush and then pounce. The second technique is more dramatic: they fly through open woods or along the edge of a clearing, hoping to frighten a bird into flaring into the open so they can capture it.

I will probably never see the nest of a Cooper's hawk. A nesting pair requires extensive home territory and they build their nests high in large trees. After a courtship when the couple sing hour-long duets to each other, the female lays three to six eggs, incubating them for about five weeks. After hatching, the nestlings stay close for about the same amount of time before they can fly. When they are about

164

eight weeks old they commence to catch their own prey, doubtless only after many failures.

Even adults do not find it easy to catch birds that hide in tangled crotchety chaparral or duck under branches, such as acorn woodpeckers do, or shed their loose feathers as did the mourning dove. Researchers have noted that for every bird a Cooper's hawk captures, four will elude its pursuit to live another day. Now I understand why the Cooper's hawk I saw that winter morning did not pursue the fleeing dove. Losing one of its victims is not at all unusual and it was best for it to collect itself and begin a new search for food if it wanted to survive until spring.

Wee, Sleekit, Cow'rin, Tim'rous Beastie

The Scottish poet Robert Burns used these words to describe a mouse; if he had lived in the Cuyamaca mountains he would have employed them to capture the essence of the local pack rat, or wood rat, more properly the dusky-footed wood rat (*Neotoma fuscipes*), a shy, timid, Bambi-eyed creature, that runs slower than a man walks and avoids sunlight like a cat avoids water.

In fact I suspect that few people have seen a pack rat, or wood rat, the preferred name. This is because they are nocturnal and usually spend their daylight hours in trees up out of sight. But nearly everyone who has been in the woods has seen their houses, large piles of sticks and leaves as much as five feet high; smaller ones are in tree crotches near the ground. Providing shelter from the weather, the houses are riddled with tunnels, some leading to ground burrows. At the center of the pile is a nest, a tightly woven core where the animal rests or raises her young.

Wood rats are solitary, finding each other for their moment of passion only in passing and then going their separate ways. Females raise the young alone, like Navy wives. The houses, though, are more or less permanent, the animals moving in whenever they find one vacant. Researchers have observed that these large structures are more correctly apartment houses than single-family dwellings. In them they have found three species of salamanders, Pacific tree frogs, alligator lizards, shrews, and surprisingly, king snakes and rattlesnakes. But still, in each house will be usually only one male wood rat or a female and her litter.

These inoffensive creatures don't fear humans very much; biologists can remove them from their live traps without resistance. Predators must find them easy taking because they are so slow of foot; their only hope is to find safety in a tree.

My dog Bella discovered them early. Upon our arrival in the mountains, she dashes from the truck with a single mind: to catch and kill as many wood rats as possible. She finds them lurking under boards or planks or sometimes in their houses. Like all orderly people I once felt the obligation to stack my firewood neatly so it would dry properly and to impress my neighbors. Bella strewed the wood over a garage-sized area ten by thirty feet in pursuit of her gentle prey. Now I fence the firewood. Her hunting is often successful; I

166

find the wood rats' sodden corpses where she has left them along the paths. Other predators dine on them as well. They make up a major part of the diet of bobcats and great horned owls, particularly, and larger snakes must take them with ease.

Wood rats are well adapted to life in the mountains. They live on leaves and berries of all sorts, but especially coastal live oak leaves and acorns. They don't hibernate, but are active all year. They seem to get adequate water from the vegetation they eat. Their favorite habitat appears to be brush with an over-story of trees, especially live oaks, and so they must be happy in the Cuyamacas where this is a common landscape. Our species is not local; *Neotoma fuscipes* occurs in northern Baja, most of California, and in Oregon.

They are moderately prolific rodents. A female has usually one to five litters a year, with, however, only one to three young in a litter. This means that a female produces perhaps six or eight young a year, sometimes more, mostly fodder for predators.

Wood rats have not had a very good press. First of all, they are not related to the infamous *Rattus rattus*, eater of filth and carrier of disease, in spite of their common name. Alas, it is their naked tails that put them into the same class as rats in the public mind.

People usually call them pack rats because of their habit of collecting random objects that they place in their nests. This human-like custom of collecting "treasure" has attracted much attention and numerous observers have written about this curious habit. Theodore Roosevelt wrote the wildest account: "From the hole of one, underneath the wall of a hut, I saw taken a small revolver, a hunting knife, two books, a fork, a small bag, and a tin cup." It takes courage to question the words of a president of the United States, but I wonder if human hands had not placed these objects in the hole. It requires a vivid imagination to see the small rodent I know moving a knife, a small revolver, and two books (hard bound or paper backs?). Maybe Roosevelt's memory betrayed him and the account was hearsay. The cowboys loved to deceive "Four Eyes" as they called Roosevelt because he wore glasses. Maybe it was a second-hand tall tale the president remembered as his own observation.

The world of science, by an odd turn of events, owes a debt to the wood rat's habit of building commodious houses. They sometimes build them in rock shelters or caves where they are protected from the elements. Aridity and the animals' urine preserves these brush heaps for centuries. Paleobotanists, scientists interested in the past history and distribution of plants, disassemble the houses where they sometimes find twigs and leaves from plants that no longer grow anywhere near the house site. This is firm evidence for the past occurrence of these plants near the house. Of course, Paleobotanists still rely on the fossil record for most of their evidence for past plant distribution, but these wood rat houses are invaluable for filling in the historical record for recent times. In this field of study these wood rat accumulations are not called houses, but rather middens, a term usually reserved for the accumulations of debris that humans leave behind them. This is another thing that endears the little creatures–like people, they leave trash, sometimes valuable, behind them.

These slow-moving shy mammals in the woods near our cabin provided me with another example of animal behavior that at first I found baffling. One spring day I heard Bella making her way toward me through the woods emitting a strange high-pitched whine. When she approached, 1 could see she was carrying in her jaws a wood rat, still alive.

Why was Bella bringing me this animal and why was she whining in this strange way? Then I realized she was only responding to instinct. She was bringing live food to her pups and her whine was to summon them to the experience of dealing with living prey.

Of course, we had her spayed when she was still young and she never was a mother and never will be. But instinct commanded her to follow the ancient way, in spite of the fact that she had no pups to feed or train. So she brought the wood rat to me as a substitute for her non-existent offspring because she had nothing better.

August

August

   This, to my mind, is not the happiest time of the year. True, the deer flies have left us, but it's still as hot as it was in July and the dust accumulating on leaves and grass is deeper every day. Spring flowers are gone and vegetation looks weary; oaks and pines are growing visibly, but their greens are paler and less vibrant.

   If only it would rain! But this summer the thunder showers have failed us. I read in the papers about torrential monsoon rains south of Tucson and heavy showers are falling over the whole state of New Mexico; the run-off must be filling the washes and the squat Indian corn is thriving as its roots take up water from the sandy moist soil. If only a few of those great anvil-shaped clouds would drift our way to drop two or three inches of rain, to wash clean the vegetation, to lay the dust which daily grows deeper on our unpaved roads, and to revitalize the plants that are struggling to make it through these hot dry months. Last week I saw heavy clouds to the east of San Diego and the next day I eagerly checked the statistics for the previous day at the east county locations. Not a drop had fallen in Julian but Borrego Springs reported .19 of an inch of rain. As so often happens, the shower was well east of the mountains. Maybe next week...

   One reason I'm apprehensive about this time of the year is because I have unpleasant memories from the events of a dry hot August four years ago when pine beetles moved onto the land and we lost half a dozen mature Coulter pines and worried about losing more.

   The entire state was suffering from a lengthy drouth, and I'd read that vast areas of forest as far north as Lake Tahoe were dead. In our own area whole hillsides had turned that ominous reddish-brown that indicated pine beetles were flourishing and leaving uncounted dead trees in their wake. So far, the beetles had not reached our land, but I could see the consequences of their attacks on nearby hillsides and we would be fortunate if our trees somehow escaped their inroads.

   In July trees were dying on our neighbor's land only a few hundred feet away, although as yet our trees were apparently still healthy. But then in August some of our pines took on that repellent reddish cast that was undeniable evidence that the beetles had at last established themselves on our property.

   It was no accident that the beetles had reached our land toward

171

the end of a long hot dry summer after a dry winter. Beetles are always present in the forest, but so long as rains are adequate the pines produce enough sap that the beetles have to struggle to invade the trees; the pines flood them out with abundant resin. But now the pines were stressed because of the drouth, the flow of sap had fallen, and the beetles had found congenial quarters in their host trees. This was the situation in thousands of square miles of forests in California, not only on our small plot.

It was probably western pine beetles which flew to our trees from our neighbor's land. Not much more than an eighth of an inch long, they bore through heavy pine bark and dig tunnels through the tree's inner bark (sometimes they are called engraver beetles), the vulnerable layer carrying nutrients to support the life of the tree. The first beetles to attack a tree emit odors into the air, chemical messages called aggregation pheromones, which attract other beetles in the vicinity. It's like a party, with early guests calling their friends to say "Hey, get over here! What a pad! Plenty to eat! And girls!" The girls are female beetles which not only enjoy the food offered by the inner bark, but also become pregnant (these things happen). They dig out niches along their tunnels for the several dozen eggs which each female deposits there.

When the eggs hatch into larvae, they promptly begin eating their way through the inner bark at right angles to the tunnel their mother had excavated, producing the curious comb-like engravings which are common on logs on the forest floor. Their tunnels further reduce the essential flow of nutrients to the branches of the tree. If the tunnels of the adult beetles and larvae girdle the tree, the vegetation above that point dies. If their depredations are close to the ground–and this is usually so–the tree is doomed. If the damage is higher in the tree, then perhaps only a branch or the top of the tree dies and with time the tree recovers. To make the situation even worse, the beetles carry microscopic fungi in their guts that flourish within the tree and obstruct the upward flow of sap even more. Beetles deliver a right uppercut and the fungi follow with a left jab. In most cases the tree is down for the count.

After dining for a few weeks or months on the tree's inner bark, the larvae become pupae, which are transformed into adult beetles. These climb to the surface of the bark, their receptors alert for the aggregation pheromones telling them it's time to fly to a new tree and

172

a new party with their friends.

The speed with which the beetles advanced into our trees was not at all unusual. At low elevations the beetles' reproductive cycle repeats itself three to five times during the warm months. As the fall advances, the pupae remain under the bark waiting for the coming of spring.

About six or so of our Coulter pines died late that summer. Most of them were large, about thirty inches in diameter and about eighty years old, as I discovered from counting the annual rings on the stumps. Some, though, were much younger. Apparently the beetles had an open field; any pine was a potential banquet table and nursery.

Still, most of our pines survived. Those that died were close to the neighbor's property where I first saw evidence of the beetles' presence. This suggests that the beetles are not very strong flyers and tend to go to nearby trees when they abandon their natal pines. But I leave this puzzle for entomologists to solve.

After we had survived the anguish of seeing our pines die (and the expense of having the trees cut up for firewood), we could see, unexpectedly, some benefits from the die-off. Kellogg oaks, which compete with the Coulter pines for light and water, got a new lease on life and grew in girth and reach. Increasingly, oaks dominated slopes where mostly pines had grown. Our view to the west improved as pine groves died and fell of their own weight; wind brought most of the dead trees down within a year. Surviving pines thrived as their neighbors died and lessened competition for water and light made the survivors healthier and better prepared to resist the attack of future pine beetles.

And yes, the pine beetles will return. Perhaps next year the drouth will come back and within a few years I will again see dead pines on the mountain. But this time, certainly older and hopefully wiser, when I see dying pines during a dry hot August, I will be less concerned. I know that some pines may die, but the forest will live.

A Satisfying Half

In 1895 the American naturalist John Burroughs, tiring of the splendid house he had built overlooking the Hudson, decided to seek out a site for a more modest residence. He wrote this about his choice, justifying his enthusiasm for a place that he called "not the most ambitious spot in the landscape."

> Scenery may be too fine or too grand and imposing for one's daily and hourly view. It tires after a while. It demands a mood that comes to you only at intervals. Hence it is never wise to build your house on the most ambitious spot in the landscape. Rather seek out a more humble and secluded nook or corner, which you can fill and warm with your domestic and home instincts and affections. In some things the half is often more satisfying than the whole.

Burroughs' words capture our mood when we purchased our cabin site on North peak. We had spent several months looking at lots all over the east county but this was the place we wanted. I'm sure that Burroughs, in his bearded way, if he had been present would have given us his blessings.

Because the mountains rise so steeply above San Diego's coastal plain there are many backcountry sites with magnificent views, particularly looking towards the sea. We visited some of them, driving over eroded tracks through the chaparral and to windy hill tops on county roads. But somehow these spectacular view sites left us uncomfortable.

One reason for our uneasiness was obvious: a site with a splendid view is a site where the wind blows, and in a region with ferocious east winds, to say nothing about the nagging south winds of springtime, this worried us. People can sit out days of rain so long as the roof is sound. Endless cloudy weather, while depressing, can be outlasted. Shade and air conditioning offer relief from heat and humidity. But winds that howl for days push anyone to the breaking point. The insistent force of the wind, its shrill and hiss, drills into the brain; there's no escaping it.

Something more than the wind made us shy away from sites with expansive views, something that Burroughs sensed and captured nicely: scenery can tire and demand too much. We wanted a piece of land with a view, well, because everyone sometimes needs to allow his spirit to expand, to free himself from limitations and restraints, to grow inwardly. But a limited view can have special appeal, and the land we were considering had a half view, just as Burroughs recommends. We found it to our liking.

Behind us, North Peak's shoulder shelters and protects the hollow and the meadow where we hoped to build the cabin. A wall of oaks and pines that follows a ravine through the property blunts the east wind.

To the west we could look down the valley of Sandy Creek to see a long ridge that blocks, it seems, the distant view. However, along it are two shallow gaps, almost as though the ridge sags, unable to bear its weight, and these greatly enhance the half view. At these low points on the western horizon stand mountains. In the first gap rises Iron Mountain, a pleasantly evocative name—is it rust colored or are there iron deposits on the mountain? Next to it lifts Woodson Mountain, named for a pioneer settler, useful to us as an orientation point alongside the state highway. Its tuft of electronic towers makes it instantly recognizable. Situated at the center of the second notch on the long ridge is the symmetrical triangle of Starvation Mountain. Its name describes the tragic condition of the American survivors of the Battle of San Pasqual, exhausted and hungry after the battle.

I like mountains in our view. For me, raised in the west, no view is complete without a mountain to tell me something about the weather, if nothing else. If I can see the summit of Woodson Mountain, then visibility is twenty miles and I don't have to listen to the weather report to know that coastal haze is only moderate. But a mountain's presence means more than a way of interpreting the weather. It is reassuring to have within my view something that offers constancy and consolation when transience and decline shadow my life. For people who live on a plain, the Russians, for example, it is the rivers that sustain; for us westerners it is the lift of mountains that makes our spirits soar.

Through these gaps on clear days, especially when a steady north wind blows, we can see something that is so much a part of our lives in California, the Pacific Ocean. Behind Woodson Mountain and suspended over Starvation Peak runs the ocean horizon, with the shifting bronze and blue of the water reflected in the westering sun. Like mountains, the ocean is a source of beauty and consolation. To live by the ocean is the dream of a lifetime for many people. To walk by the ocean gives pleasure to residents and visitors alike. And here is the ocean at my doorstep, thirty five miles removed, a distant neighbor.

But best of all in our satisfying half view, best because it is rare, and therefore, as Burroughs says, never tiring, is the sight of San Clemente Island, a hundred miles from our cabin. Perhaps one day in twenty, when the wind has been blowing for days and enough rain has fallen to cleanse the air and fog does not mask the face of the ocean, we can see the island's broad back.

The apparition of this land on the horizon is always startling. Has it always been out there? I have to tell myself that it must have been, although at first I don't think this is possible. But reason assures me that it could not have risen during the last few days. It must be a permanent feature of the landscape. Isn't it on all the maps? Well, then, I admit grudgingly, that is San Clemente Island and it has been there all the time.

Newlyweds

"I knew I would buy the house before I even saw it." It was my neighbor, Dick Storekeeper, who said these words. He was responding to the casual non-scientific survey I have been conducting for the last few years, namely, why do people move to the Cuyamacas to live?

"When I drove up the lane, after leaving Engineers Road and the pavement, and we went through the trees, and I couldn't hear any noise from cars any more, I felt as though I was coming home. I really didn't care what the house had to offer. I'd already made up my mind," he continued.

The house Dick bought is not far from our property. With two floors and a deck with an expansive view from El Cajon Mountain to San Clemente Island and Santa Catalina island on clear days, it's one of the older houses around–rumor has it that a group of doctors built it about twenty years ago as a getaway. Even today it isn't hard to find spent shotgun shells where they practiced shooting skeet in front of the house. Since the nearest residence was then some distance away, this was harmless, if noisy sport; now it would be too hazardous to the neighbors who have built nearby. Because several owners were involved in its construction, the house has a large number of bedrooms, four, a living room with a view to the west, a small kitchen, and a bath.

Dick was planning to build a house in the San Diego suburbs when a real estate agent told him he'd heard of a mountain house for sale that Dick might consider buying. Dick had been thinking about leaving the city to escape its noise. Like most of my neighbors who have chosen to move to the mountains, it seems to be the city's din he could least of all tolerate. "Noise in the city never seems to stop," he says.

As a matter of fact, it was the quiet at the mountain house where Dick spent two days before making the final decision that clinched the deal, but there were other reasons as well, perhaps dimly felt reasons. A native of San Diego, he was a Boy Scout and a volunteer for the YMCA at Camp Marston in Pine Hills. So, like many of us for whom memories of adolescence seem to possess particular poignancy and longevity, Dick's return to the hills was also a return to boyhood.

Dick's work had prepared him for an independent life at a house a mile from the pavement and ten miles from the nearest town. Trained in electronics in the Air Force after the Korean War, upon his move to the mountains he began to make improvements at the house. Solar cells, batteries, and a back-up generator that he installed guarantee reliable electricity far from the nearest power line and pole. A satellite dish and a new television set provide excellent reception; distance doesn't necessarily mean complete isolation. Talking with him, I concluded that breakdowns in the electrical or water systems won't cause him much concern; He'll take them in stride.

Dick's retired now. For many years an employee at one of San Diego's biggest electronic firms, he witnessed its slow decline during the last decade. The volume of work slid downhill as the Cold War ended, and the number of workers at the plant sank lower and lower. Seeing the shrinkage, Dick decided he would retire before he got a pink slip with his paycheck. He was happy to leave, jumping to solid ground as the ship crashed onto the rocks and sank under his feet.

Another reason he took to the mountains was because he felt it was time for a change. His wife of thirty years had died of cancer and his two sons were grown and independent. This was also the time he grew closer to the woman who became his new bride.

Marge Storekeeper was born in the town of Trail in the Kootenay district of British Columbia deep in the Canadian Rockies; like Dick, mountains are in her earliest memories. When she was eight years old her parents moved to Vancouver where she trained as a nurse, an excellent occupation for someone in the backcountry. Coming to Long Beach to work, in Southern California she met her first husband. After thirty-one years of marriage he died of cancer in 1990, leaving her a widow with three grown children.

Dick and Marge had known each other for two decades before they married. With their respective spouses they met as members of a rock-hound club that made excursions to the desert to collect gemstones and to share their experiences grinding and polishing their finds. Dick now uses one of the former bedrooms in the house to display his rock collection from those years.

They married in December 1995 at the home of Marge's daughter in San Diego with members of their two families as the only guests. They found the lady minister at "Anytime Weddings" in the Yellow Pages. She, as promised, provided a dignified and appropriate service anytime and anywhere.

They have grand plans for the house. A contractor has expanded the living room and enlarged the windows to the west. Next, they will have a mud-room built (Marge's idea) to make space for a washer and dryer lacking in the present house. After this is completed, they will have a garage built to provide protection for Dick's pickup and Marge's Escort. I don't think the doctors who built the house will recognize it when the Storekeepers finish their remodeling, including a new roof and a balcony off the second-story bedroom.

After the wedding Dick and Marge left San Diego to spend their honeymoon on Santa Catalina Island. I asked Dick why they chose this place to celebrate their marriage. "Well," Dick said, "I've always wanted to visit Catalina, and besides, if the weather was clear, we thought we might have a view of the Cuyamacas. Sort of keep an eye on things at home," he said.

Not a bad idea, when you stop to think that the newlyweds will spend the rest of their lives together in the house there on Starlit Way, on North Peak.

Mystery Ditch

Born in the western United States, by the time I was five years old I was confident I knew all I needed to know about ditches. They all fell into two categories: irrigation ditches brought water to crops, and drainage ditches removed unwanted water from fields or marshlands. What else did I need to know?

But later my confidence was shaken when I discovered the Kelly Ditch which runs for more than a mile west to east along North Peak above Boulder Creek, passing under Highway 79 just north of Cuyamaca Dam, and that once delivered water into Cuyamaca Reservoir. (The Kelly Ditch trail follows it.) It wasn't an irrigation ditch because there is no farming in this mountain district at 4,600 foot elevation with meager soils and brief growing season. In Southern California there is almost no such thing as unwanted water, and so it did not qualify as a drainage ditch. Clearly, here was a ditch that did not fit into my classification scheme, learned early, for western water management.

Only after I read a little in early San Diego County history did I understand the purpose of this five-foot by twenty-foot trench excavated along the mountain's flank. Until El Capitan Dam was completed in 1933 Cuyamaca Reservoir was the only water storage facility on the San Diego River or its tributaries. This meant that any water falling into Boulder Creek below the dam flowed unused to the sea. Someone conceived the idea of digging a ditch to intercept the run-off down North Peak where more than thirty-six inches of precipitation falls every year and divert it east to the reservoir for storage. So properly speaking, it was neither an irrigation nor a drainage ditch. It collected surface water and transferred it elsewhere rather than allowing it to flow its natural course.

I also discovered there were other such ditches in the west. In central Utah engineers have dug ditches along the eastern crest of the Wasatch mountains that capture surface water that would otherwise flow into the Colorado River and divert it to streams draining into the Great Basin for irrigation. But the most famous collection ditch in the U. S. is the Grand Water Ditch that the Denver Water Board dug athwart the Mountain of the Holy Cross, to the horror of today's nature lovers, to divert surface water from the Colorado River to the front of the Rockies. So I discovered that the concept of a collection

180

and transfer ditch is not unique to the Cuyamacas.

Another question, and a more difficult one, was who dug the Kelly Ditch and when? While some have written on this subject I was not satisfied by their answers. One newspaper account dated May 5, 1985, states that the ditch was completed in the 1860s, but this was impossible because the dam was not erected until the 1880s. Without the dam the ditch had no purpose. Further, the article says Kelly's ditch was named for an unknown Irishman. About 1872 James Kelly, part-owner of Julian's Owens Mine, established a ranch west of North Peak; the ditch must have been named for the Kelly family or the ranch. Another individual told me that he believed the ditch was dug in the 1880s when the dam was built, but he had no evidence to support his theory.

Initially, I was convinced that the ditch was dug between 1910 and 1916, probably in 1915. In June 1910 Ed Fletcher and his associates bought out the San Diego Flume Co., and that same year he bought the Kelly Ranch. It seemed reasonable that the new owners would want to increase the watershed of the newly acquired system, utilizing Fletcher's new land holdings. When I visited the Fletcher Family papers at UCSD I found what seemed to be confirmation for this theory.

First of all the ditch was not listed among the properties that the Cuyamaca Water Co. acquired from the old owners in 1910. Probably, it seemed to me, this meant that the ditch did not yet exist. Furthermore, Chester (Chet) Harritt, who was Fletcher's hydraulic engineer, displayed detailed knowledge of the ditch, noting for example in a 1919 report that the Hatfield flood of January 1916 had severely damaged it. What's more, in the same report he wrote that the excavation of the ditch required the removal of three kinds of material: moist clay and small boulders at 65 cents a yard, loose rock "dragged out of the trench by chain sling and mules" at $1.25 a yard, and solid rock removed with the aid of explosives at a cost of $3.00 a yard. In a report dated 1923 Harritt stated that the ditch occupied fifty acres, was one and a half miles long, and required the excavation of approximately twelve thousand cubic yards of material.

But in a report in which Harritt described all the expenditures on the water system from June 1910 to January 1915, he said not a word about excavating the ditch. It looked as though I could conclude that Harritt supervised the digging of the ditch between January 1915 and

181

the Hatfield flood of January 1916.

But still I did not feel confident to make this claim in print. All my evidence was indirect and I had not found proof that the Cuyamaca Water Co. had dug the ditch.

At this point, when I seemed to have come to a full stop in my efforts to solve this problem, I got a telephone call from the San Diego Historical Society Archives that they had found some maps which might be of interest to me. Two maps, dating from the turn of the century, showed some kind of a channel northwest of Cuyamaca Reservoir. My theory was wrong and the San Diego Flume Co. had dug the ditch before 1910. But when and under what circumstances?

This led me back to the files of the *San Diego Union* and a series of articles which its editors wrote in August 1895 about the status of the San Diego Flume Co.'s water system. And here after four months of digging at four local libraries I struck pay dirt. Writing in the *Union* on August 22, 1895 an editor said:

> The watershed is only eleven square miles, although $8,000 was expended last autumn [1894] on a ditch that is supposed to drain three miles more. During the heavy rains last January the ditch broke, and little water was caught, which will always be the case unless the company spends a large sum in cementing the sides and lower bank, so that it will stand overflows. There seems to have been an error of judgment as to this ditch, for its capacity is not half the flow of the three miles of extra draining during heavy rain.

The San Diego Flume Co. completed Kelly Ditch in the fall of 1894. From the first year, run-off from storms damaged the ditch so that its flow was much below expectations. The Company spent no more money to maintain the ditch, so that by 1910 when it sold out to the Cuyamaca Water Co. no one even bothered to list the useless ditch among the properties sold to the new owners.

Recently I walked the Kelly Ditch, beginning near the reservoir. At times I had to clamber over obstacles where floods have washed away the ditch or filled it with rock. At times I detoured around oaks that grow in its channel. I must admit I felt a certain satisfaction in knowing that I was the only person in the world who knew that the ditch was 101 years old–but now you know too.

September

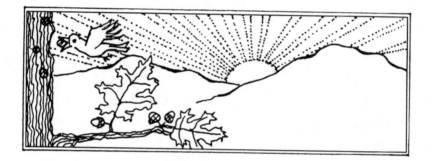

September

Last night in the mountains we had an unexpected and welcome September shower. Now the air feels different, somehow, and the ground has a new spring to it. The wet dead grass has a strange smell, faint and pleasant, like old straw, or a stable that has stood empty for years, well after the horses are gone. Not much rain fell, barely enough to cover the bottom of the rain gauge, just drowning the summer's accumulation of dead spiders and flies in the glass. But the shower was heavy enough to trigger the hatch of some aerial insects, and while they're too small for me to see, acorn woodpeckers are aware of them and they're busy this tranquil September morning, snatching them from the air.

Three of them are perched gregariously in a dead Coulter pine, filling the air with their frenetic "wack-a! wack-a! wack- a!" From time to time a bird darts out from a dead branch, flashing black and white and red briefly as it snares the insect, then returning to the tree to eat its invisible prey. Acorn woodpeckers get about a quarter of their food this way, behaving more like flycatchers than woodpeckers, making use of their unusually broad wings; when the young hatch in the spring their exclusive diet will be insects that the adults bring to them in a hollowed out nest.

Usually acorn woodpeckers haunt oak trees, to which they have a close attachment. As early as January they find food in the oaks: they drill small holes in the bark and then return to feast on the sap. They won't let me forget that they are first cousins to sapsuckers. In spring, as soon as the acorns are big enough to eat, the birds pull them green from the trees, breaking them loose sometimes with twigs still attached.

Now it's September and the woodpeckers' harvest season has commenced. Acorns are ripe and the birds collect them to deposit in their granaries. Choosing a sturdy tree, but sometimes a telephone pole or even a wooden building, they excavate an acorn-shaped hole and ram an acorn into it, butt out. These granaries contain thousands of acorns; the prize winner is a California sycamore seen in 1923 that held an estimated twenty thousand acorns in its bark. (A recent source raised the count to "forty-fifty thousand." Hans Winkler, et al, *Woodpeckers,* 1995). These granaries are crucial to the birds' well-being, because they enable them to survive the winter when aerial

185

insects are rare, oak sap has not yet begun to flow, and the acorn crop has not yet ripened.

Granaries are not hard to find. I can hear the woodpecker cries and see their flashing colors near the tree at a considerable distance. Sometimes I pause on Engineers Road just above the reservoir to inspect a huge incense cedar close to the pavement that serves as a granary; it holds thousands of acorns. In its vicinity hover and swoop a swarm of acorn woodpeckers–the granary's proprietors. They ignore me, devoting their time to sparring with each other, all the while repeating their raucous calls.(Recently the birds seem to have abandoned this granary–August, 1997.)

Acorn woodpeckers are the most social of northern birds; even the casual observer knows that he will rarely see only one or two birds together. What's more, this is not an aggregation of birds, like a flock of crows or sparrows. From cradle to grave acorn woodpeckers lead an intensely social life.

Because they are communal, or cooperative, ornithologists have studied them very closely, hoping to find aspects of their behavior that might contribute to the theories of Sociobiology, especially popular since E. O. Wilson published his book with this name in 1975. Cooperative societies in the animal world offer intriguing challenges to the traditional theories of evolution, most of which are grounded in the idea of individual competition.

How do ornithologists conduct their studies of this bird? Through close observation of individual birds which they have captured, examined, and marked. For example, before Walter D. Koenig and Ronald L. Mumme, and their assistants, wrote their *Population Ecology of the Cooperatively Breeding Acorn Woodpecker,* they captured and marked over eight hundred birds. They followed this with thousands of hours of field observation.

Their book and those of their predecessors reveal some surprising facts about the cooperative life of acorn woodpeckers. Investigators discovered they live in groups of two to fifteen birds (a pair is a rarity). The group settles in the vicinity of its granaries which they defend vigorously along with their adjacent territory. This group is divided into two classes. On the average two to six birds are "breeders" while the rest of the birds are "helpers" who do not breed at all.

All the females among the breeders are sisters or a mother and

186

her daughters; all the male breeders, who are not related to the female breeders, are brothers or a father and his sons. What's more, when egg-laying time comes, female breeders deposit all their eggs in one nest; this is the cooperative spirit with a vengeance.

When a female breeder visits the nest and finds an egg preceding her, she removes it to another location where the members of the group quickly puncture and eat it. Only one female, with perhaps another female joining in, lays all the eggs in the nest.

At first ornithologists had difficulty analyzing the birds' breeding patterns, but lengthy observations indicate that sexual choices among the breeders are broad, to put it nicely. They discovered that some breeders are faithful to one mate, some females have several mates, some males have several mates, and some males and females breed indiscriminately. These breeding choices are described as monogamy, polyandry, polygyny, and polygynandry, respectively.

When for some reason there are vacancies in the group new sets of brothers or sisters are recruited from the outside; this assures that family inter-breeding does not occur. New breeders first destroy all the eggs and nestlings of any preceding breeders; this means that they alone contribute to the group's gene pool.

Helpers, as noted, do not breed. When they are a year old they leave to become breeders elsewhere. But there is an exception to this: if all the breeders of one sex die, then helpers of the *opposite* sex can become breeders within their own group. This assures that a male bird does not breed with his mother or his aunts, nor a female with her father or uncles. The former helper may now join his father as a breeder; the same principle holds for females that may join their mother as breeders.

Helpers, while they do not breed, have a place within the group. They defend granaries and the group's home territory. They incubate eggs and feed nestlings, none of which of course are their own offspring. Ultimately, they can become breeders abroad or at home under special conditions.

Two questions have especially intrigued biologists who investigate the social life of acorn woodpeckers: why do they live in groups and not as isolated pairs like most birds, and why do helpers help?

The answer to the first question seems to be related to the existence of granaries, which provide a reliable food source during the winter. In other words, the social system seems to have arisen because of the presence of this rich food supply which is best accumulated and maintained by a group of birds. In some places acorn woodpeckers live in environments that do not provide acorns for granaries; here they live as independent pairs, like most birds.

The answer to the question of why helpers help is more difficult. One theory is that helpers, while they do not pass on their own genes, are satisfied to see close relatives pass on their genes successfully. (Recently I asked a middle aged woman if she'd ever had children. "No," she responded, adding proudly, "But I have three nephews!") Secondly, the principle of reciprocity may perhaps explain what some see as the helpers' altruism: helpers help because they know the communal system with its granaries aids them. Another theory has it that helpers are too young to breed competently.

Still, biologists cannot decide the why of acorn woodpecker social life to everyone's satisfaction. Theory is more challenging than the task of collecting data. Observers in folding chairs with binoculars have established the facts of acorn woodpecker behavior beyond much doubt, but analyzing that behavior still presents difficulties.

I, for one, cannot see an acorn woodpecker without, for a moment, asking myself: is that a male or female breeder or helper? If it is a breeder is it involved in monogamy, polygyny, polygamy, or polygynandry? Did it take its place within its own group or was it an outsider? If it's a helper, does he or she yearn to leave the group, in some birdish way, to enter a new group? Does he or she follow the mortality within the breeders of the opposite sex in the group, hoping, once more in some birdish way, for a vacancy within its class? Human life is heavy with uncertainty, but so, too, it seems, is the noisy life of the acorn woodpecker.

Unfriendly Fire

This year in August we held our annual property owners' picnic. As always, it offered a pleasant occasion to renew acquaintances with neighbors, to chat, to gossip. The mood was, as always, light and casual. People talked and ate potato salad at the same time. But this year unexpectedly a neighbor raised the question of fire safety, asking, if fire should break out, what would be the best escape routes from our district? Instantly the mood of the gathering changed. Talk ceased and the speaker had the rapt attention of everyone seated around the long food-laden tables. A lively discussion followed. If there is any subject that the mountain people take seriously it is fire.

With good reason. Hillsides holding decades of accumulated rotting trees and brush, vegetation rich in highly combustible oils, long dry summers that convert green wood to tinder, Santa Ana winds that blow across the range, driving fire before them–these elements raise fire danger to a very high level in Southern California. Every summer and fall wildfires dot the countryside here. And growing population in the rural areas only increases the odds that some hand may provide a spark to set off a holocaust.

I have never been able to find any evidence of fire on our property. If there had been fire in recent decades, then I should find burned stumps or fire scars on some of the oaks and pines on the property, but there's nothing of the sort. Recently, pursuing this question, I visited the County Planning Department to see if it had any records of fire in our area. I found that county officials also have a lively interest in the subject of wildfires. As a matter of fact, specialists in the Cartography Section have compiled maps showing all the fires in the county since 1910, each indexed to help find more detailed information about how the fires were fought, if at all. What I had before me on these maps was eighty-five years of fire history in the county.

The maps confirmed my assumption that our property has not burned, at least since 1910. But several fires have come very close. In the late 1920s a huge fire burned the upper watershed of Boulder Creek, but it did not sweep to the north over Engineers Road. For thirty years there were no fires nearby, but in the 1950s a large fire

189

scorched the summit of North Peak; today, because so many homes have been built overlooking Cuyamaca Reservoir, such a fire would destroy many structures. In the same decade a small fire also burned a patch of woods near Azalea Creek, but it did not spread far.

In November 1956 the most tragic fire in the county's history began some five miles southwest of our property. Strong Santa Ana winds pushed the so-called Inaja fire away from our land. Later in its course it changed direction and crossed Boulder Creek Road eastward at several points; however fire fighters were able to control its advance in our direction without too much difficulty.

On October 30, 1967, fire broke out in Pine Hills to the north of us. Ultimately, it scorched 20,000 acres of hill country. Crossing Cedar Creek southward it advanced up the slope towards our place, but bulldozers contained it not more than a half-mile from our property; as I walk down the chamise and manzanita covered slope to the north I can see faint traces of the fire breaks they cut across the hillside. Not far away stand pines with blackened bark, testimony to the fire that burned nearly thirty years ago.

Since the 1920s the Pine Hills, North Peak, Boulder Creek, and Inaja Fires have burned in a noose around our land. I suppose the question remains whether our woods will burn next, but that's no certainty. It is reasonable to, say, though, that if our woods burn, and perhaps the cabin in it, the fire will be very hot, thanks to the fuel accumulated in the last four score and ten years.

Only since early in the 20th century has government taken an active role in the suppression of fires in the Cuyamaca mountains. Before that, lightning-set fires burned out of control until rain or lack of fuel extinguished them. Indians set woodland fires to improve deer browse, to make travel easier, and to remove cover for enemies. Nineteenth century ranchers continued the Indian policy because open woods provided better grazing, as well as easing the problem of controlling their livestock.

In 1957 Charles Kelly, once an employee of Cuyamaca Rancho State Park and former part owner of the Kelly Ranch on North Peak, gave an interview that is preserved in the San Diego Historical Society archives. Born in 1881, he describes conditions at the turn of the century and later, when fire was still friendly in the Cuyamaca Mountains:

190

My dad [James Kelly, rancher, who died in 1902] always had four or five men working for him. Then he'd hire twenty or twenty-five Indians and all during the late fall they'd go over the country burning up old logs and brush piles. Then if a fire got started in the heat of the summer it would run into something that had burned the year before and they'd put it out. It's nothing like it is nowadays....

...But the old-timers really did control burning. They'd clean up one place this fall and next fall another place, so if a fire started in the summer it would run into one of those cleaned-up places and never get started or go any further. And now the Cuyamaca mountains are going to burn off and it can't be helped. The timber will go if a fire gets started with the right wind because the underbrush and the dead timber and oaks on the north, middle, and the south peaks is so dense. Where I used to go through on horse-back you can't crawl now on your hands and knees, because of the underbrush and the dead timber that's fallen.

Today such free use of fire is impossible, if nothing else because of the numerous houses in the backcountry. And so fuel continues to build up and everyone watches for a disastrous fire in the mountains, with dread.

Many of us would like to think that a disastrous fire could not sweep through our district because of the quick response that modern technology provides at the first appearance of smoke in the hills. Cellular phones are now commonplace, so that observers notify the authorities at the earliest hint of fire. Fire fighting forces are well organized at the local, state, and federal level, guaranteeing that manpower will be on hand to put down any fire in short order. Aerial tankers are waiting not far away; these old four-engine bombers and new helicopters deliver thousands of gallons of flame retardant liquid within the hour. The latest innovation, "Super scoopers," airplanes that onload water directly from lakes, are also on the ready.

About ten years ago the mountain people had a close opportunity to see modern fire suppression at work. At Memorial Day weekend, 1984, a teenager was target shooting not far from Mountain Meadows, old Indian country with grasslands and a modern apple orchard. One of his bullets ricocheted off a boulder and sparked a blaze that an east wind blew down into the meadows. Even though vegetation was still springtime green, the bullet produced a wall of flame that witnesses still talk about today. State and federal fire forces responded very promptly; helicopters dipped water out of the nearby farm pond to drop on the fire.

In spite of the fact that the fire was in a very accessible site, an early alarm was sounded, and response was prompt, the fire consumed thirty-five acres; it's estimated that it cost between $40,000 and $50,000 to suppress the blaze. Old-timers still shake their heads when they recall the fire, asking each other what might have happened if the fire had reached the hills beyond the meadows and advanced up the slopes where an up-draft might have driven the fire at break-neck speed; this is where many people have built houses to take advantage of the expansive views.

Noting improvements in fire fighting techniques, plus better communications, an optimist might conclude that fire is no danger in the hills. A more realistic attitude is that fire danger, except during the cool moist winter months, is always high in Southern California. All that is necessary is that appropriate conditions of heat, high winds, and a spark coincide–and fire will explode. To the west of our district, these conditions existed in November, 1956, leading to the Inaja fire. This wildfire deserves a second look because it offers an example of the combination of elements that brought about a terrible conflagration, a fearful model for wildfire in the Southern California hills.

*****

The fall of 1956 saw little rain. The gauge at Lindbergh Field in San Diego showed less than half of average rainfall for the five months from July through the end of November–.68 inch, instead of 1.54 inch. In the hills, rainfall probably measured between one inch and two inches for these months.

What's more, the weather map for Saturday, November 24, showed high pressure over the Intermountain West, and as a result air was flowing over and down the coast ranges towards the Pacific, Santa Ana winds blowing between twenty and fifty miles an hour.

At 9:00 that morning a fifteen year old boy at the Inaja Indian Reservation thought he would do something "crazy" and threw a match into damp grass to see if it would burn. It did, with a vengeance. Fanned by the wind, within a few minutes it swept across Boulder Creek Road, heading southwest, the direction of the wind.

By sundown that day the fire had spread with appalling speed as far as the Barona Indian Reservation, which was evacuated but only after the fire had destroyed twelve homes. The fire also extended west and north, but not so rapidly as in the direction the wind was blowing; flames spread to within three miles of Pine Hills and five miles from Ramona. Late in the day fire reached El Cajon Mountain, ten miles or so from Inaja, and the *San Diego Union* estimated that in one day the fire had consumed 25,000 acres of chaparral and forest. This means it was burning more than two thousand acres of hillside every hour, or more than three square miles.

On Sunday a man-made break between El Capitan Dam and El Monte Park stopped the fire's advance for the time. Eventually the fire crossed El Monte Road, leading to the dam, at several points. It burned within three and a half miles from Ramona on the old Julian highway. By now the authorities estimated the fire had burned 33,000 acres; this figure was to grow to 38,000 acres the next day. Nineteen hundred men worked on the fire lines, particularly on the western advancing edge of the fire.

Here, in a narrow steep ravine close to the dry bed of the San Diego River at a site below Eagle Peak Road, occurred the greatest tragedy in the history of fire in San Diego County.

In this place Sunday night about 9:00 p.m., well after sundown, eighteen men were digging a fire line. They believed they were not in danger because the nearest flames were about a half mile to the east, but darkness no doubt limited their ability to estimate the distance and advance of the fire. Suddenly, the wind increased to gale force, probably over fifty miles an hour, and the fire swept over the crew. Seven men scrambled to safety up a steep rocky hillside, but eleven men were burned to death, their clothes consumed by the flames. A monument on Highway 78 below Julian honors their names. Today, if I stand on the knoll above the monument and look down the straight valley carved by the San Diego River, perhaps close to the patch of blue water marking El Capitan Reservoir I can see the place where they died. Of the eleven men, eight were prisoners who had volunteered to fight the fire; it's appropriate that inmates of the honor camps in the county paid for the erection of the monument to their fellow prisoners, and the other victims, by the roadside.

By Wednesday, November 28, crews had nearly controlled the fire, although some still feared it would cross Highway 78 and advance into the Volcan mountains above Julian, since sea breezes were pushing it eastward, the Santa Ana winds having abated. However, by the end of the week, fire crews had it completely contained. The Inaja fire burned 43,000 acres within a ninety mile perimeter. It was the largest fire in memory within the county, although the Laguna fire in 1970 was larger and caused more property damage. But the Inaja fire remains by far the most tragic in the county's history.

*****

What can we learn from the Inaja fire? Everyone in the mountains must give high priority to reporting fire promptly; a skeptic might respond by saying, in the case of conditions such as existed at the time of the Inaja fire, this would be of no avail. Perhaps so. Fire fighters know they must answer wildfires as energetically as possible, employing overwhelming resources in men and equipment. Recently, when a sixty-acre fire broke out in Pine Hills to the north, they did just that, sending in five helicopters and six aerial bombers in a short time. If the authorities want to contain a fire, they know they must do it in minutes, not hours.

But in spite of these measures, it seems undeniable that if the right (or wrong?) conditions of drouth, wind, and flame meet, nothing can stop a wildfire in the Cuyamacas. Nor am I the only one in our district who takes this view. One of our neighbors who lives at the end of a gravel road with his wife and children has gone to the expense of building a permanent fire shelter, a six by eight foot windowless block house with a dirt roof and low entrance doors. Here his family will take refuge in case of fire. It's rumored that another neighbor will soon build a shelter like it.

Everyone in our family agrees that if smoke appears anywhere in sight of our cabin, particularly to the east whence come Santa Ana winds, everyone must leave as soon as possible. Because of the discussion at our annual property owners' picnic we and our neighbors know the escape routes from our mountain homes very well, although we don't talk about them very much. I hope we never have to use them, our hearts in our mouths, wildfire red and fuming over our shoulders, but it's only common sense to be prepared.

Fire in the mountains is nothing new, and like so many things here we must know how to live with it. Or how to run from it.

Orchard in the Wilderness

When we bought land in the Cuyamacas I never thought I would establish a mountain orchard. We bought land as a retreat, a place to watch animals and birds, and as a site for a cabin, perhaps. But as a place to maintain an orchard, never. Only with the passing of time did I think that it might be pleasant to dig and rake mountain soil, eat mountain fruit off the tree, and drink a glass of wine fermented from grapes grown in a mountain vineyard.

One of the sights which turned me in this direction was a glimpse of a grape vine flourishing on a roadside fence not far away from our acreage, In mid-summer it displayed robust leaves even without care or irrigation. If a grape vine was growing in total neglect, perhaps I could obtain a grape harvest myself without too much trouble. And of course, this mountain region is famous for its apples and pears. I had no illusions about growing vegetables; fruit could be protected from birds and animals, but I knew that mice, gophers, wood rats, foxes, ring-tail cats, raccoons, and birds would pounce on any corn and tomatoes I was foolish enough to plant.

Very tentatively I cleared a little space in the brush near the cabin site and planted the beginnings of an orchard-vineyard, an apricot, a cherry, and six grape vines. I chose a cherry and an apricot because these trees won't produce fruit in coastal San Diego; here fresh cherries and apricots are as exotic as mangos, papayas, and bread fruit. I planted six varieties of grapes because I wanted to see which of them would prosper; some varieties of grapes are notoriously finicky about where they will grow. But thrive they did, the trees and the grapes, and I began to expand my little orchard. Eventually, it would include about one hundred grape vines and fifteen apricots, cherries, apples, pears, and a plum tree.

But it wasn't easy. First I had to clear a space roughly sixty feet by sixty feet, densely overgrown with scrub oak, Palmer's ceanothus, chamise, manzanita, poison oak, and miscellaneous creeping and crawling vines. These I cut off with a hand-saw, dragging the corpses off to concealment in a nearby ravine. With some uneasiness I painted the stumps with brush-killer; the directions said dilute one part brush-killer to a hundred parts water, but I used the chemical straight, knowing that the chaparral plants are survivors. In a year or so I had a clearing, sort of, but even today I keep an eye open for brush reviving in the orchard. When a blade of green emerges from a stump I leap into action, shovel in hand, brush-killer at the ready.

One May morning a few years ago I drove up to the mountains to inspect my growing orchard. To my shock I discovered that while I was absent someone had pruned my grapes and trees with a dull hedge shears, lopping off nearly every vigorous shoot. The malefactors, of course, were deer who relish the freshest, the most succulent spring growth. Recovering, I purchased and applied deer repellant; it doesn't work. I tried wrapping every plant in protective chicken wire. But when an adventurous shoot pushed its way through the meshes, a hungry animal promptly nipped it off. Gritting my teeth, I had to admit that the answer was to build a deer fence around the orchard.

Three different garden manuals recommended six foot, seven foot, and eight foot heights for a deer fence. I took no chances and built an eight foot fence with a matching gate. When I had completed it, I stood back and looked aghast at what I had wrought: one of the ugliest things I have ever seen. Chain link, aluminum poles, looping wires. Even Frank Gehry couldn't have done anything with those materials. The only saving grace is that this eyesore is surrounded by woods that screen it from the lane; at least, only few people have seen this monstrosity. But it has kept out the deer.

The following spring I thought my fence had let me down. One fine day I visited the orchard to find that some one had pruned off many of the shoots on the grapes. At first I assumed that deer had leaped the fence and I hurriedly reinforced it at low points. But then I realized that the cuts were cleaner than those deer inflict and they were all close to the ground. Cuddly, adorable, black-eyed bunnies, otherwise known as brush rabbits, had been here. Peter Rabbit, along with Flopsy, Mopsy, and Cottontail had abandoned Mr. McGregor's garden and moved to mine. I could not possibly screen them out of the orchard; it was too easy for them, like Peter, to squeeze under the fence. My response, and it was mostly successful, was to erect screens around the tenderest grapes until their leaves were out of the rabbits' reach. I began to understand that gardening in the wilderness has its special challenges.

But the clash between the wood's fauna and my flora had not yet reached its climax. I'd noticed that there were low mounds of fresh earth from time to time in the vineyard. What was even more ominous, sometimes a small grapevine would disappear without a trace.

I suspected gophers.

The next spring I planted a few more fruit trees, the prize being a Rainier cherry with creamy fruit blushed pink which the catalog said the birds would not eat. That was for me. I ordered it from an Oregon nursery; it cost nearly thirty dollars. The young tree grew well, putting out energetic new growth. One day I noticed that its leaves had wilted. Checking to see if it had rooted firmly, I tested its branches: its trunk lifted clear of the ground. My pretty little tree was now a dead stick. A gopher had decapitated it at the base of the neck. When I recovered from this loss, I wrote these verses to express the raging fury and impotence I felt when a lousy gopher cut short the life of my beautiful thirty dollar Oregonian:

I am a nature lover
I love her dawn, her dusks,
The sadness of her seasons,
Her gentle murmurs.
    I am a nature lover.

I tremble at her voice.
Keen to her message,
My soul waxes and wanes with her moon.
I know her every way. Her pages
    Are mine to read, a book without a cover.

But today the cherry tree is dead,
Cut off at the roots
By the Felco incisors of a little monster.
Where's the axe! Where's the fire hose!
    This is the Year, I swear, of the Dead Gopher!

(If you are not a gardener you may not know that the Swiss company Felco makes the world's best pruning shears.) I added gophers to deer and rabbits as yet another creature which feeds on my garden. According to David Rains Wallace in his book, *The Untamed Garden,* (an endearing title!) in which he describes his own adversities with gophers, the best course is to ignore them. If you kill them, others will simply move in to take their place. With crossed fingers I'm following his advice; I hope he's right. But to be safe, I'm taking the

197

precaution of planting new trees in wire baskets to protect their roots from the gophers.

In my simple verses, besides my rage, I also tried to express the idea that it is possible to love nature in the abstract (I hope that the reader comprehends that the emotional excesses of the first two stanzas are meant to be ironic), but not so easy to love her when you try to make a living from the land and so must resort to artificial methods to have your way. No doubt farmers have committed grave errors to "maximize production," but it's undeniable that sometimes firm measures are necessary to restrain unfriendly nature. For example, no one in the world could enjoy a glass of wine if its makers did not use sulphur to control mildew on grapes and mold on wine, something the French discovered centuries ago. Reasonable, cautious, restrained use of chemicals in agriculture seems to be unavoidable.

Another thing I have acquired from my novice mountain orchard is a great admiration for anyone who can make money from the land. Me, my orchard soaks up money like its soil soaks up rain. If I calculated what each grape and apple I have harvested in the mountains has cost me, I'm certain I would be reduced to speechless horror, and my wife, who is even thriftier than I, to anger.

She'd insist that it is her right to take a trip to Italy as her fair compensation for my horticultural excesses. I don't know how I could argue with her.

I'm happy to say that I have begun to enjoy the fruits of my labors. The birds and I both like the fresh grapes. This year I will have a few McIntosh and Braeburn apples, with more to come next year. After making some adjustments for the four-footed fruit lovers, I think the garden is a success. It is gratifying to eat your own fruit, as garden books have been saying for years

As a trade-off for the wildlife and its inroads, because of the orchard's isolation, I have had very few insect or fungus pests on my trees and vines.

Now if I could only think of a way to hide the deer fence.

Home on the Range

The big cat sniffed at a patch of sandy ground sparkling with mica that lay below a huge gabbro boulder, bigger than most houses on the mountain. Wizened pine needles and tobacco-brown oak leaves the wind had blown into the alcove yielded to her broad paws. She lay down heavily, panting, noting that the south wind roaring in the pines up the mountain here did not even whisper. Pulling a few soft hairs from her underbelly, she made a sort of bed. Her three blond and spotted kittens were born that evening, just as the sun fell below the distant Pacific.

Next morning, exhausted after giving birth and nursing her kittens, she dropped onto the top of the giant boulder, luxuriating in the warmth of the April sun. She knew that below her in the sandy-floored den the kittens were sleeping, their bellies as round and hard as young puff-ball mushrooms emerging under pine trees in the spring sun.

From the flat rock she had an expansive view of her home territory, about fifteen square miles, that she knew as well as a suburban housewife knows her ranch house with its picture window and recently remodeled kitchen. Most of her home territory lay on the broad front of North Peak leading down to a narrow canyon where flowed Cedar Creek. Over the ridge to the south a steep slope declined to Boulder Creek. Behind her rose the mountain's summit with its steel towers and dirt roads where pickup trucks often growled their way up to the crest.

From where she drowsed in the sun she could see the territory belonging to two other female lions. To her left and behind rose Middle peak that another female hunted and called her own. Sometimes the two of them met near Paseo de Coscar where Boulder Creek pierced the range. Far to the west in rolling hills where Cedar Creek turned toward the sea another female claimed her home territory. The three female lions in this quadrant of the Cuyamaca Range had a deferential relationship, something like mutual respect. They left each other alone. All they shared were the favors of an old male lion that endlessly and tirelessly patrolled the huge expanse the three females occupied, partaking with them in the game the hills provided and watching for signs that one of the three had come into estrus.

The landscape she surveyed was good mountain lion country.

Deer flourished in most of it; they were her major source of food. Ground squirrel colonies riddled bare rocky slopes. Sometimes she caught one of the mountain's gray squirrels that ventured too far from its home trees. On occasion she tore wood rat nests apart to catch their succulent owners. Brush rabbits went down her gullet whole. Very rarely, she pursued a fox or bobcat successfully; these small predators were hardly enough to provide the nutriment her hundred and twenty pound body required.

After returning conscientiously to nurse them, she left the kittens in the rock shelter. Quickly they grew, doubling their weight, their blue eyes opening and their hearing becoming more acute. When she was gone they slept or played together, fierce little contests with mock attacks, their needle sharp claws extended, tumbling and rolling down the slope close to the shelter, but never departing too far from the protection of the great rock hanging over them.

When the kittens were two months old she led them away from the den to new shelter under an oak that had collapsed, its base rotted, in an early snow storm. Here the soil was dry and the kittens in a tangle of dead leaves and branches could not be seen a bobcat's leap away. She had sensed it was time to move them, fearing a predator might find them playing in the sunny spot below the rock.

Hawks spiralled over the mountain, coyotes ventured into her territory, and either of them might make a quick meal of a kitten. But most of all she feared stray male cougars that sometimes invaded her territory—she found their scrapes, piles of dirt and leaves topped by feces or urine, along prominent trails. Without hesitation they would kill and eat the kittens if they chanced on the rock shelter. Now she and the kittens deserted this place pungent with their smell and littered with scat, the kittens half-covering it with leaves and sand, like all good cats.

That evening, confident that her kittens were safe under the oak's sheltering trunk and hidden in branches and twigs, she hunted up the mountain. She paced deliberately, stopping to sniff the air, but mostly watching attentively for any signs of movement in the night forest heavy with shadows. Her progress was slow and the moon was high when she neared a clearing that canyon live oaks and incense cedars surrounded. Through the trees she sensed movement in the meadow bright under the moon.

Dropping to the ground, her eyes intense and her long tail held low, she crept towards the clearing. On its far edge a spike buck was feeding on new chaparral growth, but the deer was still four hundred feet from her–much too far. For a quarter of an hour she slid towards it, hiding behind trees, shrubs, and boulders, avoiding dry branches or twigs whose snapping would warn the deer; automatically, her rear paws descended in her front paw tracks, reducing the possibility of breaking a twig or dislodging a stone.

She was fortunate to find a solitary buck; a herd of feeding deer is much more difficult to approach. This animal had drifted away from the two other spike bucks with which it usually consorted. Nervous, it seized only a few mouthfuls of succulent green shoots at a time, then peered about in every direction, instinct crying that solitary feeding demanded high attention. Once or twice it started, ready to flee, but hearing nothing in the silver meadow it returned to its feeding.

By now the cougar had made its way to within fifty feet from the buck. Taking cover behind a low boulder at the clearing's edge, she slowly gathered her long back legs under herself. Longer than the front legs, they had immensely powerful muscles. This was the crucial moment–either she killed the deer or it would vanish. She could not hope to run it down in open pursuit. Her lungs were small in proportion to her body and she could exert herself only for a moment; her endurance was not much greater than that of an Olympic sprinter.

In two blinding leaps she bulleted across the meadow in the time it took for the buck to lift its head. Hitting it broadside, she wrapped her wickedly clawed paws around its chest, held fast, and plunged her huge incisors into the back of the buck's neck, bulging jaw muscles closing down. Like twin daggers, her upper incisors slid between the vertebrae and sliced the spinal cord; the buck crashed to the ground. This kill had been swift and certain, but one of five deer she essayed managed to escape; deer had a fighting chance against a cougar attack, more so if they were in a herd with all eyes inspecting the surrounding woods for danger. As she grew older and her attack slowed, more and more deer would elude her, until finally she might die of hunger, all prey escaping her feeble grasp.

Slitting open the deer's abdomen, she extracted its stomach and intestines. These she dragged into trees some distance away from the kill. Next she removed heart, lungs, and liver, quickly devouring them. These were the most nutritious part of the body. Even if she

201

had to abandon the carcass, she had consumed them—not that she had any concept of nutrition, for it was instinct that directed her actions.

Seven days had passed since she had last killed, and she was hungry. Nursing her young made great demands on her body. Before her kittens were born she need kill only one deer about every two weeks to feed herself. Now that the kittens were ready to shift from mother's milk to meat, she must quicken her kills until she was catching a deer every three days to feed the four of them.

Dragging the carcass well into the brush, she covered it with leaves and soil. From the air, scavengers could not detect it, and the same was true for a passing coyote or fox. Once her labor was done, she returned down the trail, walking purposefully now. Finding the kittens, she led them back to the prey. They promptly attacked the animal, trimming off bits of flesh and gulping them down. Although they had eaten small prey she had brought them—squirrels and rabbits, once even a wild turkey—this was the first occasion they could eat all the meat they wanted at a sitting.

When they had gorged, she led them not far away to a dense tangle of manzanita and saw them bedded down. Here they remained until the deer was reduced to a bedraggled hide and staring skull. Three days later, when they abandoned the kill, the kittens had beaten down all the vegetation for a lion's leap around the carcass and deer hair littered the ground. She had established a pattern that would persist until the kittens were nearly eighteen months old, their blue eyes becoming the tawny gold of adult cats: after making a kill, she led the kittens to it, and they stayed in the vicinity until they exhausted all the sustenance it had to offer.

The cougar knew she shared the mountain with humans. Besides the roar of pickup trucks at the summit of the peak, she could hear vehicles passing on the county road that bisected her home territory. She saw that houses rose high and low on the mountain. She sensed that humans were different from her kind because, well, they looked different: they were taller than wide and their colors did not resemble anything else she knew. And their necks (she observed necks very closely) were short and went the wrong direction.

One day she ensconced the kittens in a thicket of willows and poison oak near Cedar Creek and ventured up the north bank of the stream to where stood many old spacious houses, a district that people knew as Pine Hills. As the sun set, she happened to be close to a stone house when she saw a barking dog emerge from its back door opening into the woods. She had a terrible fear of dog packs, a deeply imprinted instinct from the time when lions' most feared enemies were wolves; when she encountered barking dogs a primal force told her to climb into a tree or onto a boulder until danger passed. But this dog was alone, and did not bark much after it had eaten a heaping bowl of food that a young woman put out for it on the stoop.

He was a lean lithe eighty pound registered Doberman named Graf Herrnstein von Herrnstein, but everyone called him "Fritz." He zigzagged down the long driveway, leaving his mark on bushes and stones along the way. The lion, crouched in the brush, watched him as he passed. Moving closer to the drive, she awaited his return. As he passed by through the trees, in one bound the cat attacked. The dog never knew what happened as the cat hit him and the deadly incisors cut through his spinal cord.

From the house, the cougar carried the Doberman in her jaws down the long slope to her hungry kittens. Years later, a pack of adventuresome Boy Scouts tramping down the stream found a rotted dog collar half buried in sand, tags still attached. One husky lad threw it as far as he could up the hill. The dog's owners liked to think that someone had lured the dog away to take him to the city. They imagined he had found a happy, if lowly, life as a junkyard dog–his size and strength qualified him as the most fearsome creature on any block. But he had met his match in the mountains.

Sometimes, for reasons known only to herself, the big cat liked to watch the comings and goings of human beings. Walkers she often saw on the mountain, but they never saw her. On weekends, she saw hikers crossing the mountain's shoulder from the State Park to the County Park five miles away. Sometimes she even followed them.

One day, for half an hour from a sunny hiding place in the chaparral she lazily watched a bearded man and a little boy delving in the sandy bed of an oak-shadowed ravine; they were seeking pebbles studded with black tourmaline crystals. Finding a feldspar pebble, the six year old hummed with delight. It was destined for the mineral collection on his bedroom window sill. He never went very far from his grandfather because his parents had told him there were mountain lions in the woods.

Driven by curiosity, the lion one day silently approached the site

203

of an unfinished house rising in the woods at the base of the mountain. Her tawny eyes, acute at day and night, followed the movements of vehicles and gestures of two carpenters engaged in building the cabin. Several times a day the men would stroll into the woods, shovel in hand, passing a hundred feet from where the lion lay under a dense live oak. Of course, they did not notice the cat whose golden pelt merged with the broken shadows and dead leaves under the tree.

Watching that day, the lion kept a desultory eye on one of the carpenters passing through the woods. Suddenly, though, the man stopped and bent over to tie a shoe lace, resting his foot on a stone. The cat's ears lifted as she saw the figure taller than wide transform itself: now it was low and long and its neck was stretched out horizontally. Triggered by the instinct to attack, the cat's muscles tensed and her eyes narrowed. But then, the lace now tight, the man arose, becoming again a strange tall multi-colored figure. The lion yawned and lay her head back on her paws.

The kittens were now nearly as large as their mother and the spots they had sported since birth had faded, leaving only faint patches inside their legs and on their bellies. Their appetites were prodigious, greater than their mother's, and she was driven to make enough kills to support them and herself. One day, after killing a deer and eating her fill, she failed to go in search for the youngsters to share the kill. She simply put them out of her mind.

The kittens waited a full two days for their mother's appearance, growing ever hungrier. They whined and became irritable. Hunger gnawed at their bellies. Finally, the three of them separated, each driven by a vision of food. Four years earlier this had been the fate of their mother, born and abandoned twenty miles away on Mount Palomar. Like her, they began a time of aimless solitary wandering in search of something to eat. Without a home territory, driven by hunger, they might wander a hundred miles as transients until they found a place they would call home.

One of the three, a male, turned northward towards Pine Hills. He made futile attempts to catch quail, even towhees, in the chaparral. A brush rabbit escaped him by darting into an impenetrable chamise thicket. By the end of his first day of wandering he had gone five miles to an unknown land of fields, broken woods, orchards, and houses. The odor of food drew him toward a house behind which in a little corral bleated a pair of goats. The house's owner, who had lived in the country all his life, had covered the pen with heavy netting to protect them from predators. During the night the hungry cougar charged the pen, but he could not penetrate the stout wire. In the morning the house's owner saw the cougar crouching fifty feet from the pen near a pile of old tires in the shade of a maple tree.

Returning to the house, he took his 30.06 from its rack and went into the yard. Resting the gun barrel on the hood of his pickup truck, he took careful aim and at one hundred feet killed the cougar with a single shot. Later that day he buried the body where it fell. This mountain lion would never appear on any of the mortality records for lions that California Fish and Game maintains to guide public discussion of the status of the mountain lion population in the state.

Another cub, a female, turned southwest. Driven by hunger, she paced on and on. Descending a long slope she came to Boulder Creek. Desperate for food, she pounced on frogs that hid in streamside grasses and even caught two salamanders she saw swimming in shallow water. The next day in her wandering she had great good fortune: she came upon a range cow with a dead calf. Standing disconsolate over the calf's body, at the sight of the cougar the cow bolted and ran. Pouncing on the carcass, the young cat ravenously chewed the meat with a characteristic sideways motion–her sharpest back teeth were adapted to cutting, not tearing.

Now ten miles southwest of North Peak, she could see the distant lights of the city at night. She found a new source of food at a vast ground squirrel colony where foolish young abounded near the shallow burrows. While each rendered her only a mouthful of food, they helped maintain her strength.

Something about this area attracted and held her. As she roamed the huge rounded mountain above the ground squirrel colony that night, she found no sign of any other lions, except for an old scrape left by a passing young male transient lion a month earlier. She saw lots of deer sign too, and heard a buck plunging off through the chaparral when it sensed her presence. This was territory that might become hers.

The mountain had no resident female because a few months before, the female who claimed it as her home territory chose one night to leave her kittens and range southward in pursuit of food. Easily surmounting a five foot chain link fence, she saw at her feet a broad strip of concrete down which from time to time passed great hurtling shapes with bright lights. Waiting until the highway was dark, she began to trot across it. She never saw a sports car speeding at eighty five miles an hour as the driver hurried from his home in Phoenix to a long weekend in San Diego. He caught only a glimpse of a tan shape in his lights before the blunt smash of something against the fender of his car. When he managed to stop a half mile down the road, he was aghast to see the fender smashed flat and a huge crack across the windshield. Assuming he had hit a deer, he never reported the incident. Actually, he was preoccupied by the thought of a girl in Tijuana he remembered from his last visit to San Diego. The lion's kittens starved to death in their hiding place on the mountain. The lion's body was found a month later in a roadside ditch by a weekend crew working off traffic tickets. Now the mountain was open to any wandering young female lion that might claim it.

The third kitten, a male, also turning south when his mother deserted her family, stayed in the Cuyamaca mountains, traversing high across the slopes of the range. Five miles from his natal territory, hungry and confused, in the midst of a fern-filled meadow, he suddenly saw another lion. Sensing danger, he turned to run, but the big male lion with torn ears charged instantly.

He bowled the kitten over and his long incisors clamped down on his neck. The kitten died quickly. Neither lion in this uneven contest was aware that they were father and son. The old male acted to protect his home territory. Perhaps if the kitten had been small and with his mother, and recognizing the kitten as his own, he would not have attacked. But the interloper was a growing male far from his mother and a rival.

So long as the mother lion had kittens with her, she did not come into estrus, but now she was no longer nursing and they were absent, her reproductive cycles commenced anew. Normally, the cycle repeated itself every twenty-three days; she was receptive to males for only eight of those days. Conception and birth might occur any time during the year. She knew that the old male regularly patrolled her home territory because she noted his scrapes and sometimes she heard or saw him. Searching for his scrapes, now in estrus, she watched and waited for him.

When they found each other, the amorous couple passed a week together, preoccupied with mating fifty to seventy times a day, one of the highest levels of sexual activity for any mammal known. Frequent intercourse was essential if the female lion was to ovulate; without constant sexual stimulation she could not conceive.

The week over, she drove the male lion away and fled up the mountain to find solitude. Recognizing the inevitable, he abandoned her to search for another receptive female, driven by his raging libido, as always. Three months later the female gave birth to two kittens in a safe place within her home territory

During her life span she might have five litters, but few, if any, of her dozen progeny would survive to become parents. Injuries from deer hooves, guns, automobiles, starvation, combat with other lions, and disease would eliminate nearly all of them when they were still young, inexperienced, and foolish. Few, if any, would enjoy a long life with a full cycle of birth, reproduction, and late death that their mother knew on North Peak amidst oaks and pines with a distant view of the sea.

October

October

John Burroughs was born and spent nearly his entire life in the Catskills, a gentle region of wooded mountains and farms with a temperate northern climate. The highest point in the mountains is Slide Mountain, at 4204 feet the same altitude as our cabin on North Peak, but of course his home territory is much further north than our site; if the Catskills were in California they would be on the Oregon border. Nor do the Catskills enjoy the moderating effect of the Pacific Ocean which contributes to our benign climate in an important way.

In 1875 he published an essay, "Autumn Tides," displaying his distinctive combination of nature observation and literary embellishment colored by his enthusiasm for Emerson, whose works he admired extravagantly. Reading his essay, I'm reminded that we so often see autumn through the eyes of nature writers from the east, especially New England, that it sometimes hinders from seeing the Southern California mountain autumn as it really is. Burroughs' October, it has to be admitted, is not the October I know on North Peak.

At length he describes the arching rhythm of his year, the pulsing beat of spring, summer, and fall, which determines the year's growth. Spring brings growing roots, summer's heat produces expansion and stem, and early autumn delivers flowers and fruit which must ripen before killing frosts. Or as he puts it: "In the growth of most plants and weeds, April and May represent their root, June and July their stalk, and August and September their flower and seed. "

The event that terminates the growth cycle is frost, coming as early as September. After this blow to the plant world follows a period when warmth alternates with frost until cold finally wins the struggle and winter becomes king for at least a quarter of the year.

On North Peak the rhythm of plant growth is very different. Moisture, not cold, is king. Growth begins slowly in December after the arrival of November rain. Some plants begin to bloom in January, or even earlier. The volume of growth and flower reaches a crescendo in late spring, but then it diminishes in July. The last flowers fade in August. Autumn flowers are with us a rarity.

So too is the east's famous display of autumn leaves, what Burroughs calls "the big show," that brings tourists to the countryside,

209

especially in New England, in the fall. Not that we don't have changes in leaf color as the season wears on. As early as August the most casual observer will see splashes of fine pink or even crimson in the woods or on the margins of meadows. Poison oak, close to the ground, knee-high, or sometimes a vine climbing into brush or up the columns of the Coulter pines, is the harbinger of autumn. The leaves display an attractive range of color. I suspect we would admire the plant more if it did not have such uncomfortable associations –sometimes I wish that one of our mountain booster organizations might convince us to give it a more appealing name such as "flaming mountain woodbine." Who knows, we might even have Woodbine Festivals to attract tourists and their spending money, like the current Apple Festival, but of course the tourists would have to be reminded not to pick the woodbine.

The most distinguished autumn foliage in the mountains is on the Kellogg or black oaks, large handsome deciduous oaks often with picturesque broken trunks. In October its leaves begin to turn a faintest yellow. As time passes, the yellow turns darker, sometimes almost orange, sometimes an earthen russet. As with most trees, individual plants vary and some have more brilliant leaves than others. Where stands of this tree are extensive they form mild spreading yellow clouds across the mountain slopes.

Other leaves change too in our autumn in the mountains, but the most colorful flaunt themselves along stream beds which are rare in our district. Willow turns a brilliant yellow and dogwood becomes scarlet. A special treat for those who know where and when to look is a stand of Lombardy poplars that grows near the lake. For a week they are the strongest proudest yellow, but I can hardly claim Lombardy poplars as mountain trees. Other shrubs and trees such as alder change colors too, but their hues are not vivid, but studies in olive, mauve, tan, humus, and ash. For someone who is willing to pause to inspect them, these leaves, with their subdued nuances of color, offer rewards, but they must be sought out. They whisper, they don't shout.

When cold finally conquers summer heat in the Catskills, it will leave only bare branches and conifers. On North Peak, even after hard frosts, the slopes do not display many naked stems, aside from Kellogg oaks. Many chaparral plants such as chamise, manzanita, and scrub oak, are evergreen. So too are coast live oak, canyon live oak, and Engelmann oak, even though their leaves may hold accumulations of snow. Variety rules our winterscape: evergreen chaparral plants and live oaks are mixed at random with bare Kellogg oaks, the bright green of cedars, pines, and rare white firs. This is not the austere northern winter scene, but a landscape which declares the south, warmth, and mild ocean air.

In Burroughs' essay frost speaks with a commanding voice. In our mountains it can almost be ignored. It comes late to the mountains, usually in November, when foliage is dessicated, even after the first rains have fallen. It is a kind of afterthought, not of much importance compared to the arrival of rain after a five-month drouth. And because the autumn rains overshadow the late frosts, we don't have the season which so entrances Burroughs, a mild interval between frost and winter–Indian summer. This time of the year, "soft and hazy" without "a breath of air and not a ripple on the river," has been a favorite for eastern nature writers. Burroughs follows the convention of identifying this mild season with the Indians: "It is red and yellow and dusky like him. The smoke of his camp-fire seems again in the air. The memory of him pervades the woods. His plumes and moccasins and blankets of skins form just the costume the season demands. It was doubtless his chosen period. The gods smiled upon him then if ever..." He can romanticize and poeticize Indians because white men had mostly eliminated them in the east by Burroughs' time, leaving only a literary myth. Western writers, living where Indians have persisted, cannot employ such conventions with any confidence, I think to the benefit of western writers. The muddled image of the gods smiling upon the Indians, "then if ever," leaves me uneasy, or worse.

No, our October is not John Burroughs' October. Summer heat has subsided, so that in the afternoon the temperature rises only into the 70s or low 80s, and the nights are measured. Frost has not touched the meadows or the groves. Records show that an inch of rain may fall this month, but then again it may not–this year no rain at all fell in October. If a brief northern storm passes by, it may bring cold, even frost before morning, but this is as rare as rain.

The sun rises in a sky without fogs or clouds. It burns steadily, calmly, warmly, as it progresses through the waning days. The air is still and the yellowing leaves on the Kellogg oaks hang long on the trees, slowly darkening. No wind blows to free them.

Shadows are much longer than they were at the summer solstice. Because the sun no longer hammers the earth the way it did in July, at noon I can sit comfortably for an hour in the October sun, my hat tipped over my eyes and my feet on the deck railing, and watch the long slender blue shadows of the pines easing across the meadow.

North of the house a young apple tree that for the summer was flat under the high mountain sun now rests in the comfortable shade cast by the house. Its leaves, close to lime green in the summer, now look almost turquoise. It is assured of a six month respite before the April sun claims it once more, welcoming it to the world.

Time seems arrested and the season is suspended between summer's heat and winter's chill. This is a month of patient waiting, of restraint, of measure and moderation, a moment lacking violent skies or violent events. It is a time of contemplation and reflection over the days of the year, of taking accounts. Above all it is a time when expectation rules–the old year is ending, not at the conclusion of winter on the eve of spring and renewal, as in Burroughs' northern world, but after the season of summer heat and drouth that imperceptibly slipped into October.

One night I will hear rain on the roof and know that soon the mountain earth is about to stir and heave. In the meanwhile I am strangely drowsy and content to savor the last days of October, for mountain people the most favored month, the most blessed month, of the year.

The Death of a Young Man

At last something that I dreaded had occurred: pine beetles had invaded our property and a third of the Coulter pines had sickened and died, rapidly, in less than a month.

Eager to have them cut down to halt the beetle invasion, I made inquiries and got the names of two woodcutters, father and son, James Streamer and Little Hawk Streamer. Over the telephone I spoke with James Streamer. I told him the sick trees were obvious–their needles had become pale with a reddish cast and they were falling from the trees. I instructed him to cut the pines close to the ground with as little damage as possible to the surrounding vege-tation. He agreed, seeming to think my conditions were reasonable. For the work of him and his son he asked for only a modest payment. In fact, his estimate was so low that for a moment I even thought of offering him more, but I knew this would only contribute to the widespread mountain conviction that flatlanders are crazy, so I said nothing and accepted his estimate. I would pay him when the trees were cut and disposed of.

Later I realized that they would be earning more than the price we had agreed on, because the father had shyly asked me if I wanted the wood. No, I had no use for it, I told him. I had no tools to cut or split it, and besides, I thought, like sour grapes, Coulter pine is poor fuel, being notoriously quick-burning.

I had given him the wood and he would sell it for a profit. I wasn't angry because I had been deceived and cheated (I hadn't–my cost for the job was still very low), but rather I felt a kind of pity for Streamer's lack of business acumen. He could have gotten much more from me for difficult and dangerous work, as well as pocketing the money from the sale of the wood I didn't want. Now, I thought, if the Streamers lived in the city where business practices are sharper they could have doubled their earnings and then, I later thought, they could pay their rent.

*****

213

The day they finished the wood cutting, I met the Streamers in the woods to give them their money. I thanked them for the low stumps they had left and the minimal damage done to the trees around them. They had a certain family resemblance, I thought, the father in his forties and the son about twenty, but I felt a kind of tension between them, a stiffness, an absence of give and take. I decided that they were not father and son, but step-father and step-son, but I was wrong, as it turned out; they were rightly father and son.

We chatted as they finished their lunch. The son led the conversation to the question of whether I wanted any trimming done, particularly on some of our Kellogg oaks which often have broken snags. He spoke of the work enthusiastically as though it would bring real improvement by preventing the spread of decay. He seemed young for his age, fair, innocent, almost as though he belonged in the woods, a shy animal. He fitted in, a comfortable part of the landscape, in worn levis and a faded plaid shirt, with sawdust in his thick hair.

No, I answered that this wasn't a suburban yard or a public park. I liked the woods wild and untamed. But I was a little concerned about the dead lower branches on some of the pines. These might serve as ladders to lead a brush fire into the crowns of the trees. I might cut some of them off, if I was too concerned, I told them. "Oh, I wouldn't do that!" Little Hawk said. "Climbing trees is dangerous and you might hurt yourself!"

His concern touched me. Why should he care if some flatlander chose to risk life and limb by climbing a ladder with a chain saw? I agreed that I'd think it over, and I would let them know if I wanted any tree trimming done. In fact, a few years later I wanted the father and son to trim my pines, but I was too late then.

* * * * *

"For the past six or seven weeks, he'd been sliding more to the side of unreality," Streamer said. "I had told him so many times that he was welcome here anytime (at the Streamer home on the Los Coyotes Indian Reservation), but that the only thing not welcome was methamphetamine and alcohol abuse."

These words are part of an interview James Streamer gave to reporters from the *San Diego Union* for an article on March 9, 1994.

He asked his son, age 23, because of his son's drug and alcohol abuse, to leave his home. Little Hawk found a cottage to rent for $400 a month near Lake Henshaw.

On March 3 the rent on the cottage was due. When the manager asked Little Hawk for the money, he gave him only five dollars and kicked a pot of noodles he was cooking off an open fire in front of the cottage, his manner defiant and abusive. The manager phoned the Sheriff's substation to report a disturbance. Deputy Sheriff Jeff Hamm, who knew the Streamer family, drove to Lake Henshaw where he tried reasoning with Little Hawk, but the conversation disintegrated. Little Hawk became combative and Hamm sprayed him in the face with pepper spray, but this seemed to have no effect at all on the young man. In the background from the cottage came the sound of the rap song "Cop Killer" played on a borrowed tape recorder.

Streamer said his son's problems with drug and alcohol abuse began in his teens after his parents divorced when the elder Streamer began serving a prison sentence. "To Hawk, his family was everything," Streamer said. " When that happened, he was devastated."

At sixteen, the boy dropped out of Julian High School and began working. At the time of his death he was self-employed as a tree trimmer. His father proudly displays photographs of his son sitting atop a huge downed tree.

To the cottage came a second vehicle, driven by Deputy Sheriff Keith McClanahan to serve as a backup for Deputy Hamm.

Little Hawk emerged from the cottage with a bottle of liquid and a shotgun. He poured the liquid down the driveway towards one of the patrol cars. A neighbor who was looking on shouted "He's got a Molotov cocktail!" Hastily a deputy moved one patrol car and both of them took refuge behind the second car. Little Hawk raised his shotgun and fired a single shot, hitting a spotlight mounted on the patrol car behind which the deputies huddled. They immediately returned fire, striking Little Hawk several times. When the deputies' fire hit him, he was standing on the cottage porch, for when the reporters from the *Union* arrived to interview James Streamer he was scrubbing down the cabin's porch and steps. Little Hawk died a short time later.

"Hawk was as honest as the day is long," Streamer said. "There wasn't a violent bone in his whole body. This wasn't his personality.

The drugs just warped him. It's terrible stuff."

Sometimes people say that San Diego County is the methamphetamine capital of the United States, although they sometimes grant this odious distinction to nearby Riverside County. Meth laboratories are often located in rural houses because manufacturing the drug produces foul odors which invite complaints from neighbors to the police. Apparently, these rural laboratories have stimulated local drug use: there appears to be a correlation between the existence of the labs and the use of the drug in the backcountry.

James Streamer says he does not hate the deputies who killed his son. He said that although he thinks there may have been other ways to handle the situation he believes that when an officer is fired upon the result almost always will be fatal.

*****

In my mind's eye I see the morning scene at the cottage: last night's noodles spilled over a cold fire, broken glass from the sheriffs' car, shotgun casings scattered about, gasoline stains spilling down the driveway, and James Streamer washing his son's blood from the porch. I want to remember Little Hawk when he was a few years younger, alert to the people around him, attentive, and working in the woods where he belonged. This was where he was alive, happy, and close to the outdoors he loved.

But wherever he is, may the sun shine in a cloudless sky, his chain saw be forever sharp, and the wood of the tree turn true and easy to the blade.

The History of Two and a Half Acres

Location pertains to feeling; feeling profoundly pertains to place; place in history partakes of feeling, as feeling about history partakes of place.
                    Eudora Welty

When searching through records at the San Diego County Recorder's Office in an attempt to identify the earliest settlers in the Cosmit for the essay "Uninhabited and Uninhabitable," I made a serendipitous discovery. Looking for something else, I stumbled on the names of the first owners of our land: on February 9, 1877, Herbert and Martha Crouch, along with other tracts, homesteaded eighty acres, the S 1/2 of the SW 1/4 of Section 19, Township 13 S, Range 4 E, San Bernardino Meridian, that includes our two and a half acres.

Crouch and his wife, like their good friends, the Sawdays, the earliest settlers in the Cosmit, were English. Born in Lambourne, Berkshire, in 1841, Herbert Crouch first emigrated to Australia and then came to San Luis Rey in 1869. At a time when nearly all the county's hill country was open range, Crouch amassed a herd of four thousand sheep, according to Richard Pourade's *History of San Diego,* that he pastured near Oceanside and in the Laguna Mountains. Pourade asserts that the county was then mostly sheep range–he cites records indicating there were 150,000 sheep in the county but only about ten thousand beef cattle.

Delighted by the discovery, it occurred to me that by using this as a starting point, I might be able to trace all the past owners of our land. Not only did I think this might be satisfying–building an emotional foundation under our legal ownership of this bit of mountain land–tracing the chain of ownership might also provide a history, not only of our property, but of land use in the Cuyamacas. Our few acres of land might serve as a microcosm for all of the San Diego backcountry; following its history, I could read the story of land ownership in the district, beginning twenty years after California became a state to when we bought the land and on it built our cabin in the last decade of the twentieth century.

A few years after the Crouches acquired our land, they sold it and cattle replaced the sheep that grazed in the hills above Sandy Creek. James Kelly and his bride of 1873, Narcissa Ann Bunton

Kelly, bought up all the land on the front of North Peak, creating the Kelly Ranch, or, as it was known, "Kelly Country."

It's not easy to follow exactly how Kelly acquired his land, since the only source of information is the early handwritten, poorly indexed records in the County Recorder's Office, but I did succeed in finding the record of Frederick Sawday's sale of his land to Kelly's wife in December, 1881. He had held it only six years. An 1890's plat map at the San Diego Historical Society shows that by that date the entire mountain side was in Kelly's hands, including, of course, our land. About the time that Sawday sold out, the Crouches probably sold their homestead to James Kelly and his wife.

James Kelly came to Julian about 1870, the time of the earliest gold discoveries, where he developed the Owens Mine, named for his friend, Barney Owens, in partnership with others. Contrary to the rumors that he was an Irishman (although he might have been of Irish descent), he was born in Hartford, Connecticut in 1845, according to James A. Jasper, the chronicler of early Julian history. Active in civic affairs, including the defense of the Julian mines against the claims of the owners of Cuyamaca Rancho, about 1873, after his marriage, he sold his mine holdings and began to acquire ranch land. Eventually, he owned somewhere between three thousand and four thousand acres of North Peak land; his ranch headquarters was at Anahuac spring, west of the Inaja Reservation not far below today's Boulder Creek Road.

A plat map dated 1891 shows an unexpected event in North Peak real estate history. That year, an individual named Emil Honniger acquired eighty acres of land on the mountain in the center of Kelly's ranch that included our land. Honniger—and I know nothing about him except his name—retained ownership of the plot for two years only. Why did he buy the land and hold it for such a brief time? The explanation may be that in the same year the Gold King Mining Co. also purchased eighty acres directly east of Honniger's land. It seems reasonable that Honniger was speculating on the possibility of a gold strike on North Peak, and so bought adjoining land, holding it only long enough to become convinced that the property had no value. At any rate, Honniger was the third party to own our land, if only briefly.

These two land purchases and Hayes' mention of prospectors at Inaja provide the only evidence I have ever found that miners

218

believed there was gold on the west front of North Peak. To the north prospectors searched for gold in Pine Hills where outcrops of Julian schist are everywhere, and to the south the Boulder Creek Mining District was modestly active from 1885 to about 1940, but with these exceptions, North Peak has never attracted the attention of gold-seekers, yesterday or today.

James Kelly died in 1902 and the ranch passed to his widow, his son, Charles, and his two daughters. They retained the ranch for only eight years until they sold it to the developer, Ed Fletcher, who with his backers had only recently purchased the San Diego Flume Co. that delivered water from their Cuyamaca Reservoir to San Diego and its suburbs.

After the sale of the ranch, Charles Kelly continued working as a cowboy in the Cuyamacas, first for George Sawday, eldest son of Frederick Sawday, and later for the Dyar family who owned Cuyamaca Rancho. In the 1950s he recorded an interview for the San Diego Historical Society, a colorful account of cowboy life on the range at the turn of the century. I quoted from it in the essay "Unfriendly Fire."

Fletcher described his purchase of the Kelly Ranch in a chapter of his *Memoirs*, 1952, entitled "Our Beautiful Cuyamaca Mountains." In his account he declares he bought the ranch when he heard that Charles Kelly intended to sell it to a lumberman for timbering, Fletcher typically combining, with some justification, what he considered public service with personal gain. The price he paid was more than $30,000, or about ten dollars an acre.

To obtain the money Fletcher went to Pasadena where he got $10,000 from the F. and W. Thum Co. whose owners were the brothers William, Ferdinand, and Hugo Thum (He named one of his sons for Ferdinand Thum). He got the same amount from C. A. Canfield of Los Angeles, and also from Senator James A. Murray who had backed him on the Cuyamaca Reservoir purchase. Not yet a wealthy man, Fletcher contributed a smaller amount–he usually provided one-sixth of the total cost of a project in his own money–in this case, perhaps $5,000.

When Fletcher bought the ranch he mostly divided the land among his backers, giving each legal title; a plat map dated 1933 shows that the W. and F. Thum Co. held title on all the land above Sandy Creek, including our two and a half acres, thereby becoming

219

the sixth owners of our land.

Fletcher managed all the land for the new owners of Kelly Country, leasing out grazing rights to George Sawday, born on the Cosmit in 1876. The younger Sawday, the "millionaire rancher" from his home at Witch Creek controlled great herds of cattle that grazed from the Pacific Ocean to Imperial County, usually, as in this case, preferring to lease rather than buy land. Perhaps when he rode on North Peak, he visited the site of the cabin near Sandy Creek where he was born,

According to his nephew, Charles F. Sawday, during the years that his uncle leased Kelly Country, he had wells dug and stock ponds excavated. Some of the land he fenced also, and at places today near our land rusty barbed-wire still trails from post to post through the oaks, buried under fifty years' accumulation of leaves and rotting logs, surviving long after the cattle it once enclosed have disappeared.

Fletcher's purchase of the Kelly Ranch for himself and his backers marked a new era in the history of the Cuyamacas. Before 1910 ranchers such as the Sawdays or the Kellys owned the land and on it grazed their sheep and cattle. Now, entrepreneurs like Fletcher realized that handsome profits could be obtained by purchasing properties and holding them for re-sale or development. The large sums of money needed to buy land nearly all came from outside investors, either from booming Los Angeles or from out of state. A new period of what might be called regional or national land finance had begun. I suspect that this generalization is valid: anywhere in the United States where profits were to be made in large scale land speculation, money to finance the deal would be found, even if the source was hundreds or thousands of miles away.

Fletcher eventually exercised options to buy out some of his partners, purchasing Canfield's interest and Senator Murray's for an unspecified amount. However, he writes that the Thum brothers sold their interest not to him, but made a good profit selling to "outsiders." This was certainly before 1952 when his memoirs appeared and after 1933 when the plat map shows our land still in the possession of the Thum brothers or their heirs. Who these "outsiders" were, I have not been able to ascertain in the county property records for this period. It is not even clear what Fletcher meant by "outsiders." Were they someone outside the land development industry? Some mountain residents believe that ranchers named Chamberlain purchased the land, but others assert they only leased it for grazing.

In the twentieth century the automobile brought enormous changes to the Cuyamacas, only forty miles from the coastal cities. To reach Julian from San Diego in a buggy required a two day ride; now the journey by automobile consumes about an hour, less if you are seventeen and driving your father's car. To ease the way for the automobile, back country secondary roads were upgraded and paved. Finally, the completion of Interstate 8 in the 1960s so reduced driving time to the mountains that anyone in the city whose heart was set on a picnic under Cuyamaca oaks could do so quickly and almost effortlessly. To provide a site for these picnics and others forms of mountain recreation, Cuyamaca Rancho State Park was established in 1933 and William H. Heise County Park in 1970.

Someone with a job in San Diego can reside in Julian if he (or she) does not mind a hundred mile commute, not so rare in Southern California. A retiree in Cuyamaca above the reservoir can see his internist in La Mesa for a ten o'clock appointment after a leisurely breakfast on the road. The same internist can own a second home in Julian Estates, knowing he can relax Saturday evening in front of his fireplace with a Martini in his hand after only a brief drive. The mountains' isolation was no more; the automobile had shifted San Diego's city limits sixty miles to the east, *de facto*.

Realizing the improved highway access available to the mountains, and sensing money to be made, on December 29, 1967, a lawyer/developer in nineteen transactions bought six hundred acres of ranch land along Engineers Road from "William F. Derbonne, unmarried man and Betty Lou Derbonne, unmarried woman." I know nothing about these two individuals. Perhaps they were the "outsiders" Fletcher had in mind, or perhaps there were intermediate owners who bought from the Thum estate.

Using a technique known to surveyors as "4 x 4 x 4 lot splits," dividing his six hundred acres into many parcels that he "sold" to family members, repeating the process many times, the developer carved out 220 lots of about three acres each. Attempting to trace the "chain of ownership," I struggled to identify the early owners of our land. After 1967 the problem changed shape, for now I was overwhelmed by the frequent changes of title I found. Our land was bought and sold in 1967, 1970, 1972, and 1979.

The lawyer/developer limited his lot splits to four "sales" each because any higher number would have automatically qualified as a legal subdivision, and this was something he wished to avoid. Legally sub-dividing the land would have entailed large expenditures for roads, utilities, etc. all under supervision by county authorities. He did organize a small mutual water company to provide water to some of the lots–but it was not large enough to provide water for all of them. This does not seem to have concerned him. He offered the lots for sale at prices between $7,000 and $9,000; twenty-five years later they sell for about five times as much.

Twenty-one years after the developer filed his nineteen legal documents in 1967, my wife and I bought one of those lots, becoming, according to my calculations, the twelfth attested owner of our two and a half acres since 1877.

The nineteenth century in the mountains was an age of animals–horses, cattle, sheep. The twentieth century gave us the automobile, with its advantages and disadvantages. And if the futurists are correct, the trend towards decentralization, including the dispersal of population away from the city, will persist and intensify thanks to the automobile and jet planes and work-at-home computer stations. More of us will want to live in places like the Cuyamacas.

More and more of us will seek surcease in something like nature, one foot on the pavement and one foot under an oak tree in the Cuyamacas, where if we look closely we see Indian morteros or strands of rusted barbed-wire, vestiges of the mountain past. To that history contributed Indians, ranchers, developers who made a handsome profit, moneyed men from Pasadena, and a city lawyer who understood how to buy and sell mountain land to his greatest advantage. Now our two and a half acres belong to city folk who on it have built a cabin. What will be the future events in its history and who will be its future owners? But that is a question, certainly, that only time can answer.

The National Bird Finds a Neighboring Niche

Last winter circumstances forced me to park and wait for a half an hour next to the highway at Cuyamaca Reservoir. Because, among other things, the Recreation District maintains a stable water level so it has no unsightly "bathtub ring," the reservoir is a pleasant, pretty place, popular with tourists, fishermen, and, not without controversy, duck hunters in season. While I waited above the lake on this cloudy winter day, I saw the reservoir's glory and pride, a magnificent mature bald eagle. Not a hundred yards from me, it rested in a tree by the lake shore, gleaming white head and tail, chocolate body and wings, piercing eyes, formidable beak, all in plain view.

I understand it is one of a small flock of these birds that winter in the county; there are more of them at Lake Henshaw to the north. Assuming it is the same bird, I also saw it a year ago as I drove past the reservoir. The Audubon Society reported one bald eagle at the lake at Christmas, 1994, but they failed to see it in 1995. It seems likely that we are all watching the same bird.

Like most people, I associate bald eagles with wilderness and Alaska, killer whales, snow spinning into old growth cedars, salmon-rich rivers and giant white-eyed birds fiercely and wildly independent. This bird rested comfortably a few hundred yards from a busy restaurant with an even busier parking lot. Yet closer, a cluster of fishermen, seated in colorful plastic folding chairs, dropped their lines in the water. Other men, women and children tried their luck from boats on the tiny lake. As best I could see, they ignored the bird and it returned the favor. The picture I saw was one of magnificence against the most ordinary background, people dining, riding past in their cars, fishing, in general enjoying a mild winter day in the mountains, the kind of things people like to do on a day off.

How did the eagle find a niche in this unlikely setting, I asked myself. Certainly permanent water drew it here; bald eagles, as is well known, want the presence of water in their world. More than a hundred years ago a water company built the dam at the site of The Lake That Dries Up, Laguna que se seca, pools and marsh with an outlet that disappeared with summer's heat. The lake appears to hold only one eagle, though. Seemingly, it can provide food for only one bird and at that the bird is here only for the winter: one eagle on a small lake for the winter months only.

I also asked myself how the bird supports itself during its sojourn here on open southern water. Below the tree where the bird perched, ducks rafted–mallards, mostly, I think–also electing to ignore the bird of prey. I doubt the eagle could catch one of these speedy birds, unless it was wounded or sick, and I suspect it does just that at times. Coots, though, collect at the shallow south end of the lake. Notoriously weak flyers, I surmise that many of them become food for the eagle; I doubt whether anyone mourns the passing of any of these homely and prolific waterfowl, the bane of water hazards on golf courses and children's duck ponds.

But I doubt there are enough coots and other slow-flying birds to support the eagle, although at times it may supplement its diet by capturing ground squirrels on nearby meadows. No, most of its food must be fish, its primary food wherever it lives. And the irony is that open-handed humans, with whom it deigns to share the lake, supply these fish to the bird.

During the course of the year, men pour tons of trout into the lake that are raised at considerable expense and trucked in from God knows where. Fishermen, and their wives and children, promptly catch most of them, but no doubt, the eagle takes its share, thriving on what man provides.

Every day, it seems, the media remind us how we are exterminating wildlife here or there, or depriving it of food or nesting sites, and in general making life difficult for it. At Cuyamaca we have a magnificent wild creature dwelling on a body of water that would not exist had humans not impounded it. It flourishes on a rich diet that humans serve to it with much expense and trouble.

Perhaps it is only small compensation, but I must admit that the sight of Lake Cuyamaca's free-loading eagle, besides the pleasure it gives me to follow its form and flight, makes me feel a little better about wildlife in the world we humans increasingly control, not always wisely. As in political affairs, accommodation and co-existence are preferable to war and slaughter. An eagle on every lake, a fox at every window, a toad under every board, I say.

Bibliographic Essay

Sources that I have cited in the essays will not be repeated here, except to clarify details, as needed.

The epigraph that opens the book is from Wallace's essay "The Nature of Nature Writing" in *The Untamed Garden* (Columbus, Ohio U. Press, 1986) p. 118. It was originally in the *New York Times Book Review,* July 22, 1984.

Birds Obscurely Understood
The quote is from Philip Unitt, *Birds of San Diego County,* (San Diego, San Diego Natural History Society, 1984) p. 101. R. G. Jeffrey, "Band-tailed Pigeon" in G. C. Sanderson, ed., *Management of Migratory, Shore, and Upland Game Birds in North America.* (Wash., Assoc. of Fish and Wildlife Agencies, 1977). Quote on p. 215. On band-tails in California see W. M. Smith, "The Band-tailed Pigeon in California" in *California Fish and Game,* 54 (1) 1968, p.4-16. For the band-tailed pigeon in the Florida Keys see John K. Terres, *The Audubon Society Encyclopedia of N. A. Birds,* (N. Y.,Wings Books, 1980) p. 733.

Battle in View
Letters of William James and Theodore Flournoy, (Madison, U. of Wisconsin, 1961) p. 175. As a source for the facts of the battle, I have employed Peter Price, *The Battle at San Pasqual (*San Diego, Pembroke Publishers, 1990). Thoreau writes about the Battle of Concord in *Walden* in the essay "Brute Neighbors."

Three Long Mountains
The basic sources on Cuyamaca mines and geology are F. S. Hudson, "Geology of the Cuyamaca Region" *U. of California Pubs. in Geology,* Vol. 13, p. 177-252, 1922. The quote is on p. 190. M. G. Donnelly "Geology and Mineral Deposits of the Julian District" *California Journal of Mines and Geology,* Vol. 30, 1934, p. 331-370. Donald Everhart, "Geology of the Cuyamaca Peak Quadrangle" in *Crystalline Rocks of Southwest California.* California Division of Mines and Geology, *Bulletin,* 159, 1951, p. 51-115, The quote is on p. 60. F. H. Weber, "Mines and mineral resources of San Diego

County" Report 3, California Division of Mines and Geology, 1963.

Why the Road Goes Thisaway

Ed Fletcher, *Memoirs* (L. A., Prelude Press, 1982) p. 279. Fletcher's book is an invaluable source for information about development in the Cuyamacas.

Rain and Snow, Sun and Clouds

As a source of data I have used *Climates of San Diego County ed.* by Daniel H. Close (San Diego, U. C. Agric. Ex. Service, 1970) This publication gives data for many stations in the county. For geographical data see Philip R. Pryde, "Climate, Soils, Vegetation, and Wildlife" in his *San Diego. An Introduction to the Region.*(Dubuque, Kendall/Hunt, 1984) p. 31-49.

Mountain Quail

As a source of general information I have utilized P. A. Johnsgard, *Grouse and Quail of North America,* (Lincoln, U. of Nebraska Press, 1973) D. D. McLean, *The Quail of California* (Sacramento, Calif. Fish and Game, 1930) and S. Mastrup, *Guide to Hunting the Quail of California* (Sacramento, Calif. Fish and Game, 1993). The recipe is in Mastrup, p. 93.

Engineers Road

For road construction data see   J. E. Reading, *History of San Diego Highway Development* (Highway Development Assoc. of San Diego, 1977) Fletcher describes the purchase of the Kelly ranch in the chapter in his memoirs entitled "Our Beautiful Cuyamaca Mountains."

Community Spirit

There will probably never be unanimity in defining California's many diverse biological communities. While I follow Schoenherr in seeing our land as an ecotone where Upper Chaparral and Mixed Forest meet, Bakker has Coulter pine forest as a subdivision in the Lower Montane Pine Forest. *Island Called California* (Berkeley, U. C. Press, 1984) p. 354. In the language of the profession, Schoenherr appears to be a "lumper" while Bakker is a "splitter."

February

As a matter of fact, the observation about chaparral birds and song appears in Schoenherr, *A Natural History of California* (Berkeley, U. C. Press, 1992) p. 375.

First Man into the Country

Benjamin Hayes' voluminous papers are at the Bancroft Library; they deserve full editing and publication. For the time being, the only printed source on his Cuyamaca sojourn is the short and unsatisfying article "Notes on the Indians of San Diego County. From the manuscripts of Judge Benjamin Hayes." Foreword and Notes by Arthur Wood. *The Masterkey,* Vol. VIII, no. 5, September, 1934. Pages 140-150. The most convenient source on the Cuyamaca Rancho litigation is Charles LeMaster's *Julian City and Cuyamaca Country* (Eagle Peak Pubs., 1992), Pages 59-79.

Two Blue Jays

A. C. Bent *Life Histories of N. A. Jays, Crows, and Titmice.* U. S. Nat. Mus. *Bulletin* 191. Sylvia Wilmore, *Crows, Jays and Ravens* (Middlebury, Va., Eriksson, 1977) G. E. Woolfenden, *The Florida Scrub Jay* (Princeton, P. U. P., 1984) On Steller, see Leonhard Stejneger, *Georg Wilhelm Steller,* (Cambridge, C. U. P. 1936).

North Peak Trail

The purchase of the land for the park is described in an article in the *San Diego Union,* Dec. 25, 1975. The sawmill fire is described in an article in the same paper for Aug. 16, 1897. The map is in the San Diego Historical Society archives. Fletcher describes his intervention for the sake of the forest in his *Memoirs*, p. 674-675.

I Design a House

The epigraph appeared in the essay "Designs for Escape" in the *New Yorker*, Oct. 16, 1995, p. 160.

Men and Mountains Meet

The Blake verse is in his *Complete Poetry and Prose* (Berkeley, U. C. Press, 1982) p. 511. The manual I bought is by Ralph Wolfe, *Low-Cost Pole Building Construction* (Pownal, Vt., Storey, 1980).

Four and a Half Fine Trees
Most of the facts in this essay are from *Oaks of California* (Los Olivos, Calif., Cachuma Press, 1991) by Bruce M. Pavlik, et al. The quotation from John Muir is also in this book, p. 32. Another excellent source of information is *Fremontia*, Vol. 18, no. 3, July, 1990. "The Year of the Oak."

Our Very Own Mining District
Besides Petrone's article, see A. J. Mroz "Geology of the Boulder Creek Mining District" (San Diego State University Geology Dept, Undergraduate Repts. 1968) W. B. Tucker wrote the section on the mines of San Diego County, including Boulder Creek, in the *Reports* of the Calif. Mining Bur, 1925. See Everhart "Cuyamaca Peak Quadrangle," 1951, p. 109-11.

Selective Annihilation
The Ingles quotation is on p. 147.

Uninhabited and Uninhabitable
President Grant's executive order, dated Dec. 27, 1875, was in the *San Diego Union* on Jan. 23, 1876. For information about Frederick Sawday see "F. R. Sawday, My Grandfather" by Charles F. Sawday in Julian Historical Society *History of Julian*, 1969, p. 64.

June
For Paeoniceae, see F. A. Novak, *Pictorial Encyclopedia of Plants* (London, Hamlyn, 1966) p. 113. Also P. A. Munz et al, *A California Flora* (Berkeley, U. C. Press, 1968) p. 78. For Xantus, see Howard Ensign Evans, *Pioneer Naturalists* (N. Y,. Holt, 1993) p. 234-239.

The View from Cuyamaca Peak
Little has been written about Van Dyke. For a brief biography see Joe Stone's "Paved Way for San Diego Water," *San Diego Union*, Aug. 13, 1973. p. 3. See the 19th century index to this paper for many references to Van Dyke.

One Tough Tree
The prime source for western botanical history is S. McKelvey,

Botanical Exploration of the Trans-Mississippi West, 1790-1850.
(Cambridge, Harvard U. P., 1955) For information about the pine see
B. Zobel, "Geographic Range and Intra-specific Variation of Coulter
Pine." *Madroño*, XII, no. 1 (Jan. 1953) p. 1-7. Also ,the same
author's "The natural hybrid between Coulter and Jeffrey Pines."
Evolution, 5: 405-413, 1951.

July

H. E. Evans provides the origin for the name of Anna's hummingbird, in *Pioneer Naturalists*, p. 24. For phainopeplas see R. S.
Woods, "Phainopeplas" in *Life Histories of N.A. Wagtails, Shrikes,
Vireos and Their Allies,* ed. by A. C. Bent. U. S. Nat. Mus. *Bulletin,*
no. 197, Washington, 1950. G. E. Walsberg, "Ecology and energetics
of contrasting social systems in Phainopepla nitens." *U. C. Pubs. in
Zool.* 108, p. 1-63. For interpreting the meaning of scientific bird
names see James Jobling, *A Dictionary of Scientific Bird Names*
(Oxford, Oxford U. P., 1991)

Woodland Raptor

See P. A. Johnsgard, *Hawks, Eagles and Falcons of N. A.,*
(Washington, Smithsonian Institution Press, 1990) especially p. 171-
175. James Cooper's article is entitled "Animal Life in the Cuyamacas." Vol. 8, p. 14-18. See also C. Asay, "Habitat and Productivity of
Cooper's Hawks Nesting in California." *California Fish and Game*,
(73) 2, p. 80-87. 1987.

Wee, Sleekit, Cow'rin, Tim'rous Beastie

See J. M. Linsdale and L. P. Tevis, Jr., *The Dusky-Footed Wood
Rat* (Berkeley, U. C. Press, 1951) and J. Dixon,"Notes on the Natural
History of the Bushy Tailed Wood Rats of California. U. C. *Pubs. in
Zool,* 21, no. 3. p.49-74. 1919. The Roosevelt anecdote is from H. E.
Evans *Pioneer Naturalists*, p. 146-147. For wood rat middens, see
Schoenherr, *Natural History*, p. 380.

August

For information on pine beetles see *Bark Beetles in California
Forest Trees,* U. C. Division of Agricultural Sciences, Leaflet 21034,
n.d.

A Satisfying Half

The quotation from Burroughs is in his essay, "Wild Life about my Cabin," in *Birch Browsings* (N. Y. Penguin Books, 1992) p. 95.

September

In addition to the book by Koenig and Mumme (Princeton, P. U P.,1987) see B. R. MacRoberts and M. H. MacRoberts *Social Organization and Behavior of the Acorn Woodpecker in Central Coastal California* (Baltimore, Amer. Ornith. Union, mon. 21, 1976).

Unfriendly Fire

The San Diego County Planning Department, Cartography Dept., has "Fire History" maps dating from 1910. The Inaja fire was the subject of numerous articles in the *San Diego Union* in November and December, 1956.

Home on the Range

I have used two sources for this essay: Chris Bolgiano, *Mountain Lion. An Unnatural History of Pumas and People.* (Mechanicsburg, Stackpole, 1995) and Kevin Hansen, *Cougar. The American Lion.* (Flagstaff, Northland, 1993). My only questionable conjecture is the father lion killing his son, but research seems to show that lions, including family members, kill each other more frequently than expected See Bolgiano, p. 97.

October

Burroughs' essay, "Autumn Tides" is in the volume *Deep Woods* (Salt Lake City, Peregrine Smith, 1990) p. 89-104.

The Death of a Young Man

The *San Diego Union* published three articles on the Streamer incident, dated March 4, 5, and 9, 1994.

The History of Two and a Half Acres

Eudora Welty, "Place in Fiction" in *The Eye of the Story* (N. Y., Random House, 1977), p. 122. Richard F. Pourade, *History of San Diego,* IV, (San Diego, Union-Tribune Publishing, 1964) p. 152, p. 149. The best source of information about James Kelly is James Jasper, *Trail-breakers and History-makers of Julian,* ms., at the San Diego Historical Society Archives. Plat maps are at the same institution.

About the Author

Leland Fetzer taught Russian language and literature for nearly three decades. He has published three volumes of translations from Russian and articles on 19th and 20th century Russian literature, but he is proudest of an essay he wrote in 1971 on Bernard DeVoto's western origins. He lives in San Diego but spends as much time as possible at a cabin in the Cuyamaca mountains. At the present time he is writing *Three Long Mountains: A History of Cuyamaca Country.*